Shaking Up the City

Shaking Up the City

IGNORANCE, INEQUALITY,
AND THE URBAN QUESTION

Tom Slater

UNIVERSITY OF CALIFORNIA PRESS

University of California Press
Oakland, California

Library of Congress Cataloging-in-Publication Data

Names: Slater, Tom, author.
Title: Shaking up the city : ignorance, inequality, and the urban question /
    Tom Slater.
Description: Oakland, California : University of California Press, [2021] |
    Includes bibliographical references and index.
Identifiers: LCCN 2021007244 (print) | LCCN 2021007245 (ebook) |
    ISBN 9780520303041 (hardback) | ISBN 9780520386228 (paperback) |
    ISBN 9780520972643 (ebook)
Subjects: LCSH: Cities and towns. | Sociology, Urban.
Classification: LCC HT151 .S487 2021 (print) | LCC HT151 (ebook) |
    DDC 307.76—dc23
LC record available at https://lccn.loc.gov/2021007244
LC ebook record available at https://lccn.loc.gov/2021007245

Manufactured in the United States of America

26 25 24 23 22
10 9 8 7 6 5 4 3 2 1

Publication supported by a grant from
The Community Foundation for Greater New Haven
as part of the Urban Haven Project.

For Woody (2009–2019),
who walked me out of pain
and into my best thoughts

Contents

Illustrations

Foreword

URBAN POLARIZATION
AND EPISTEMIC REFLEXIVITY

Loïc Wacquant

Over the past three decades, social inequality and marginality have grown in concert in the metropolis, spawning a deeply polarized class structure that has beset central and local governments with a host of thorny administrative challenges and pressing policy quandaries: homelessness and gentrification; the involution of districts of dereliction and the return migration of bourgeois families hungry for public amenities, street policing, and infrastructural rebuilding; rent control and skyrocketing real estate; and bureaucratic upheaval spawned by fiscal retrenchment and the neoliberal revamping of the state. New discourses have correspondingly swirled about the city, themselves bifurcated into a buoyant celebration of urban "renaissance," diversity, and technology, on the one hand, and dark tales of festering crime, uncontrolled immigration, creeping surveillance, and the crystallization of "ghettos" of ethnic secession and social perdition, on the other.[1]

Surveying the landscape of urban studies at this pivotal moment, *Shaking Up the City* tackles many of these issues head on and sounds an urgent clarion call for *epistemic reflexivity*, that is, the critical examination of the core categories, questions, methodological moves, and discursive tropes informing scholarly and policy debates on the metropolis. Where do the problems that urban sociologists, geographers, and economists pose come from? Why do they pose them in just these terms? What symbolic forces and institutional processes cause them to diffuse across the academic field and become hegemonic topics, absorbing disproportionate research funding, brain power, and administrative resources? What are the questions that students of the city *could* be raising instead with a different set of theoretical constructs and observational foci? Finally, moving into the normative register, what are the issues urban scholars *should* be articulating, based not only on a more sober and independent assessment of social trends and historical transformation, but also on grounds of social justice in the city? (Fainstein 2010).

Slater's treatment of the moral panic around the "sink estate" and its policy consequences is methodologically exemplary in these respects. Instead of deploying the notion to capture the devolution of social housing or settling for a moral critique of its negative connotations, he queries its origins, painstakingly retraces its trajectory, and maps out its semantic range and uses by cultural elites and state managers. Charting the travels and travails of the sink estate from the science of ethology to journalism to the world of think tanks, philanthrocapitalists, and policy makers, and back into scholarly discourse allows Slater to demonstrate that this construct is, properly speaking, not a scientific category but a *social categoreme*, that is, an instrument of public accusation that skews both science and policy: science by fixating the scholarly gaze on the estate itself at the expense of locating it in the structure of objective positions in symbolic, social, and physical space that makes up the city; and policy by fostering programs of demolition of social housing and geographic dispersal of the poor that disregard the social fabric of their existence and treat their neighborhoods, anthropomorphized as so many urban bogeymen, as the self-standing cause of their social predicament. Moreover, it emerges from this genealogy that the symbolic denigration of public housing and its residents partakes of a broader discourse of devaluation of the *public*, the collective, the common, and thence of the state as the institutional incarnation and guardian of the *urban commons* (Stavrides 2016). Indeed, many of the categories in the reigning lingua franca spoken by fashionable urban scholars and au courant city policy analysts and decision makers is stamped by an overt or covert antistatism that bespeaks the corroding influence of neoliberal thinking.

The rich case studies in the politics of urban constructs that compose this book converge to remind us of what should be the first commandment of every working social scientist: *thou shalt construct thy own concepts and formulate thy own problematic*, instead of borrowing ready-made notions and social problems prepackaged by policy experts and government elites. They also suggest that one should be especially wary of the importation of language from the natural into the social sciences, as with the falsely neutral notion of urban "resilience." The idiom of nature has for inescapable effect the paradoxical *dehistoricization* of historical reality and the *elision* of the relations of material and symbolic power that constitute the city as the site of accumulation, differentiation, and contestation of capital in its different forms (and not just economic capital, as Tom Slater would have it). The deft theoretical move whereby Slater joins Robert Proctor's agnotology, the historical science of the fabrication of collective ignorance, with Pierre Bourdieu's theory of symbolic power, the sociology of the realization of categories, gives us the necessary tools to thwart this danger.

But the effort to free ourselves from policy fads and academic bandwagons and to avoid the deadly *lemming effect* that has struck urban studies over the past few decades, enticing so many students of the metropolis to jump with bravado from the "underclass" to the "creative class," from "gentrification" to "revitalization," and from "resilience" to "data-driven innovation," will only succeed if it is a collective endeavor, carried out by a community of scholars committed to helping one another forge and keep their intellectual tools clean, so that they may marry scientific rigor and civic relevance without ceding to political subservience (Bourdieu [2001] 2004).

Berkeley, December 2020

Acknowledgments

This book is a synthesis of over twenty years of research and teaching in the field of critical urban studies. I am very grateful to Naomi Schneider for approaching me to write such a book, for her confidence in my work, and for her remarkable patience. Naomi's editorial assistant, Summer Farah, has been wonderfully efficient and kind throughout. I also want to acknowledge the remarkable work of the wonderfully eagle-eyed copyeditor, Sharon Langworthy.

It would not have been possible for me to write this book without the support and kindness of many friends and comrades all over the world, and it is a pleasure to acknowledge them here. Marsha Henry and Paul Higate helped me survive over five years in a thoroughly bizarre and unsettling policy studies department at the University of Bristol from 2003 to 2008. They are both very special to me. From 2008 to date, I would not have coped in a very challenging workplace without my dear friends and colleagues Jan Penrose and Julie Cupples. Jan is the consummate teacher and brilliant scholar, whose enormous generosity (not least in drams!), integrity, and friendship mean more to me than I could possibly express. Julie always inspires me to fight the neoliberal university and geoscientization, rather than succumb to or retreat from such exhausting problems.

Her awesome knowledge of feminist, critical race, and decolonial theory (and praxis) has opened my eyes to what a truly global and critical urban studies might look like. The Cape Town field course that Jan, Julie, and I devised and teach together has become a highlight of my professional life.

Thank you to Simon Kelley for improving conditions at the workplace, and especially for granting me overdue sabbatical leave when others would not. Hamish Kallin, formerly my undergraduate, master's, and PhD student, and now my colleague, has been a joy to work with for so long, and I learn from him all the time. Much of my grasp of the agnotology of rent control in chapter 4 is indebted to him. I also want to thank Eva Panagiotakopulu, Krithika Srinivasan, and Mike Summerfield for demonstrating on multiple occasions what it means to act with integrity in difficult circumstances. Sarah McAllister, Faten Adam, and Rosie Russell believed in my dream to take students to Cape Town annually and played a huge role in making that happen. Thank you also to Duncan Phillips, Paul Thomson, John Binnie, and Colin Kemp for some fantastic times on the Scottish links, miles away from the "pure pish" of academia, and thank you to Ché Moore and Phil Greenwood for nearly forty years of friendship and laughter. Sharon Dunn is a huge inspiration and the most generous and kind friend anyone could ever wish for.

My PhD students over the years have inspired and educated me in ways I am not sure I could ever match in return. They are Paul Kirkness, Junxi Qian, Yunpeng Zhang, Yannick Sudermann, Hamish Kallin, Ioanna Papadopoulou-Korfiati, Emma Saunders, and Eoin Palmer. I must acknowledge all those scholars who allowed me the honor of serving as external examiner of their brilliant PhD work; in reverse chronological order they are Hannah Holmes, Alistair Sisson, Mika Hyötyläinen, Liev Cherry, Gergo Pulay, Csaba Jelinek, Melanie Nowicki, Marieke Krijnen, Marc Morell, Aseygul Can, Viktoria Vona, Debbie Humphry, Lidia Manzo, Tom Gillespie, Antonis Vradis, and Lee Crookes. Literally thousands of undergraduates and master's students over nearly two decades and across two institutions have attended my lectures and/or interacted with the ideas and materials that constitute this book. While some embraced and deployed those ideas, others took issue with them, and those latter occasions were when I learned the most as a teacher and scholar.

During the 2018–19 academic year I was fortunate to secure two visiting fellowships, where many of the arguments in this book were clarified. At the University of Cape Town, I will never forget the warmth of Sophie Oldfield, Gareth Haysom, and especially, Tanja Winkler. Tanja's immensely kind and beautiful soul helped me recover from some bruising times in Edinburgh *and* remember what matters most. She is such an inspiring example of a passionate, dedicated teacher and scholar. At the University of Chile, Ernesto Lopez-Morales is a longtime friend and comrade in the battle to imagine a world after neoliberal urbanism, and along with the leaders of COES, Dante Contreras and Maria-Luisa Mendez, provided me with a supportive institutional base.

Ever since I made the questionable decision to pursue an academic life, it has been a privilege to encounter some remarkable scholars (in addition to those already mentioned), who have not only taught me a great deal but consistently offered words of encouragement and support. They are (and I am so sorry if I have forgotten anyone!): Manuel Aalbers, Abel Albet, Alfredo Alietti, Jorge Omar Amado, Ntsiki Anderson, Isabelle Anguelovski, Sonia Arbaci, Martine August, Sara Jane Bailes, Nuria Benach, Lawrence Berg, Matthias Bernt, Nick Blomley, Katherine Brickell, Gavin Brown, Alice Butler, Felicity Callard, Brett Christophers, Eric Clark, Anne Clerval, Veronica Crossa, Steve Crossley, Winifred Curran, Martina Cvajner, Mark Davidson, Jonathan Davies, James DeFilippis, Kristian Nagel Delica, Jatinder Dhillon, Nick Dines, Joe Doherty, Rowan Ellis, Akwugo Emejulu, Mary Gilmartin, Giovanna Gioli, Kevin Glynn, Sara Gonzalez, Kanishka Goonewardena, Sarah Green, Neil Gray, the late great Anne Haila, Dan Hammel, Anders Lund Hansen, Stuart Hodkinson, David Howard, David Hulchanski, David Imbroscio, William Jenkins, Tracey Jensen, Paul Jones, Sinead Kelly, Rob Kitchin, Tuna Kuyucu, Bob Lake, Henrik Gutson Larsen, Troels Schultz Larsen, Phil Lawton, David Ley, Rob MacDonald, Kate Maclean, Gordon Macleod, Gordon Maloney, David Manley, Jose Mansilla, Peter Marcuse, Miguel Martinez, Jon May, Margit Mayer, Heather McLean, Zoe Meletis, Luis Mendes, Nate Millington, Don Mitchell, Gerry Mooney, John Morrissey, David Nally, Kathe Newman, Cian O'Callahan, the late great Phil O'Keefe, Eoin O'Mahony, Martin O'Neill, Kris Olds, Sue Parnell, Kirsteen Paton, Rob Penfold,

Stefano Portelli, Libby Porter, Martin Power, Joao Queiros, Dallas Rogers, Damaris Rose, Javier Ruiz-Tagle, Kanchana Ruwanpura, Bahar Sakizlioglu, Graham Scambler, Ted Schrecker, Giuseppe Sciortino, Kate Shaw, Hyun Shin, Dan Silver, Bev Skeggs, Susan Smith, Susanne Soederberg, Ebru Soytemel, Kate Swanson, Catharina Thörn, Mario Trifuoggi, Imogen Tyler, Justus Uitermark, Mathieu van Criekingen, Michiel van Meeteren, David Wachsmuth, Alan Walks, Paul Watt, John Western, and Carolyn Whitzman.

When Joe Schaffers showed me around the ruins of District Six, Cape Town, in April 2004, neither of us could have imagined what it would lead to. When we met again in April 2016, it was the start of a memorable and ongoing pedagogical collaboration. It is a massive privilege to know Joe, to watch a master of the educational craft, and to learn so much from him about so many of the issues in this book. Jo-Anne Schaffers is a wonderful soul who has enriched my life immensely in the short time we have been friends. Loretta Lees got me started in academia a long time ago and has always been a very supportive friend and ally. Javier Auyero, Virgilio Borges Pereira, Neil Brenner, and David Madden are four of the most enthusiastic, supportive, and kind scholars anywhere, and their consistent intellectual generosity before and during the process of writing this book has been a source of great strength. The same goes for Elvin Wyly, a great friend, role model, and shining example of how studying the histories of ideas and methodologies has massive relevance in the fight for a better world. Loïc Wacquant is an incomparable mentor, a sharp yet fantastically supportive critic, and truly an intellectual inspiration. Neil Smith has his awesome fingerprints all over this book and my academic life, and even though he never feels very far away, his support is so greatly missed. I hope Neil would have approved of how I tried to follow my "instinct, guts, politics" in this book. The final academic acknowledgment must go to David M. Smith, my undergraduate teacher at Queen Mary's geography department. How lucky I was to have my entire life changed by David's astounding lectures and brilliant writings, and by his August Losch–inspired insistence that "the real duty . . . is not to explain our sorry reality, but to improve it." Delivering in November 2016 the annual lecture that carries David's name will always be the greatest honor of my career.

My parents, Sue and John, and my sister Holly (and her family) have always been so interested in and supportive of anything that I do in my life; together with their unconditional love, a son and a brother could not ask for more. Finally, thank you to Sara, Zach, and our dogs (past and present) for somehow tolerating my forgetful, sleep-deprived and absent-minded self, for all the moments of joy in the beautiful landscapes of East Lothian, but above all, for their patience and love.

.   .   .   .   .

Some of the chapters in this book are substantially revised and extended treatments of working texts published at different stages in the advancement of the research. These are the original sources:

Chapter 2: "Rent Gaps." In *The Handbook of Gentrification Studies*, edited by Loretta Lees with Martin Phillips, 119–33. London: Elgar, 2018.

Chapter 3: "Unravelling False Choice Urbanism." *CITY* 18, no. 4–5 (2014): 517–24; and "Planetary Rent Gaps," *Antipode* 49, no. 1 (2017): 114–37.

Chapter 4: "The Myths and Realities of Rent Control." In *Rent and Its Discontents: A Century of Housing Struggles*, edited by Neil Gray, 139–52. London: Rowman & Littlefield, 2018 (with Hamish Kallin).

Chapter 5: "Your Life Chances Affect Where You Live: A Critique of the 'Cottage Industry' of Neighbourhood Effects Research." *International Journal of Urban and Regional Research* 37, no. 2 (2013): 367–87.

Chapter 6: "The Invention of the 'Sink Estate': Consequential Categorization and the UK Housing Crisis." *Sociological Review* 66, no. 4 (2018): 877–97.

Chapter 7: "The Reputational Ghetto: Territorial Stigmatisation in St. Paul's, Bristol." *Transactions of the Institute of British Geographers* 37, no. 4 (2012): 530–46 (with Ntsiki Anderson).

1 Challenging the Heteronomy of Urban Research

If you're unwilling to muster the courage to think critically, then someone will do the thinking for you, offering double-think and doubletalk relief.

Cornel West (2008, 9)

At a time when doublethink and doubletalk relief are very widespread, this book responds in the form of a double move. It addresses the causal mechanisms behind urban inequalities, material deprivation, marginality, and social suffering in cities across several international contexts, and while doing so, it scrutinizes how knowledge (and all too often *ignorance*) on these issues is produced by a range of urban actors (such as intellectuals, policy officials, journalists, planners, urban designers, think tank writers, and economists writing for popular audiences). The motivation for this double move is not only the urgent problem of widening urban inequalities, but also the striking deficit of collective intellectual reflection on the social and political organization of urban research. The allure of fashionable concepts and policy buzzwords (e.g., *resilient cities*, *regeneration*, *smart cities*, and *placemaking*), and especially the worries of politicians, business leaders, university leaders, and the mainstream media, has meant that urban scholarship often fails to call into question the prefabricated problematics and imposed categories of urban policy. This has led to analytic neglect of the changing balance of state structures and institutional arrangements that shape, and in turn are shaped by, the evolution of capitalist urbanization.

Throughout this book I offer many examples of urban buzzwords in action, but for now let's consider *placemaking*, which has become something of a cottage industry among architects, "sustainable" urban designers, neoclassical urban economists, policy officials, and urban planning gurus. Many of those involved display a near-evangelical belief in the physical appearance and feel of neighborhoods, parks, and streets as the principal determinants of economic and social life in them (not vice versa), and that the way to address all existing and future urban problems is via engaging local communities in hands-on placemaking (i.e., facilitating urban design and functional use from the ground up). One illustration comes from New York City and the Project for Public Spaces (PPS), founded in 1975 to mobilize the visions of celebrated urbanists Jane Jacobs and William H. Whyte vis-à-vis what makes for "livable" neighborhoods and "inviting" public spaces. Building on the commercial success of its 1980s transformation of Bryant Park in Midtown Manhattan, PPS has grown into a hugely influential organization working in all fifty states in the United States, with a set of values that have spread very widely on a global scale (policy makers in multiple international contexts, too numerous to list, have jumped on the placemaking bandwagon). The PPS is guided by a conviction that "a strong sense of place can influence the physical, social, emotional, and ecological health of individuals and communities everywhere" (Project for Public Spaces n.d.). Upon reading some PPS pronouncements, it is easy to see why its notion of placemaking has traveled so widely: "When people of all ages, abilities, and socio-economic backgrounds can not only access and enjoy a place, but also play a key role in its identity, creation, and maintenance, that is when we see genuine placemaking in action."

At first glance, such a scenario seems impossible to dislike. But on closer inspection, although placemaking is usually rolled out through a notion of people-centered inclusivity, what often emerges is a process that disavows the realities of politics and power in which it is embedded (Montgomery 2016). There are uncomfortable parallels with colonialism: in any context where placemaking is planned, *what if there is a place already there*, one to which residents might be deeply attached and might not want transformed? What if local communities take exception to external placemaking professionals arriving and engaging them in a process they never wanted in the first place? It is well documented that placemaking can be deeply undemocratic and dismissive of resistance and can amount to a strategy of *placebreaking* to serve vested interests (MacLeod 2013). On a structural and institutional level, who stands to reap the financial rewards that an attractive new place might bring, and at whose expense? Place-making normalizes, if not naturalizes, the claims of particular institutions with profit interests in urban land and real estate and reframes them as if in the urban public interest. For instance, in 2017 CBRE (the world's largest commercial real estate services company) and Gehl Architects authored a document entitled *Placemaking: Value and the Public Realm*, which opened with the following: "Placemaking happens when buildings are transformed into vibrant urban spaces that offer wellbeing, pleasure and inspiration. Its success can be measured by improved lives, greater happiness and, when done successfully, an uplift in property values."[1]

Furthermore, people's experiences of urban life are not solely deter-mined by the appearance and vibrancy of the public spaces they use. They are determined, to a far greater extent, by people's ability to make a life in the city. Concerns over making rent (harder when there is an "uplift in property values"), feeding your family, accessing health care, childcare, and a reliable network of support are of much more immediate impor-tance than the appearance and vibrancy of public spaces. For policy elites, embracing and trumpeting placemaking as a panacea for all urban prob-lems is a very convenient way to sidestep the difficulties of addressing material deprivation. Grassroots struggles and social movements tend not to march to city hall with banners demanding placemaking as an end to their problems. Their cries and demands are for much more profound changes.

This book, therefore, articulates a critical approach to urban studies that *guards against the subordination of scholarly to policy agendas* and weds epistemological critique with social critique, with a view to opening up alternatives and formulating research-driven ideas, as a counterpoint to mainstream, policy-driven approaches to urban research. It goes against the grain of established research orthodoxies to dissect multiple aspects of urban division, to diagnose and challenge the hegemonic economic and political order of the metropolis, and to critique the categories of urban research that serve the interests of state elites and big business. This approach is nourished by a combination of abstract theory and concrete empirical evidence from multiple sources and across multiple urban contexts to critique existing conceptual formulations—while extending and advancing what I see as more helpful ones—vis-à-vis the themes of urban "resilience," gentrification, displacement and rent control, "neighborhood effects," territorial stigma, and ethnoracial segregation.

In the pages that follow, I take aim at a fast-moving and expanding target: the *heteronomy of urban research*. At first glance this may seem like abstruse academic jargon, but it is really rather simple: it refers to the condition of scholars being constrained in asking their own questions about urbanization, instead asking questions and using categories invented, escalated, and imposed by various institutions that have vested interests in influencing what is off and on the urban agenda. These institutions range from major arms of the state to philanthropic foundations, to university research centers, to urban design consultancies, to think tanks across the political spectrum. In the next section I provide a detailed example of heteronomy in action by focusing on the explosive growth of recent interest in "urban science" prioritizing "data-driven innovation." But for now, it is important to note that the heteronomy of urban research is not a brand new development. It was present in rounds of twentieth-century urbanization, for instance during the Fordist-Keynesian era and its subsequent mutation into post-Fordist entrepreneurialism. But why has it expanded and intensified in the twenty-first century? Given the enormous pressures on university finances (which are the outcome not just of state disinvestment in higher education but also of the warped priorities of university leaders), scholars are under greater pressure than ever before to secure substantial external research funding, and it is frequently to government funding bodies that many apply. The result is the rise of *policy-driven research at the expense of research-driven policy*, and with it, *decision-based evidence making at the expense of evidence-based decision making*. Within the field of urban studies and in public debates outside it, what has been emerging for some time now is what we might call a *vested interest urbanism*. This book is a critical response in the form of an analytic intervention, one that is positioned against the prevailing political wind: the steady erosion of intellectual autonomy. This seems necessary because the moment that we cannot ask our own questions about cities due to the priorities of the state (which are all too often in dialogue with the priorities of big business), what we are doing ceases to be research and becomes propaganda.

The ethical problem of heteronomy versus autonomy has a long history that predates urban studies. In moral philosophy, the problem stretches back to Jean-Jacques Rousseau (1712–78), who saw most of his contemporary philosophers as little more than rationalizers of self-interest and spent considerable time arguing that personal autonomy is achievable "only if citizens surrender part of their status as individuals and think of their social membership as essential, not merely accidental, to who they are" (Neuhouser 2011, 478). Rousseau's famous liberal musings on the formation of this social contract informed the writings of Immanuel Kant, who argued that possessing autonomy of the will is a necessary condition of moral agency (his overriding goal being to explain what autonomous moral reasoning would look like). He argued that in contrast to an autonomous will, a heteronomous will is one of obedience to rules of action that have been legislated externally to it, and the moral obligations it proposes cannot therefore be regarded as binding upon the person(s) being obedient. Kant presented an understanding of heteronomy as something that precluded any sustained consideration of where such obedience stems from in the first place, which was, for him, a poor foundation for ethical reasoning.

Much more helpful in thinking through the *political* ramifications of autonomy and heteronomy are the writings of Pierre Bourdieu in the field of cultural production. Bourdieu analyzed societies as consisting of a series of fields in which people jostle for status and control vis-à-vis the economic, social, cultural, and symbolic capital at stake in the particular field. For instance, Bourdieu (1993, 1996a) described the field of cultural production (arts, music, television, film, etc.) as having autonomous and heteronomous poles. Taking the example of the arts, he explained how, as they gain distance from political, economic, and religious dictates, they become rich in symbolic capital but poor in economic capital. Producers in the field struggle among each other to accumulate symbolic capital such as prestige, with those showing a deep commitment to art for art's sake (or "restricted production," as Bourdieu put it) gaining the most status. Such a commitment is "founded on the obligatory recognition of the values of disinterestedness and on the denigration of the "economy" (of the 'commercial')" (Bourdieu 1996a, 142). He argued that this was an inversion of practices occurring in the economic field:

> In the most perfectly autonomous sector of the field of cultural production, where the only audience aimed at is other producers . . . the economy of practices is based, as in a generalized game of "loser wins," on a systematic inversion of the fundamental principles of all ordinary economies: that of business (it excludes the pursuit of profit and does not guarantee any sort of correspondence between investments and monetary gains). (Bourdieu 1993, 39)

By contrast, Bourdieu defined the heteronomous pole of the field of cultural production as one that is ruled by commercial and business interests. To Bourdieu, heteronomous arts range from the "bourgeois arts," which sell to and gain a following among more privileged social classes, to lowbrow commercial works, or "industrial arts." These are poorer in status than the autonomous arts but much richer in economic capital (or in the potential to accumulate it).

Bourdieu's student and collaborator Loïc Wacquant has expanded this understanding of heteronomy as deriving from penetration by commercial interests to include a consideration of penetration by the *state*.[2] When responding to and extending the argument of a paper I wrote many years ago on the eviction of critical perspectives from gentrification research (Slater 2006), Wacquant pointed to the "growing subservience of urban research to the concerns, categories and moods of policy- and opinion-makers," where intellectual inquiry is "guided primarily by the priorities of state managers and the worries of the mainstream media" (2008a, 200–201). He offers several examples of this, including this particularly powerful one:

> In France, the Netherlands, Germany and Belgium, political tensions around postcolonial immigration and the deterioration of public housing have fueled a wave of studies and policy evaluation programmes on "neighborhood mixing," "community-building" and crime-fighting centered on working-class neighborhoods, but studiously avoiding the socioeconomic underpinnings of urban degradation, in keeping with the design of politicians to deploy territory, ethnicity and insecurity as screens to obscure the desocialization of wage labor and its impact on the life strategies and spaces of the emerging proletariat. (201)

As I demonstrate in several chapters of this book, what Wacquant calls "the common malady of heteronomy" (201) that afflicts urban research has strengthened over the years since he penned those words. A great deal of urban scholarship has not resisted the "seductions of the prefabricated problematics of policy," nor has it advanced what Wacquant hoped for: "research agendas sporting greater separation from the imperatives of city rulers and carrying a higher theoretical payload" (203). Instead, political and media worries and the funding bandwagons they create appear irresistible to many urban scholars, especially the institutions that employ them. The moral philosopher Christine Korsgaard contended, "When you are motivated autonomously, you act on a law that you give to yourself; when you act heteronomously, the law is imposed on you by means of a sanction" (1996, 22). If we replace *law* with *concept*, her contention applies to much contemporary thinking about cities, and intervening in this state of affairs is what, I hope, animates much of the analysis in the pages of this book.

This is not to say that the pendulum between autonomy and heteronomy has become firmly and irretrievably stuck on the latter. Critical urban studies, as a multidisciplinary field combining multiple theoretical approaches and methodologies, is very vibrant and ensures that a tug of war is underway between autonomous and heteronomous approaches. It is simply that, at the moment, the heteronomous side is pulling harder. Helga Leitner and Eric Sheppard (2013, 516) provided a helpful definition of critical approaches to the urban question as "presaged on a vigilant examination and critique of the logic and assumptions underlying preexisting mainstream theoretical accounts of cities, narratives of urban process and urban life, and the urban policies reflecting these." In the same article they were quick to caution against "othering the mainstream," which they felt might "undermine the vitality of critical urban geographic knowledge production" (517). They saw the mainstream as quantitative urban scholarship in the positivist tradition of validity, reliability, replicability, verification, and falsification, the knowledge produced by which, they felt, could not be glibly dismissed as lacking in radical potential, an argument subsequently extended by Elvin Wyly (2011) in a riveting essay tellingly entitled "Positively Radical." I have much sympathy with this argument, and rather too many scholars identifying as critical are quick to shun quantitative analysis as positivist/empiricist number crunching without delving into the details or the findings that statistical analyses produce (the majestic work of the Radical Statistics Group over four decades being a case in point).[3] I see the "mainstream" as something characterized not by methodology, but rather by an *atheoretical, unquestioning embrace of the structural and institutional conditions (and concepts and categories) favored by city rulers and the profiteering interests surrounding them.*

Over a decade ago, in introducing a special issue of the journal *CITY* entitled "Cities for People, Not for Profit," Neil Brenner, Peter Marcuse, and Margit Mayer (2009, 179) offered a helpful articulation of five core concerns of a critical urban studies:

- To analyze the systemic, historically specific, intersections between capitalism and urban processes;
- To examine the changing balance of social forces, power relations, sociospatial inequalities and political-institutional arrangements that shape, and in turn are shaped by, the evolution of capitalist urbanization;
- To expose the marginalizations, exclusions, and injustices (whether of class, ethnicity, "race," gender, sexuality, nationality, or otherwise) that are inscribed and naturalized within existing urban configurations;
- To decipher the contradictions, crisis tendencies, and lines of potential or actual conflict within contemporary cities, and on this basis;
- To demarcate and to politicize the strategically essential possibilities for more progressive, socially just, emancipatory, and sustainable formations for urban life.

This is by no means an exhaustive list, and the authors acknowledged that fact, saying that critical urban studies is not "a homogenous research field based on a rigidly orthodox or paradigmatic foundation." However, this list of concerns does help identify a distinctively critical branch of thinking about cities that "can be usefully counterposed to 'mainstream' or 'traditional' approaches to urban questions" (179). To this I would add that it can be usefully counterposed to heteronomous approaches, which leave unquestioned and sometimes even thrive upon the structural and systemic problems that lie behind the stubborn inequalities in cities of the twenty-first century. A clear example of an emerging heteronomous approach is the recent interest in "urban science," to which I now turn.

THE FALSE PROMISES OF "URBAN SCIENCE"

In June 2018 the Department of Urban Studies and Planning at the Massachusetts Institute of Technology (MIT) tweeted that it had "discovered a new kind of science" when announcing the launch of "a novel sort of program": an undergraduate major in "urban science." The tweet was in fact a quote from an article in *Wired* (a magazine focusing on digital technologies vis-à-vis society, culture, and the economy), which celebrated MIT's new program as one in which students would "examine patterns mined from data, explain them in ways any urban dweller can understand, and transform them into effective, helpful policy—the guidelines that make cities go" (Marshall 2018). The message from both MIT and *Wired* was that teaching students to analyze urban "big data" would have genuine benefits for policy, planning, and practice in urban communities, as it would lead to "an increased supply of workers—the kids who are interested in civics and willing to go through the urban programs and then fan out into city governments." The *Wired* article also referred to similar new programs in other universities across the United States, barely containing its excitement that informatics students across the country might start thinking about the wider implications of their work, guided by instructors asking them: "How do you create a good citizen *and* a good computer scientist?"

It did not take long for the MIT tweet to generate backlash in the form of a staggering range of tweeted responses from urban scholars all over the world, with a vast majority angered that a prestigious academic institution could claim, with colonialist arrogance, to have "discovered" a field of study that has existed for well over one hundred years. The scientific study of cities is not a new development. Perhaps more powerful still were the responses of scholars who were distressed by the increasing hard scientization and data-driven obsessions of a multidisciplinary field, to the elision of theory and the exclusion of all other existing approaches, methodologies, and forms of knowledge within that field. For instance, the urban geographer Ayona Datta, a renowned critical analyst of "smart city" boosterism, tweeted eloquently on July 3, 2018: "The 'urban' is not 'science'. It cannot be measured, replicated and forecast like other sciences. The urban is an imaginary, a relationship between multiple spaces and scales from the personal to the global, a site of politics and governance. The urban is much more than 'science.'" MIT chose not to respond to any of the tweets—perhaps having achieved its publicity goals—and the program admitted its first cohort of students in the fall of 2018.

The hype surrounding the relationship between big data analytics and cities, and the central role of universities in it, is certainly not limited to the United States. In 2017 the university where I work signed the Edinburgh and South East Scotland City Region Deal and became a major institutional player in a strategy to "identify new and more collaborative ways that partners will work with the UK Government and Scottish Governments to deliver transformational change to the city regional economy" (City Region Deal n.d.). The City Region, in the eyes of those behind the deal, comprises six local government authorities, containing a total of 25 percent of the Scottish population. The deal was justified along two fronts, first, to "accelerate economic growth through the funding of its infrastructure, skills, and innovation" (City Region Deal n.d.), and second, because "prosperity and success is [sic] not universal across the city region. 22.4% of children are living in poverty; there is a lack of mid-market and affordable housing; and too many people are unable to move on from low wage/low skill jobs. The City Region Deal will address these issues" (City Region Deal n.d.) Very substantial sums of money are behind this deal, which was announced during a protracted period of austerity that caused enormous misery. The UK and Scottish governments will each invest £300 million over fifteen years, and numerous regional partners (a mix of public, private, and third sector organizations) committed to adding more than £700 million over the same time frame. The money is to be spread unevenly across five themes: research, development, and innovation (receiving well over half the total investment); employability and skills; transport; culture; and housing.

The University of Edinburgh's involvement (and stated aim) in this deal is "to work with partners to establish the region as the *data capital of Europe*, attracting investment, fuelling entrepreneurship and delivering inclusive growth" (University of Edinburgh n.d.). Boasting about its "world-leading expertise in data science," the university claims that it wants to "help all citizens adapt to the data economy," including "less advantaged groups," for whom it aims "to develop skills and employability, and increase their potential to access good career opportunities." The overarching message that comes from all the deal documentation and public statements across government, private, and higher education sectors—in the form of what can only be described as a declamatory bombardment—is that "data science" is the solution for poverty, inequality, and disadvantage in the City Region, all of which are apparently due to a lack of data innovation and digital skills among people who have been left behind by the "data revolution." For example, under the heading "Let's Unlock Growth," the university argues that there is "a digital skills gap that is holding back growth" in the City Region. The key to unlocking growth, apparently, can be found in producing "an extra 12,800 workers each year with digital skills." These workers will be central to a "Data-Driven Innovation (DDI)" strategy, to "harness the economic, social and scientific benefits of data . . . ensuring the benefits are shared across the whole city region" (University of Edinburgh n.d.)

To provide various home bases for this data science, the university is currently creating a range of new research institutes, one of which is the jazzily named Edinburgh Futures Institute (EFI), "a global centre for multidisciplinary, challenge-based DDI research, teaching and societal impact" that will "provide thought-leadership in cultural, ethical, managerial, political, social and technological DDI issues, and help to transform the application, governance and benefits delivered from the use of data" (housed in a very expensively refurbished old hospital building scheduled to be opened in 2021, part of the university's increasingly grand real estate and rent-seeking ambitions). The EFI website states in rather nebulous fashion that it will "assemble experts who can tackle issues from different and unconventional perspectives, gathering many hands to untangle the world's knottiest problems" (Edinburgh Futures Institute n.d.). As I write these words in 2020, I have just received a circular email asking academics for secondment proposals to develop postgraduate teaching programs that are "data fluent" and will equip students with the skills needed to develop insights from computational data, in which ideal candidates are those who understand that the future trajectory of their discipline lies in data technologies and the "data society."

There can be no doubt that basic digital skills are important to acquire, and it is equally important that students interested in working with more advanced techniques to sift and sort through massive data sets related to urban issues have the opportunity to do so. Furthermore, the analysis of big data, as it has become known, when theoretically informed and cognizant of disciplinary histories and complementary approaches to the urban question, can lead to all sorts of fascinating and important insights into urban problems (perhaps best exemplified by the work of Rob Kitchin and colleagues in a large research project entitled The Programmable City).[4] But the matter of great concern is that university managers and senior science professors in several countries are bleating about discovering a new urban science, yet when we take the trouble to look closely, it is one that is robbed of its historical and intellectual context, emptied of its sociological contents, and a very particular and *exclusive* vision of what the study of cities should be.

They are doing this not only out of scientific interest, but because vast sums of money can be extracted by universities from governments and large corporations that are themselves motivated by the fast extraction of more money ("accelerated growth"). This vision of urban studies is thoroughly geared to the interests of profit, yet dressed up as being for the benefit of all urban dwellers, or "to leave no person behind," according to the convenor of the City Region Deal's decision-making body (City Region Deal n.d.). "Data-driven innovation" on urban issues, to the policy elite and business leader, is a way of producing knowledge to grease the engines of capital accumulation and circulation and a way of producing workers trained to believe that all urban problems—housing affordability, transportation maladies, environmental degradation, unemployment, ethnic segregation and so on—will be solved by crunching the data. Simply put, what disappears in the hype over data-driven innovation are the *relations of power* in and over space that constitute a city, about which *nobody* is proposing to build big data.

A much darker side to data-driven innovation has recently been subjected to a blistering and elegant critique in an article by the anthropologist Shannon Mattern (2018). Focusing on similar DDI university initiatives in the United States and trawling through the hyperbole surrounding them, she takes down the big data/artificial intelligence mantra, "With a sufficiently large dataset we can find meaning even without a theoretical framework or scientific method." Placing these initiatives in their historical context (medical scientists have long harbored ambitions to quantify the human/urban condition), Mattern is skeptical of "the blind faith that ubiquitous data collection will lead to discoveries that will benefit everyone" and demonstrates that many large-scale empirical studies actually *reinforce* urban inequalities when they are not grounded in specific hypotheses and without any theoretical or conceptual guidance, for most of these studies never articulate what class, race, gender, and culture actually mean and how such definitions are shaped by social and political forces. Even more disturbing is how data-driven models are increasingly used in law enforcement and "predictive policing," as well as how conclusions about future criminality drawn from observed correlations—never theorized nor historicized, and from data sets with high error rates riddled with demographic bias—have led to court and police decisions that further stigmatize, marginalize, and punish vulnerable urban dwellers and the neighborhoods where they reside:

> Biology, behavior, culture, history, and environment are thus reduced to dots on a map. End users don't know which agencies supplied the underlying intelligence and how their interests shaped data collection. They can't ask questions about how social and environmental categories are operationalized in the different data sets. They can't determine whether data reinscribe historical biases and injustices. (Mattern 2018)

These developments have also been exposed and critiqued by Virginia Eubanks in *Automating Inequality*. As she explains, marginalized groups

> face higher levels of data collection when they access public benefits, walk through highly policed neighbourhoods, enter the health-care system, or cross national borders. That data acts to reinforce their marginality when it is used to target them for suspicion and extra scrutiny. Those groups seen as undeserving are singled out for punitive public policy and more intense surveillance, and the cycle begins again. (Eubanks 2017, 7)

Eubanks calls this a "feedback loop of injustice" and is absolutely clear that the driving force behind it is the new regime of digital data that we all live under but are affected by to very different degrees depending on class, income and (especially in the United States—the context in which Eubanks researches) race. Perhaps most impressively, Eubanks's analysis is grounded in a deep understanding of the history of surveillance of (and punitive policies toward) the poor, and when considering her wealth of case study material on how the new age of databases, equations, predictive algorithms, and risk models curbs the life chances of already marginalized people, she argues that what has emerged is a "digital poorhouse" that encages and entraps today's poor.[5] This new poorhouse bears striking similarities to the poorhouses of the nineteenth century, in that it is undergirded by stigmatizing views of the poor as undeserving, dependent, immoral, and dangerous. Against the hype surrounding the "innovative solutions" of the urban big data age, with its grand promises of alleviating poverty, Eubanks demonstrates compellingly how "the new regime of data analytics is more evolution than revolution . . . simply an expansion and continuation of moralistic and punitive poverty management strategies that have been with us since the 1820s" (37).

The advancement of *urban science* as a catchall term for the intellectual scrutiny and solution of urban problems—regardless of all the disciplines that constitute urban studies as we know it—recently received promotion and validation via the formation and output of an expert panel on science and the future of cities endorsed by the august science journal *Nature Sustainability* (a subsidiary publication of *Nature*). The panel emerged from discussions that took place in October 2016 at the Habitat III summit in Quito, where the United Nations New Urban Agenda was launched. Before and during that conference, there was wide concern about something of a disconnect between science and policy vis-à-vis the major challenges facing cities, so the expert panel was formed to assess, encourage reform of, and offer independent advice on "the global state of the urban science-policy interface." The panel was cochaired by Michele Acuto, Susan Parnell, and Karen Seto, and together they assembled a further twenty-six eminent urban scholars from all over the world. They are undoubtedly shrewd and dynamic scholars, the work of many of whom I have admired and respected for a long time, from a wide variety of disciplines spanning the natural sciences, social sciences, humanities, architecture and planning, engineering, and computer and environmental science. In addition to meeting as one panel several times, the cochairs conducted interviews with each individual panelist. The results of these discussions were published as a report with the same title as the panel, which begins with a foreword entitled "For a Global Urban Science."

The immediate question that any nonscientist reader might ask is how a panel with such wide disciplinary expertise well beyond the sciences could subsume all this expertise under a global urban *science*: "The urban science we advocate here for is a cross-cutting field of engagement across different urban disciplines" (IEP 2018, 3). The report is in fact a very odd and inconsistent document. Admirably, it is upfront that urban science is a "loaded term" that prompts "self-critique of the way we develop knowledge about cities" (22). Mercifully, the report departs from the claims and tone of university marketing teams by noting that the scientific study of cities has a long and rich history. But then this peculiar statement appears:

> The panel, mindful of the limits and problematic associations that the term urban science invokes, cautiously endorsed a call for a 'global' urban science, not as merger or flattening of the messages from across diverse constituencies, but as field of collaboration that would open up new frontiers of inquiry and new audiences with more leverage on policy. (22)

But labeling the scholarship of humanists and even qualitative social scientists as urban science is not to flatten but to *trample* all over the enormous intellectual, analytical, methodological, and often political differences that exist between those scholars and natural science scholars. This is hardly a conducive point of departure for collaboration. It is worth imagining, for one moment, what the reaction would be if the work of natural scientists on urban questions was labeled "urban humanities" by an expert panel.

Reading on, it is difficult to avoid the conclusion that the panel felt that using the term *urban science* instead of a more generic *urban studies* would mean that urban scholarship will draw more attention and respect and augment efforts to attract research funding (of a certain sort). In fact, they are quite candid about this:

> The term [urban studies] is however relatively mute in the natural sciences, where in fact 'urban science' might currently have a greater resonance. . . . Pulling together all aspects of urban research and its encompassing areas. . . . under a common banner "urban science," has the potential to be a strong

marking and legitimization of the academic scientific community that produce urban knowledge, in order to shape practice at the local, national and
global scales. (24)

The implication of this highly unfortunate passage is that urban studies—a
term that does not privilege one form of scholarly praxis over another—is a
weak field that *eo ipso* cannot possibly produce adequate urban knowledge
or shape urban practice, at least not without a scientific branding. Far from
celebrating, promoting, and encouraging inquiry across different constit-
uencies, it reads as a surrender to physical/natural science approaches,
one that carries with it an implicit denigration of approaches that are not
somehow "science." In a recent intervention, Ben Derudder and Michiel
van Meeteren (2019, 560) view critiques of data-driven urban science as
counterproductive, arguing that the enormous diversity of approaches to
urban questions means that "there is a need to respect this diversity to its
fullest." They continue with a plea that "actively embracing pluralism needs
to go as far as respecting radically different ontological perspectives, as it is
only through cross-ontological translation skills that we can capitalize on
this diversity" (560). While there is much to admire in this necessary plea
and in the way they call for attention to the history and importance of what
Wyly (2009) refers to as "strategic positivism," it seems to me that Derudder and van Meeteren are going after the wrong target, for "urban science"
attempts to scientize the urban, to the exclusion of the very diversity they
imply critical urban scholars have been disrespecting.

As the expert panel's report proceeds, it becomes increasingly clear that
its de facto remit was to explore how urban scholars might produce practical knowledge for bureaucratic policy application, to facilitate the transition from research to state utility, and to reanimate a positivist project
within urban scholarship. Bizarrely, the interview quotations from the
panelists dotted randomly throughout the report are frequently at odds
with the report text and often highly critical or suspicious of such a remit.
There is an interesting section on confronting fads in urban research such
as smart cities, yet a peculiar lack of awareness among the report's authors
that urban science is one such fad. The report comments that the rise of
an urban data discourse was "perceived by some on the Panel as legitimiz-
ing (and even driving) a very quantitative and data-driven understanding

of cities and urbanization" (IEP 2018, 43), yet this comes after a lengthy barb against "old fashioned individual or narrow disciplinary pursuits" that are deemed "inadequate to deal with the complexity of the urban nexus," meaning that "local actors, especially local governments, often lack usable scientific knowledge about urbanization processes" (19).

Before it was released, the report was distilled into a piece published in *Nature Sustainability* lamenting that much of what is known and taught about cities is "inappropriate or inadequate to meet today's challenges," that "urban knowledge is out-dated and underfunded," that it "tends to rely on selective samples," and that it is "trapped in the twentieth-century tradition of the systematic study of individual cities" (Acuto, Parnell, and Seto 2018, 3). The authors propose "revolutionizing urban research to meet the demands of the twenty-first century" via "efforts towards repro-ducibility (and therefore accountability) in urban research if ultimately we want to produce a balanced and comprehensive knowledge through the collection of diverse topical and geographical data" (4). The keyword here is *ultimately*, and the prioritization of the positivist scientific method could not be clearer. Far from "opening up a systematic and globally ori-ented dialogue across different kinds of expertise" (4), the work of this panel (if the report is an accurate reflection of what was discussed and agreed) may well shut it down, simply by alienating urban scholars who are not scientists or positivists. My point here is not that urban scholars are somehow being brainwashed into doing urban research in a certain way, but rather that it is the structures of funding and the concomitant shape of the urban studies field that establishes the center of gravity around system-conserving concepts like urban science. Quite simply, a huge report on *critical* approaches to twenty-first-century urbanization would not have been funded and promoted in the same way as this urban science report. How individual urban scholars conceive of their own work is less important than the wider structures of careers, funding, and pres-tige, structures that promote particular research approaches and concep-tual schemas as more legitimate and valid ways of doing urban research than any others (and that usually involve disparaging and/or marginal-izing other ways of producing knowledge).

In *The Urban Revolution*, Henri Lefebvre ([1970] 2003, 181) con-cluded his analytic broadside against the professionals, specialists, and technocrats of the urban planning apparatus by tackling the question of urbanism as ideology, which establishes "a repressive space that is represented as objective, scientific and neutral." In particular, notwithstanding some celebrated urban insurrections of the past (and during the time he was writing), Lefebvre was disturbed by the far more common *passivity* among those most affected by large-scale urban planning projects and strategies, and attempted to offer some explanations for widespread political apathy. Most relevant to the foregoing account of the embrace of urban science and data-driven innovation are Lefebvre's remarks on the particular character of urbanism as ideology:

> Ideologically, technically and politically, the quantitative has become rule, norm and value. How can we escape the quantifiable? . . . The qualitative is worn down. Anything that cannot be quantified is eliminated. The generalized terrorism of the quantifiable accentuates the efficiency of repressive space, amplifies it without fear and without reproach, all the more so because of its self-justifying nature (ideo-logic), its apparent scientificity. In this situation, since the quantitative is never seriously questioned, the working class has no scope for political action. In terms of urbanism, it can offer nothing of consequence. (185–86)

The power of today's urban science lies in its strategically deployed rhetoric of reducing inequality, alleviating poverty, accelerating growth, and delivering efficiency, justified by the hyperbole and propaganda surrounding big data and finding eager audiences courtesy of the widespread popular belief in scientific practice and numerical evidence as objective, unbiased, and value free. For their part, leading urban scholars who embrace urban science may well have succumbed to what Bourdieu called the *scientific syndrome*, which he defined as "an attempt by disciplines defined as doubly negative (neither arts nor science) to reverse the situation . . . through the miraculous conjunction of the appearance of scientific rigour with the appearance of literary elegance" (1988, 121). In doing so, those scholars provide academic endorsement for an institutional embrace of urban science and data-driven innovation, one that has all the signs of what Logan and Molotch (2007) called "the same old growth machine with a decorative skin" (p. xx). This is where a constellation of powerful actors work together to ensure that urban development will proceed according to the needs of capital over the needs of people. It is very telling that, notwithstanding the illustrious intellectual pedigree of the panel membership (panelists know the history of the discipline very well; several are central figures in it, and nearly all are on the political left), the only time capitalism is mentioned in the *Science and the Future of Cities* report is in a half-baked concern about the spread of "philanthro-capitalism." The report is utterly silent on the structural conditions and institutional arrangements driving the urban inequalities that, its authors contend, urban science can reduce, and equally silent on how these conditions and arrangements have been studied in a huge literature. Silences are powerful.

CONCEPTUAL GUIDANCE: AGNOTOLOGY AND SYMBOLIC POWER

I deploy two concepts all the way through this book in order to expose and critique the heteronomy of urban research. First is agnotology. It's a troublesome and perhaps off-putting term, but like heteronomy, it is simple to understand. Some context is necessary before we arrive at a definition. We have been living through times when rigorous investigative journalism was dismissed by the forty-fifth president of the United States, Donald Trump, as "fake news"; when clear evidence of small presidential inauguration crowd numbers in 2017 was ridiculed by a senior adviser to Trump as "alternative facts"; and when a scandalous yet successful 2016 campaign to encourage people to vote for Britain to leave the European Union was aided by a false statement, printed on a campaign bus, that a "Leave" vote would save £350 million per week that could instead be spent on the National Health Service. Rigorous scholarship has traditionally and justifiably been concerned with epistemology, the production of knowledge. But for some time now, this by itself seems insufficient. How is *ignorance* produced, by whom, for whom, and against whom? James Baldwin's (1972, 58) famous statement, "It is certain, in any case, that ignorance, allied with power, is the most ferocious enemy justice can have," seems especially relevant in this era of truth-twisting in the face of injustice.

In his swashbuckling critique of the economics profession in the build-up to and aftermath of the 2008 financial crisis, Philip Mirowski argues that one of the major ambitions of politicians, economists, journalists, and pundits enamored of (or seduced by) neoliberalism is to plant doubt and ignorance among the populace: "This is not done out of sheer cussedness; it is a political tactic, a means to a larger end. . . . Think of the documented existence of climate-change denial, and then simply shift it over into economics" (2013, 83). Mirowski advanced a compelling argument to shift questions away from "what people know" about the society in which they live toward questions about what people do *not* know, and why not. These questions are just as important, usually far more scandalous, and remarkably undertheorized. They require a rejection of appeals to epistemology and, instead, an analytic focus on intentional ignorance production: *agnotology.* This term was coined by historian of science Robert Proctor to designate "the study of ignorance making, the lost and forgotten" where the "focus is on knowledge that could have been but wasn't, or should be but isn't" (Proctor and Schiebinger 2008, vii). The etymological derivation is the Greek word *agnōsis*, meaning not knowing, which Gilroy (2009) draws upon to argue the following: "We need a better understanding of the relationship between information and power . . . a new corrective disciplinary perspective that interprets the power that arises from the command of not knowing, from the management of forms of ignorance that have been strategically created and deployed, and institutionally amplified." Proctor's own work provided a hugely instructive conceptual apparatus for scholars interested in the production of ignorance (e.g., Proctor 1995). It was while investigating the tobacco industry's efforts to manufacture doubt about the health hazards of smoking that he began to see the scientific and political urgency in researching how ignorance is made, maintained, and manipulated by powerful institutions to suit their own ends, where the guiding research question becomes: "Why don't we know what we don't know?" As he discovered, the industry went to great lengths to give the impression that the cancer risks of cigarette smoking were still an open question even when the clinical evidence was overwhelming: "The industry was trebly active in this sphere, feigning its own ignorance of hazards, whilst simultaneously affirming the absence of definite proof in the scientific community, while also doing all it could to manufacture ignorance on the part of the smoking public" (Proctor 2008, 13–14).

Numerous tactics were deployed by the tobacco industry to divert attention from the causal link between smoking and cancer, such as the production of duplicitous press releases, the publication of "nobody knows the answers" white papers, and the generous funding of decoy or red-herring research that "would seem to be addressing tobacco and health, while really doing nothing of the sort" (Proctor, 14). The tobacco industry actually produced research about everything except tobacco hazards to exploit public uncertainty (researchers commissioned by the tobacco industry knew from the beginning what they were supposed to find and not find), and the very fact of research being funded allowed the industry to claim it was studying the problem.

When agnotology is transposed into the register of the urban, we can study the techniques and strategies of powerful institutions (such as think tanks, philanthropic foundations, and university research centers) that want people not to know and even not to think about certain urban conditions and especially their structural causes. Key techniques include the concoction of a falsely balanced debate in which there should always be two sides to every story and fostering a sense of massive controversy where actual debates are marginal or limited. As Mirowski illustrates, agnotology "presents itself as liberating, expanding the cloistered space of sanctioned explanation in an era of wrangling and indecision", and involves two steps: "One is the effort to pump excess noise into the public discussion of appropriate frames within which to approach the controversy; the second is to provide the echoic preferred target narrative as coming from many different sanctioned sources at once; ubiquity helps pave the way for inevitability" (2013, 297). By working with the concept of agnotology, it becomes possible to uncover how and why certain questions are kept off the urban agenda while others remain firmly on it.

Many scholars (and certainly, as we shall see later in the book, many think tank writers) might claim that there is no such thing as the intentional production of ignorance; all that exists are people with different worldviews, interests, and opinions, and people simply argue about and defend their beliefs with passion. This claim would be very wide of the mark. Even when there is a vast body of all kinds of evidence that is wildly at odds with what is being stated, and when the social realities of poverty and inequality expose the failures of deregulation at the top and punitive intervention at the bottom of the class structure, the technocrats of neo-liberal reason become noisier and even more zealous in their relentless mission to inject doubt into the conversation and ultimately make their audiences believe that government interference in the workings of the "free' market is damaging society. An agnotological approach seeks to dissect the ignorance production methods and tactics of these and other messengers of disinformation. There are, of course, many different ways to think about ignorance, such as John Rawls (1971) did positively in his promotion of a "veil of ignorance" as an ethical method with respect to his hypothetical 'original position" (whereby ignorance of how we might personally gain in a society's distribution of benefits and burdens might guarantee a kind of neutrality and balance in thinking about what a just distribution should look like). It therefore needs to be clarified that agnotology does not have a monopoly on ignorance studies and is just one element of that nascent and fascinating field (Gross and McGoey 2015; McGoey 2019). However, it is something of a surprise that agnotology has hardly escaped from the disciplinary claws of science and technology studies and permeated social science, less still urban studies, where the relationship between evidence and policy is always contentious and some-times tortured (for some fascinating recent exceptions, see Stel 2016; Cupples and Glynn 2018).

Agnotology, though very useful in dissecting the methods and tactics of messengers of disinformation, is less useful in explaining precisely how certain terms and categories are converted into common sense (often across the political spectrum) and become so powerful that alternative or competing terms, and the arguments they anchor, are kept off the political grid and the policy agenda. This brings me to the second concept I use throughout the book to expose and critique the heteronomy of urban research: Pierre Bourdieu's *symbolic power*, which I feel is crucial for any exploration of the categories of urban research and their consequences. As explained by Bourdieu himself, symbolic power is

> the power to constitute the given through utterances, to make people see and believe, to confirm or to transform the vision of the world and, thereby, action upon the world and thus the world itself, an almost magical power that enables one to obtain the equivalent of what is obtained through force (physical or economic) by virtue of the specific effect of mobilization. . . .

What makes for the power of words and watchwords, the power to maintain or to subvert order, is belief in the legitimacy of the words and of those who utter them. (1991, 170)

Wacquant helpfully distills these words to define symbolic power as "the capacity for *consequential categorization*, the ability to make the world, to preserve or change it, by fashioning and diffusing symbolic frames, collective instruments of cognitive construction of reality" (2017, 57; emphasis added). Bourdieu produced an enormous body of work on symbolic power; indeed, Wacquant notes that it is "a concept that Bourdieu elaborates over the full spectrum of his scientific life" (57), which runs from his early work on honor in Algeria to his late lecture courses at the Collège de France on the state, art, and science. It is especially useful in analyzing the classifying and naming powers of the state (Auyero 2012). Even when nonstate institutions such as tabloid newspapers and think tanks might be responsible for inventing and circulating particular terms and categories, symbolic power is helpful in tracing how such categories become elevated into authoritative and consequential discourses emanating from state officials and institutions: "In the social world, words make things, because they make the meaning and consensus on the existence and meaning of things, the common sense, the doxa accepted by all as self-evident" (Bourdieu 1996b, 21).

Taken together, the conceptual articulation of agnotology with symbolic power, I argue, allows us to understand the institutional arrangements and symbolic systems that fuse and feed off each other to structure the deeply unequal social relations behind the profound differences we see in life chances in cities in so many geographical contexts today.

STRUCTURE OF THE BOOK

In chapter 2 I explore and critique the production and circulation of "urban resilience." Since the famous and hugely influential writings of the Chicago School of Human Ecology, there has been a long—and disturbing—history of concepts being brought from biological sciences to be applied to the social sciences and especially the study of cities, "resilience" being the most pervasive recent example. Urban resilience has a large institutional apparatus behind it, most visible in The Rockefeller Foundation's 100 Resilient Cities competition, which from 2013 to 2019 awarded generous grants to the one hundred cities across the globe that it felt demonstrated "a dedicated commitment to building their own capacities to prepare for, withstand, and bounce back rapidly from shocks and stresses." Effectively, cash prizes were offered to the city administrations that showed the most energy in returning their cities back to market-led planning as quickly as possible following economic shocks and stresses. That there was a strong desire among urban managers to compete is evident in the fact that more than one thousand cities registered to take part in the program, and almost four hundred formally applied for inclusion.

Using examples from two of the Rockefeller Foundation's 100 Resilient Cities, Glasgow and Cape Town, I argue that urban resilience serves as a screen that deflects analytic and political attention away from the structural and institutional conditions that are forcing urban dwellers to be "resilient' the first place. Viewed through the lens of resilience, a global financial crisis morphs from being a political creation into a naturally occurring phenomenon that requires a program of public expenditure gutting—austerity—to set it back on its natural path. Working with a conceptualization of neoliberalism as "an articulation of state, market and citizenship that harnesses the power of the first to impose the stamp of the second onto the third" (Wacquant 2012a, 66), I argue that resilience is a political project to renounce responsibility for economic and environmental crises, to scapegoat people who are struggling as a consequence, to submit to "shocks and stresses' rather than address their underlying causes, and to preclude questions and practices of resistance.

Chapter 3 considers the field of gentrification research, including some of the debates my own work has ignited, and argues that a great deal of scholarship on this process succumbs to an analytically defective formula: weigh up the supposed pros and cons of gentrification, worry about threats to "social diversity" and housing affordability, and conclude that gentrification is actually "good" on balance because it represents the reinvestment that stops neighborhoods from "decaying" during a financial crisis. Informed by the (so often misconstrued) rent gap theory produced by the late geographer Neil Smith, I unravel such false choice

urbanism by arguing that disinvestment and reinvestment do not sig-
nify a moral conundrum, with the latter somehow being "better" than
the former. Drawing upon examples from numerous contexts, among
them Philadelphia, New Orleans, Edinburgh, Beirut, and Santiago de
Chile, I demonstrate that gentrification and urban decay are not opposites, alternatives, or choices, but rather tensions and contradictions in
a global system of capital circulation, amplified and aggravated by the
global crisis of affordable housing, a system that relies on propitious conditions for accumulation laid down by the neoliberal state. I contend that
the rent gap theory, understood as its author intended, is very helpful in
explaining the dramatic transformations roiling cities across very diverse
geographical, structural, and institutional contexts. It can also inform
numerous strategies of resisting gentrification that I explore toward the
end of the chapter.

Chapter 4 considers the most harmful effect of gentrification: the displacement of working-class people from urban space and the role of rent
control in mitigating against it. I examine the much-in-vogue advocacy of
housing subsidy vouchers by leading urban scholars in the United States
and critique the argument that they are a remedy for the exploitation and
displacement of tenants by landlords. This sets the scene for a consideration of what I see as a much more appropriate housing policy: rent
control. Rent control is one of the most despised yet misunderstood policies across a variety of disciplines and professions concerned with urban
issues. The hegemonic view is that rent controls—in any form, in any
context—will eventually hurt those on whose behalf they are supposedly
introduced (people struggling to find somewhere affordable to live). Like
so much agnotology, however, this view is riddled with vested interests
and grounded in deep contempt for state regulation and in veneration
of the supposed efficiency of the "free" market. Drawing on scholarship
from southern European cities, together with recent studies on the subject
from New Jersey and California, I expose and dissect three of the prevalent myths about rent control: (1) that it negatively affects the quality of
rented properties, (2) that it negatively affects the supply of housing, and
(3) that it leads to "ineffiencies" in housing markets. Once we take the
trouble to look closely at different kinds of rent control and, more broadly,
at what leads to high housing costs, then it is possible—as I attempt in

the chapter—to shift the analytical and political focus toward the urgent question of housing justice.

One of the more peculiar trends in urban studies is the ongoing popularity of scholarship exploring "neighbourhood effects," the focus of chapter 5. This scholarship stems from an understanding of society that adheres to a simple overarching assumption, that where you live affects your life chances. For urbanists writing in this genre, neighborhoods matter and shape the fate of their residents; therefore, urban policies must be geared toward poor neighborhoods, seen as incubators of social dysfunction. A belief in causal neighborhood effects is now very widespread among policy elites, mainstream urban scholars, journalists, and think tank researchers. There is an enormous literature, which keeps growing even though scholars usually find weak or no evidence of neighborhood effects. In this chapter I argue that not only is this literature tantamount to "tautological urbanism" (scholars keep getting huge grants to research something they keep finding to be not very important, and keep on concluding that we need further research), but an acceptance of the neighborhood effects thesis, however well intentioned, misses the key structural question of why people live where they do in cities. Using a framing example from Cape Town, and scrutinizing studies of neighborhood effects in the Netherlands, Australia, and the United States, I turn attention to the structural factors that give rise to differential life chances and the inequalities they produce. By inverting the neighborhood effects thesis to "your life chances affect where you live," the problem then becomes one of understanding how differential life chances in cities are produced. Such a focus highlights the problems and injustices inherent in letting the market (buttressed by the state) be the force that determines the cost of housing, and therefore the major determinant of where people live. I contend that the residential mobility programs advocated by neighborhood effects proponents—which have been influential well beyond their emergence in the United States—stand on very shaky ground, for if it is true that neighborhood effects exceed what would be predicted by poverty alone, moving the poor to a richer place would only eliminate that incremental difference, without addressing the structural and institutional arrangements that produce and sustain inequalities.

Chapter 6 tackles frontally one of the principal properties of urban marginality: territorial stigmatization. After providing an opening example of territorial stigmatization in action from Vancouver, I offer some conceptual clarification and theoretical context before critically surveying some important themes emerging in a mushrooming literature. Highlighting the need for more attention to how territorial stigma emerges in the first place, I then explore the genealogy and trace the realization of a category that was invented by journalists, amplified by free market think tanks, and converted into *doxa* (common sense) by politicians in the United Kingdom: the "sink estate." This derogatory designator, signifying social housing estates that supposedly create poverty, family breakdown, worklessness, welfare dependency, antisocial behavior, and personal irresponsibility, has become the symbolic frame justifying current policies toward social housing that have resulted in considerable social suffering and intensified dislocation. I dissect the hugely influential precursor to the sink estate designator: the "behavioral sink" categorized by the ethologist John B. Calhoun in his experiments with rats in the 1950s, in which he warned about the problems of population density for the human species in urban settings. I then explore the journalistic uptake of the *sink estate* label, especially in London, before tracing its extension into policy by way of an analytic dissection of the highly influential publications on UK housing by a free market think tank, Policy Exchange. These are scrutinized in order to demonstrate how the activation of territorial stigma has become an instrument of the state. The sink estate, it is argued, is the semantic battering ram in the ideological assault on social housing, deflecting attention away from social housing not only as an urgent necessity during a serious crisis of affordability, but also as an incubator of community, solidarity, shelter, and home.

With remarkable consistency over a twenty-year period, successive politicians and policy elites in multiple European contexts, sometimes across the political spectrum, have portrayed areas exhibiting large ethnic minority populations (especially those residing in social housing) as vortexes and vectors of social disintegration, fundamentally dissolute and irretrievably disorganized. The label *ghetto* is commonly hurled about to dramatize and denounce such disintegration. In chapter 7, therefore, I build on the critical interrogation of territorial stigmatization in chapter 6 to critique the loose and/or opportunistic use of the term *ghetto* to describe and castigate working-class territories or immigrant districts in three national contexts: Britain, Denmark, and Belgium. To do so I draw upon Wacquant's conceptualization of the ghetto as an instrument of ethnoracial closure that employs space to fulfill two conflicting functions: economic extraction and social ostracization. This robust conceptualization of the ghetto, drawn from the historical realities of the original ghetto of Renaissance Venice, is essential in order to form a coherent and powerful response to the dangerous mythology and political panic surrounding the ghetto, which has everything to do with the racialized denigration of people's lives, something that cannot be separated from the racialized denigration of the places where they live.

In the final chapter I conclude the book by specifying the connections across all the thematic materials presented vis-à-vis the conceptual frames of agnotology and symbolic power, to offer some *potential* pathways for the field of critical urban studies, extending the challenge articulated by Wacquant for an urban studies that can

> act as *solvent* of the new neoliberal common sense that 'naturalizes' the current state of affairs and its immanent tendencies, through the methodical critique of the categories and topics which weave the fabric of the dominant discourse. . . . [and] can also function in the manner of a *beacon* that casts light on contemporary transformations, making latent properties or unnoticed trends emerge from the shadows and especially reveals possible alternative paths. (2009, 129)

To this end, the conclusion offers some thoughts on the relationships between urban knowledges, urban ignorances, and urban struggles, and suggests that the reframing of urban inequalities along these lines (the subtitle of this book) carries some interesting analytical and political possibilities for critical urban studies as a vibrant and multidisciplinary intellectual field. Given the thematic content of the book, I make some observations regarding the importance of two issues at the core of each chapter: urban housing and urban land. I argue that in striving for what David M. Smith (1994) helpfully called "territorial social justice," there is much to be gained from engaging with insights from settler colonial and decolonial theory vis-à-vis Indigenous ontologies of land, and that a more complete grasp of the structural and institutional factors behind urban inequalities can be attained by holding marginalized and neglected

worldviews in productive dialogue with other, more established worldviews that are too often considered incompatible.

Before I proceed into the heart of the book, a final note about my
approach. A newcomer to "academic Twitter," as I have seen it called so
often, could be forgiven for thinking that the only way to be a critical
urban scholar these days is to use every possible theoretical and methodological approach that critical thought has ever invented, all the time
and regardless of context and topic, and to duck and run for cover if you
choose to ignore any of those approaches! So it seems important to state
at this juncture that this is not possible here, nor anywhere else. My own
work is rooted in an institutional political economy approach to urban
geography, and throughout this book I therefore focus primarily on the
political and economic structures shaping inequalities in cities.

Cities are not natural organisms but expressions and arenas of political
struggles, and by analyzing some of the more disturbing transformations
roiling stigmatized districts of unequal cities, I demonstrate how those
transformations are always connected to strategies and skirmishes tra-
versing circles of power. Where relevant and helpful to the double move
aim of this book that I outlined at the start of this chapter, I have tried
to incorporate and draw upon approaches that are often very different
from my own. More particularly, I have sought to do something that too
many other established white male urban studies scholars don't do: to
learn from and cite women, early career scholars, and scholars of color.
By my doing so, I hope that the reader will gain a sense of critical urban
studies as a vibrant and multidisciplinary field that is most progressive
when it fuses understandings drawn from the spectrum of approaches
and analytic traditions, from structural Marxism to decolonial pluriversalism. There will of course be omissions and unwitting neglect of certain
approaches and perspectives that undoubtedly would have enriched this
book, but I don't ever claim to have the last word on anything. As I see it,
critical urban scholarship is best considered as an ongoing and politically
progressive intellectual conversation, wherein scholars are learning from
each other all the time and, more importantly, learning from those who
experience and contest urban inequalities at ground level.

2 The Resilience of Neoliberal Urbanism

In September 2016 Glasgow City Council launched its resilience strategy. Supported by the Rockefeller Foundation's 100 Resilient Cities competition (2013–2019), which awarded generous grants to the one hundred cities across the globe that it felt demonstrated "a dedicated commitment to building their own capacities to prepare for, withstand, and bounce back rapidly from shocks and stresses," the council's glossy document, "Our Resilient Glasgow," sets out how Glasgow will "maintain essential functions in the face of acute shocks and chronic stresses, but also grow and thrive through them" (Glasgow City Council 2016b, 8). Based on face-to-face conversations, workshops, and online surveys with thousands of Glasgow residents, including children, the strategy identifies four pillars around which resilience is to be built: empowering Glaswegians, unlocking place-based solutions, fair economic growth, and fostering civic participation. Announcing the release of the document, Frank McAveety, then leader of Glasgow City Council, commented:

> [T]he strategy document is a staging post in the conversation between Glasgow's citizens and its institutions about resilience. The strategy points to the route ahead and I've no doubt the journey will be accompanied by robust

debate—Glasgow wouldn't have it any other way. This on-going dialogue will strengthen our resilience and allow us to face the future with confidence. (Quoted in Glasgow City Council 2016a)

In the spirit of robust debate, the first thing I argue about this document is that it is presented in a manner that is truly excruciating. For example: "During our conversations with Glaswegians on what makes Glasgow a resilient city we found that they like to talk of their 'bounceback-ability' factor—an ability to cope and even thrive through hard times" (18). I am confident that if you were to spend time in Glasgow and utter the neologism *bounceback-ability* with any frequency, you would not make friends easily. Similarly, it is highly unlikely that schoolchildren anywhere in the city will embrace being "young resilience ambassadors to develop leadership skills, share learning and champion creative new resilience ideas" (75) and find an enthusiastic reaction from their classmates. This is partly because, as the document acknowledges, many areas of Glasgow are *already* extremely resilient places: "The communities in the north of Glasgow are incredibly resilient in the face of a number of disproportionate stresses that are closely related to the post-industrial legacy of the area" (52). This excerpt brings up the questions of why a grand resilience strategy is necessary, and how people in Glasgow would feel about one being imposed. But it is in the discussion of the second pillar, unlocking place-based solutions, that we can see more of the political-economic intent behind this resilience strategy. The authors of the document are convinced that "placemaking" is a wonderful design approach, as it "contributes towards the creation of successful and resilient places, based upon balancing the relationship between the physical, social and economic characteristics of the area" (50)—apparently without taking a moment to reflect upon how people living where places are already made might feel about another vision of place being imposed on them.

The placemaking approach is perhaps to be expected, however, as the Scottish government has in recent years wholeheartedly bought into the ethos and methods of Andres Duany's "New Urbanism" (MacLeod 2013), which has placemaking and postpolitical "community engagement" at its core (and has literally bought into it, as it paid Duany £200,000 for a week's consultancy work in 2010). But a central goal issuing from the unlocking place-based solutions pillar is "to create an integrated resilience exemplar in the north of the city" (Glasgow City Council 2016b, 52). This is deemed necessary as "patterns of investment, lack of active travel and public transport networks to neighbouring areas, and low availability of local employment opportunities" have resulted in "stresses of poverty and deprivation with high proportions of young people not in education or employment and significant issues surrounding addictions and mental health" (52). It is claimed that "the high concentration of vacant and der-elict land in the north of Glasgow has also become a physical and social barrier to connectivity. It can often result in an environment that does not inspire pride in place and demotivates Glaswegians from taking advan-tage of active transport networks" (52–53).

With problems pitched in such a way, the solution—presented under the heading "Resilience Value"—is predictable:

> The community, environmental and economic potential of derelict and vacant sites in Glasgow will be unlocked. By using 3D modelling to map vacant and derelict land we will be able to de-risk development by identify-ing new opportunities above and below ground. This will promote develop-ment opportunities associated with sites in order to attract developers and promote economic regeneration, compact city development and appropri-ate services. (53)

Disturbingly, the model for unlocking such "potential" in urban land is the 2014 Commonwealth Games Athletes' Village, pitched in this docu-ment as "one of the biggest success stories," where "partnering agencies consulted intensively with local communities to build on community strengths and maximize social benefits" (56).

This is wildly at odds with what actually happened in the buildup to that 2014 mega-event: the amplification of territorial stigma already affecting the East End of the city (Gray and Mooney 2011; Paton, McCall, and Mooney 2017), which justified the forced eviction of residents, whose homes were acquired through compulsory purchase before callous demolition to make way for the Athletes' Village (Porter 2009). The complete detachment from the realities of working-class Glasgow can be read in the statement that "the Games were an opportunity to bring vitality into areas of the city" (55). As David Ley (1996, 33–34) has pointed out, the discourse of revitalization is "objectionable, implying a sense of moral superiority in the process of residential succession, and imparting a mantle of less vitality to previous land uses and users." In this Glasgow case, the positive rubric of building resilience makes acceptable and palatable the claims to "unlock economic potential" and "de-risk development" to create "opportunities associated with sites in order to attract developers." In doing so, it shuts out the question of whom the "resilient city" is for, and who is evicted to make way for it.

In this chapter I trace the recent history and usage of the term *resilience* in urban studies, exploring the arguments of those who embrace and use the notion of building resilient cities in the context of urban inequalities. My argument is that resilience serves as a screen that prevents us from asking and understanding why urban dwellers are being asked to be resilient in the first place. This argument proceeds in three steps. First, I analyze the etymology and export of the term from ecological and conservation sciences to the social sciences and urban planning. Second, I explore what happened when the city of Cape Town, South Africa, nearly ran out of water and creating a "water-resilient city" became the official policy response. Third, I explore the tensions between resilience and resistance and consider whether the former is either a precursor to the latter or precludes it completely.

THE FACT OF AVOIDING

My son is a very competitive swimmer, in a performance sport that takes enormous amounts of training and physical conditioning to improve and to remain competitive. One of the main *mental* strengths his coach teaches all the swimmers in his squad is resilience: the ability to "bounce back stronger" after any disappointment (whether it be losing out on a medal, failing to get a personal best time, experiencing an injury, receiving a disqualification due to technical infraction, and so on). Due to all the very early morning training sets and the amount of time and money spent trying to swim faster, disappointment of any kind can hit swimmers (and their parents!) very hard. Developing resilience really seems to resonate with young athletes, and I have noticed many of them become stronger swimmers and stronger people because of this notion of resilience. Why, then, would anyone be opposed to the notion of bouncing back stronger after hard times? What happens if we move resilience away from sporting excellence and into the realm of urban society and ask that very question? What happens if we ask what caused those hard times, for cities, in the first place?

About a decade ago, as cities were reeling in the aftermath of the 2008 financial crisis, I started seeing journal articles and funding calls aligned to the theme of urban resilience or building resilience in the context of either urban inequality or responses to various economic problems in cities. In a short space of time academics were suddenly falling over themselves trying to secure funding to research urban resilience, and urban policy officials and politicians could scarcely utter a sentence about their priorities and the future of cities without using the term. More generally, *resilience* was quickly found everywhere, uttered vis-à-vis national security announcements, anti-terrorism policies, disaster response coordination efforts, climate change debates, financial crisis recovery strategies, and the self-help industry. Perhaps the ultimate seal of approval for resilience applied to urban issues was the Rockefeller Foundation's 100 Resilient Cities program that I mentioned at the start of this chapter. The principal criterion for selection as one of the one hundred cities was demonstrating potential and commitment in terms of bouncing back, after shocks and stresses, to economic prosperity and environmental quality (not for one moment questioning how incompatible those two things have become). That there was a strong desire among urban managers to compete is evident in the fact that more than one thousand cities registered to take part in the program, and almost four hundred formally applied for inclusion.

The reach of Rockefeller's resilience agenda extended to the *Guardian* newspaper in the United Kingdom and its sponsorship of the "Guardian Cities" section, launched in January 2014. An introductory pitch by the editor, delivered with an intention to "start the debate," was entitled "What Makes Your City So Special?" (Herd 2014), the sort of rubric you might expect to find in a "Business Traveler" section of an in-flight magazine. More widely across the website when the "Guardian Cities" section was launched, and propping up a sense of gentrified quaintness, were uncritical nods toward the urbanism of Jane Jacobs, whose defeat of New York City's master planners is nowadays romanticized as a humanizing vision for cities, without any acknowledgment of the disruptive and cookie-cutter gentrification that such a vision has unleashed all over the world (Smith and Larson, 2007).[1] A longer article by architecture and design critic Oliver Wainwright (2014) began by parroting the irksome nugget that "more than half of the world's population now live in a city," before continuing with, mercifully, the welcome statement that "such statistics are meaningless without asking what these cities will be like, who they are for, and how they are being made." But that is where any genuinely critical impulse ended. In an essay that read more like a research center grant application, he outlined a few issues facing cities and asked what he thought were pertinent questions, concluding with: "Facing threats of flooding and earthquakes, storms and tsunamis, the resilience of cities is tested to the limit. . . . With flooding becoming an increasingly regular event, should we be retreating behind bigger barriers and steeper levees, or learning to adapt our cities to work with, rather than against, these conditions?"

The "Guardian Cities" team also ran an article on the day its website launched entitled "What Makes a City Resilient?," which recognized that resilience was a buzzword but did absolutely nothing in the way of shining a critical light on it. In fact, the article concluded in rosy and technocratic terms: "More broadly, however, the resilience movement is a global attempt to address two of the longest-standing and most vital questions facing theorists, planners and leaders. Namely, what is the purpose of society, and what is a society's responsibility to its citizens" (Watson 2014). Here urban resilience shifts meaning, from cities bouncing back from hard times to a much deeper blend of both social movement and moral philosophy. But where does the notion of resilience come from? As John Patrick Leary has explained, we can learn a lot about resilience by exploring its etymology. Its Latin root is *resilientia*, meaning "fact of avoiding." Whereas the term "seems to name peoples' ability to respond and rebound from things that strike them head-on, the term's popularity, though, derives from what it lets us avoid more clearly" (2018, 149). I return to this question of precisely *what* is being avoided in the next section, but at this juncture it is instructive to trace the import of resilience from ecological and conservation sciences into the social sciences.

Since the publication of the famous and hugely influential writings of the Chicago School of Human Ecology, there has been a long and ungainly history of concepts being imported from the natural sciences into the social sciences, and especially vis-à-vis the study of (and formation of policies toward) cities (*regeneration*, a biomedical term, being the most pervasive recent example). The Chicago School scholars took inspiration from the natural sciences and turned their city into a huge laboratory for the investigation of human beings "adapting" to their environments (to form "natural areas," as their leader, Robert Park, put it), deploying biological metaphors of invasion, succession, and dominance to describe how the demographics of neighborhoods change over time. The legacy of the Chicago School is immense and extremely divisive; the idea that a city grows and changes naturally, and that people simply sort themselves into natural areas that give rise to "moral regions," has been roundly criticized many times for its neglect of structural forces of power, politics, policy, and privilege, as well as of capital, race, gender, and class. As Libby Porter and Simin Davoudi explain:

> As past experience has shown, any framework which applies natural science thinking to social phenomena can be deeply problematic. This is partly because of fundamental ontological and epistemological divergences: natural sciences seek to explain the natural world as matters of fact. Resilience science is no different. Translating the ontological assumptions about the nature of the world into the 'socio' end of socio-ecological systems runs into problems that have been expounded, though by no means expunged, by decades of work deconstructing positivism to demote it from its domineering influence in social sciences and planning. (2012, 331)

So the use of resilience as a social category, something more than an observed quality of an environmental ecosystem, is part of an illustrious yet problematic intellectual tradition of applying natural science thinking to societies.

Resilience thinking, as it is often called, stems from the early 1970s work of the ecologist Crawford Holling. Holling's research was rooted in conservation management and represented a paradigm shift in ecological thought, destabilizing the notion that ecosystems return, via self-repair, to "equilibrium" after shock. Instead, Holling directed analytic attention to the complex ways in which an ecosystem can remain cohesive even when it undergoes extreme economic pressures (e.g., excessive deforestation and overfishing). Holling's own (1973, 21) description of his resilience framework, in the context of planning for future shocks and stresses, is telling: "The resilience framework can accommodate this shift in perspective, for

it does not require a precise capacity to predict the future, but only a qualitative capacity to devise systems that can absorb and accommodate future
events in whatever unexpected form they may take."

Holling's famous figure-of-eight diagram of the adaptive cycle of for-
est ecosystems appears in countless publications and later informed the
work of other leading ecologists (in the 1990s), building up to the formation of The Resilience Alliance in 1999, which then spawned similar organizations such as the Stockholm Resilience Centre think tank in 2007.
Holling's conceptualization of "panarchy," a framework for understanding the evolutionary nature of adaptive cycles that are nested within each
other across time and space, was instrumental in how resilience became
extended significantly as "socio-ecological resilience," wherein natural and
human systems are considered to be "interlinked in continual adaptive
cycles of growth, accumulation, restructuring and renewal" (Gunderson
and Holling 2002). As Jeremy Walker and Melinda Cooper (2011) explain,
it was Holling's later work—theorizing abstract dynamics of capital accumulation predicated on the inherent crisis tendencies of complex adaptive
systems—that aligned with leading architect of neoliberal thought Friedrich Hayek's vision of a spontaneous, complex, naturalized market order
free of government intervention and regulation:

> Although Holling never cited Hayek, we argue that it is Hayek's influential
> philosophy of free-market dynamics that has made the contemporary policy
> arena so receptive to the overtures of the Resilience Alliance. If the Mont
> Pelerin Society [the birthplace of neoliberal thought] and the Resilience
> Alliance have anything in common, it is the attempt to forge a broad trans-
> disciplinary philosophy capable of unifying nature and society under a sin-
> gle set of all-encompassing concepts. (147)

As Kathleen Tierney (2015, 1332) explains, panarchy slots so neatly into
neoliberal nostrums because it "stands in opposition to notions of hierar-
chical control, emphasizing instead the ability of systems to self-organise
across multiple scales." A similar point has been advanced by Porter and
Davoudi (2012: 332), reflecting on the newer "bounce forward" mantras in
resilience thinking (a positive extension of bouncing back): "The possibilities of transformation and the seduction of 'forward' will also neatly and
conveniently suit the neoliberal urban growth, regeneration and renewal

agendas that have persistently dominated planning discourses for the past 30 years." If we have learned one thing above all from the mutations of neoliberalism as process and practice, it fails, but it fails forward (Peck 2010a).

This brings us to the question of neoliberalism, itself a hotly contested concept in the social sciences and humanities, and its relationship to resilience agendas. It would be unnecessarily irksome to recount all the tortured debates about whether neoliberalism has analytic utility as a concept, but until neoliberalization as a process shows any sign of disappearing forever, I think it is worth clarifying the concept rather than abandoning it. I am most persuaded by Loïc Wacquant's (2012a, 66) strikingly simple definition of neoliberalism as "an articulation of state, market and citizenship that harnesses the first to impose the stamp of the second onto the third." Neoliberals have long argued that "the market" is society's primary organizing principle, something that sorts people into a natural hierarchy of winners and losers, wherein any attempt by the state to intervene hinders the efficient and ultimately utopian operation of this natural order. But the rhetorics of neoliberal intellectuals and politicians mask a critically important feature of neoliberalism: from its violent early experiments in Chile and Argentina, to its Reagan and Thatcher union breaking, to its Blair and Bush sanctimony, to its variegated zombified splintering, neoliberalism has *always* been a state project requiring continuous statecraft (Peck 2010b; Brenner, Peck, and Theodore 2010). If, as Jamie Peck, Neil Brenner, and Nik Theodore (2009, 66d) argue, cities have become "strategic targets and proving grounds for an increasingly broad range of neoliberal policy experiments, institutional innovations and political projects," it is instructive to assess the degree to which the resilience agendas embraced so widely by state officials have been central to the continuing mobilization of state power in the extension of market rule. For this, I turn to what happened in Cape Town, South Africa, when that city nearly ran out of water.

FROM THE "NEW NORMAL" TO NORMALIZED INEQUALITY

It didn't rain very much in the southwest corner of the Western Cape province of South Africa from June 2015 to June 2018. This corner contains the city of Cape Town, a fast-growing yet acutely unequal settler-colonial metropolis of around four million people, and a popular international tourist destination for multiple reasons, one of which is its pleasant Mediterranean-style climate (hot dry summers and mild wet winters). For many decades Capetonians have relied on surface water runoff from winter rainfall in the region's dam catchment area in the surrounding mountains. There are six rain-fed dams that supply not only the entire metropolitan area (58%) and its satellite towns (6%), but also the region's agricultural industries (26%) (the remaining 10% is lost due to evaporation). The three-year drought was historic by any measure; in 2017, multiple weather stations recorded their lowest ever rainfall totals since keeping records began in the 1880s.

The influence of climate change caused by human beings in the occurrence of the drought cannot be overstated (Otto et al. 2018; Tempelhoff 2019). Other factors contributing to the water crisis were rapid urbanization and population growth in the Cape Town metropolitan area, especially migrant settlement from other parts of sub-Saharan Africa (Battersby 2011), and poor management of the water system, such as alien vegetation (that could have been cleared easily) preventing runoff into the dams, together with nonoperational pumps and silted canals (Ziervogel 2019). Agricultural demand for water has increased due to the steady and significant growth of production in the Western Cape's wine industry since the end of apartheid in 1994 (Schmitt 2018).

Water in Cape Town is managed by the national government's Department of Water and Sanitation (DWS) in cooperation with the city government's Water and Sanitation Department. As the dam levels kept falling, with no significant rainfall in the long-term forecasts, these political authorities faced a mounting crisis. Political differences between different levels of government prevented a cooperative and unified response to the drought; both the city of Cape Town and the Western Cape province are ruled by the center-right Democratic Alliance (DA), while the national government is ruled by the center-left African National Congress (ANC). Both these political parties have a dismal recent track record of incompetence and corruption, not to mention considerable factional battles. In addition, the DWS is "mired in institutional challenges, including financial mismanagement, escalating debt, capacity constraints and an ensuing deterioration of infrastructure owing to lack of maintenance and investment" (Millington and Scheba 2021, 119). During the water crisis, all this was a recipe for not only enormous practical difficulties layered on top of massive inequalities in water provision across the city, but also mounting public distrust of all levels of government.

The initial response to the drought in 2016 took the form of modest restrictions on domestic and agricultural water use. In early 2017, as the seriousness of the drought became clearer, the response intensified, and the term *resilience* was suddenly found everywhere. As Johann Tempelhoff (2019, 112–13) elaborates, "Some of the keenest minds in the field of environmental and water studies in the country informed the political leadership and officials of the City of Cape Town on how to deal with extreme water shortages and how best to promote collaboration and a better understanding of the principles of resilience." The outcome was the frequent political utterance of the phrase "the new normal" in attempts to educate Capetonians about the severity of the crisis and how to brace themselves for mandatory changes in water consumption habits.

In May 2017 Patricia de Lille, the mayor of Cape Town from 2011 to 2018, formed the Water Resilience Task Team under the direction of a chief resilience officer. This team was eventually replaced in August 2017 by the Water Resilience Advisory Committee, comprised of water experts from academia, government, agriculture, nongovernmental organizations (NGOs), and the private sector. De Lille used the phrase "the new normal" in many of her speeches and explained that the response to the drought was "about building resilience, which is the capacity of individuals, communities, institutions, businesses and systems to survive, adapt and grow no matter what kind of stresses and acute shocks they experience" (quoted in Tempelhoff 2019, 131). The direct import and uptake of Crawford Holling's conceptualization of resilience was abundantly clear. The focus on "future-proofing" resulted in the (long overdue) escalation of a range of existing plans to secure sufficient water for the city: mining groundwater, expanding desalination facilities, eradicating alien plants that prevented runoff, water pressure management, and water conservation and reuse strategies. But the dam levels kept falling.

Water restrictions became tighter as the crisis escalated following very poor winter rains in 2017. In September of that year, responsibility for addressing the crisis was effectively shifted to individual Capetonians, who

Figure 1. Capetonians queue for water at Newlands Spring, March 2018. © Nate Millington.

were urged (via numerous communications campaigns in traditional and social media) to use no more than eighty-seven liters of municipal drinking water per person per day, irrespective of whether they were at home, work, or elsewhere. Toward the end of the year a new phrase emerged, replacing "new normal": "Day Zero." Initially used by the city administration to denote the day when water would be turned off in neighborhoods if the dam levels fell to 13.5 percent of capacity, in the context of mixed messages and political squabbles it quickly became understood as the day when the dams would be totally empty and the city would have no water at all, apart from that available at two hundred designated collection points across the city (see figure 1).

In January 2018 the water restrictions were tightened further, to fifty liters per person per day, amid a palpable sense of fear. As Gina Ziervogel (2019, 9) explains, this was the point at which "the burden of responsibility shifted from the City, saying they were in charge and could augment water supply, to citizens being responsible for reducing water to avoid a crisis." While the goal of "avoiding Day Zero" was drummed into increasingly concerned water users, the political leadership of Cape Town was in considerable turmoil. The DA cited de Lille's "governance failures" as the reason for stripping her of her leadership of the water crisis response (eventually ousting her as mayor a few months later on the back of fiscal scandals and a massive factional battle within the DA) and placed control with the deputy mayor, who would work in dialogue with the DWS. With de Lille off the scene, the Water Resilience Advisory Committee was immediately disbanded.

Water restrictions continued for much of 2018, in tandem with a massive increase in tariffs for nondomestic use, as well as for any domestic use above restriction levels. Changes in water consumption habits did make a significant difference in averting Day Zero in 2018, but it also began to rain more typically in the Cape Town autumn/winter of that year. Given the city's undeniable success in avoiding Day Zero, it is not difficult to see why the Rockefeller Foundation (2019, 63–64) described Cape Town as, inter alia, a "shock-ready city" and a "leading example" of "a more adaptive, inclusive and ultimately resilient city." The city's response has been lauded by numerous other water-related institutions, journalists, and think tanks, all casting Cape Town as a model of a water-resilient city. But the deployment of resilience as a celebratory label or even as an analytical device to explain Cape Town's "success" in avoiding a water catastrophe can be called into question once we start asking about the political, economic, and institutional conditions that resulted in citizens being asked to be resilient in the first place.

In a series of incisive interventions, Suraya Scheba and Nate Millington (2018a, 2018b) have demonstrated that a lack of rainfall in the Western Cape was only one element of a situation that reflects the tortured relationships between climate change, evolutions in water governance, infrastructural politics, municipal finance, and sociospatial inequality (common among water crises in the Global South, as Sultana [2015] has explained). They argue that "the appearance of crisis should be read as both rupture and continuation, revealing the inherent contradictions within the existing water governance model that has contributed to a deepening of socio-spatial inequality" (Millington and Scheba 2021, 117).

Tracing the preconditions for a crisis that should not, therefore, be read as an unprecedented or unexpected occurrence, they demonstrate that, in respect of the national DWS, it was "financial mismanagement, escalating debt, capacity constraints, and a consequent deterioration of infrastructure due to a lack of maintenance and investment" (119) that left Cape Town without the necessary resources to tackle the drought. This also created a fiscal situation in which cost recovery via, first, the removal of basic water subsidies, and second, the imposition of water demand management tariffs, became the modus operandi of water governance at the expense of water equity in this profoundly unequal city. With respect to the former, they document the withdrawal of the universal provision of the first six kiloliters of "free basic water," available in South Africa since 2001. Since July 2017 all water is now chargeable within a stepped tariff, and free basic water is available only for those households who are able to declare themselves formally indigent. Registering as indigent is extremely challenging, especially for poor residents who are required to prove their status; in Cape Town, a massive number of people living in the poorest parts of the city are undocumented migrants from all over sub-Saharan Africa.

With respect to the imposition of tariffs, the drought crisis led to a revised water tariff in order to correct for reduced water usage as a result of the drought. Wealthier consumers, whose higher volume consumption habits typically serve to cross-subsidize the water usage of the poor, were targeted by these new tariffs, and the outcome meant a lack of funds for cross-subsidization. The authors show how both these measures should be considered together, as part of the city's move to deepen "commercialisation and valuation tendencies in the context of fiscal austerity" (Millington and Scheba, 128). Questioning the celebrations of Capetonians from all walks of life united by their resilience in the face of impending thirst, the authors show how the crisis paved the way for stealthy attempts to foster *financial* resilience in the context of chronically underfunded public service delivery: "We believe that equity considerations have been subsumed under economic considerations as a result of the city having to operate within an increasingly constrained budget" (129). Water crises, notes David Olivier (2017) in his critique of wasteful expenditure and negligence in the DWS, are "rarely a matter of rainfall."

While Scheba and Millington concentrate mostly on the warped priorities of the national government, Crispian Olver (2019) dissects the abysmal arrogance and skulduggery at the municipal level of government. In a breathtaking dissection of the complete restructuring of the city administration undertaken from 2015 to 2017 by de Lille and her chief of staff, Craig Kesson, Olver reports that this restructuring was not about improving service delivery, as the DA always claimed, but rather about the total centralization and concentration of power in the mayor's office. Highly competent civil servants with years of crucial experience found themselves "restructured" out of their jobs, and their departments were then merged with others into new departments with massive and vague new remits. New senior officials with questionable qualifications and experience were appointed, who had one essential employment attribute: they would support the mayor and all decisions she made. Pushing through large private property development schemes across the Cape Town metropolis, no matter what the environmental risks or previous planning restrictions, was the tacit motivation behind this restructuring strategy. If the mayor had much more power, and with the city's top planning civil servants restructured out of their jobs, it was far easier to squash any concerns about environmental impacts, spatial integration, and equity, and to facilitate rapacious land and property deals. As Olver points out, mayors in Cape Town have always had close ties with business elites and property developers and tend to act in their overall interests. Olver explained the consequences of restructuring vis-à-vis addressing the water crisis:

> Unfortunately, the mayor's office had paralysed the line departments that were meant to be responding to the crisis by centralizing strategic policy and redistributing functions and reporting along convoluted matrices, as well as restructuring departments—including the water unit—into utter confusion. The opinion of water officials was largely ignored and their competence overlooked. The message to the line departments was clear: "you should not respond to this, we will do this centrally." This alienated the executive directors for delivery departments, who sat back and said, "Well, okay, go right ahead." (2019, 75)

As a consequence, no coherent financial plan emerged to deal with the water crisis within the city's overall budget, and de Lille was approached by all kinds of "resilience" bureaucrats promising solutions but with absolutely no capability (in terms of knowledge or finances) to deliver anything at all. Restructuring by centralization "insulated the mayor from technical expertise, which, ironically, left her unsupported when faced with a crisis" (Olver,77). It is straightforward to see the immense relevance of Neil Smith's (2006) words, "there's no such thing as a natural disaster," when reflecting on Cape Town's water crisis.

It is no coincidence that the widespread embrace of resilience has emerged at a time of widespread austerity. Over a dozen years ago, Naomi Klein (2007) advanced her devastating thesis of the "shock doctrine" to explain how neoliberals convert the crises that their policies create into further opportunities for ideological assaults on societies that they feel need to be tamed by economic deregulation and free-market discipline. The promotion of resilient cities gains traction via its frequent invocation of how citizens must adapt to shocks and stresses, whether environmental, economic, social, political, or some combination of them all.

In contexts of massive precarity, the urban resilience agenda entails, first, convincing citizens to embrace shock treatments on their own—in the Cape Town case, adhering to water restrictions and new tariffs—and second, lauding them as a form of collective heroism undergirding the creation of a shock-ready city. As Maria Kaika (2017, 98) notes, "the best these practices can do is act as immunology: they vaccinate people and environments alike so that they are able to take larger does of inequality and environmental deregulation in the future." Similarly, Julian Reid (2013, 355) points out that the creation of "resilient subjects" involves shaping citizens who have "accepted the imperative not to resist or secure themselves from the dangers they face but instead adapt to their enabling conditions." Further evidence of the shock doctrine at work in Cape Town can be seen as the drought worsened in July 2017, when the city "attracted R4.3billion from investors in the inaugural Green Bond scheme to turn Cape Town's water crisis into an investment opportunity while supporting the city in its quest to deal with climate change in a resilient way" (Tempelhoff 2019, 133).

Resilience thinking might be able to help people cope with unexpected adversity, but it cannot possibly deal with systematic oppression. In a trenchant critique of the use of resilience as an adaptive response to climate change vulnerability in Washington, D.C., Malini Ranganathan and Eve Bratman articulate how resilience discourse tends to focus on "climate proofing" the future, rather than ongoing and historical cause of harm. If the afterlives of historical oppression are erased, and/or if the "here and now" of precarity is poorly understood or willfully watered down, then resilience thinking necessarily conjures more of the status quo—with only superficial changes as recommended options. (2021, 119)

The water crisis in Cape Town happened in one of the most unequal cities on the planet, where legacies of colonial domination and racial oppression have created an abysmally divided metropolis—so divided that, for instance, the army patrols neighborhoods suffering from appalling gang violence among dispossessed and abandoned youths of color, while some of the most extravagant residences on the continent, owned largely by white people (and a tiny rich Black elite), are just a few kilometers away, sealed off and defended by elaborate fortifications and security systems.

During the water crisis there was much made of the fact that, via tight restrictions and high tariffs, wealthy white Capetonians were finally getting a taste of the water consumption realities and hardships of poor people of color in the city (Fairbanks 2018), yet building resilience offered nothing to challenge such acute disparities in the long term. As Walker and Cooper (2011, 155) contend, building up resilience to environmental crisis in the Global South "is a tacit recognition that 'development' for the post-colonial poor now consists not in achieving First World standards of urban affluence but in surviving the after-effects of industrial modernization, the Green Revolution and the financial conditions imposed under the Washington Consensus."

Resilience is an attempt to make people more tolerant of miserable situations and environments, in which the reach of realistic ambition is simply to survive. It may help people cope with sudden trauma, stress, and disappointment, accepting the things they cannot change once they have happened, but crucially, it does not help people change the things they cannot accept. Adapting to adversity in the most effective way possible is without question part of being human, but resilience pushes the emphasis back onto the victim as opposed to addressing issues of causation and questions of social (in)justice (recall the etymology of the term: "fact of avoiding").

Perhaps the ultimate marker of the faddishness of resilience, as opposed to its ability to help confront systemic injustices, is the fact that the Water Resilience Advisory Committee in Cape Town was disbanded at the height of the drought crisis, and people stopped using the term, but when the dam levels stopped falling and it started raining again, pundits, philanthropic foundations, consultants, and politicians began lauding the resilience of Capetonians, while ignoring the resilience of the massive inequalities that persist over a quarter of a century into democracy.

RECLAIMING OR RESISTING RESILIENCE?

In recent years, as the problems of the spread of resilience thinking in urban scholarship and urban policy have become clear, there have been some interesting interventions exploring the extent to which resilience can be redeemed or reclaimed in some way and used for more politically progressive urban interventions against the grain of neoliberalizing agendas. Long before resilience became such a fad, Cindi Katz (2004) had offered a formulation of resilience as the recuperation of dignity via small acts of care, mutual support, education, and retraining that allow for dominated people to cope and get by in demanding circumstances. She offered this formulation as something additional to (and working with) a standard oppositional consciousness of resistance and what she called "reworking," or the recalibration of oppressive power relations into spaces that enable new kinds of political practices.

Drawing on Katz's formulation, Geoff DeVerteuil and Oleg Golubchikov (2016) advance what they call a "critical resilience," with three theses: first, that resilience can sustain alternative and previous (e.g., Keynesian) practices that are alternatives to neoliberal ones, such as "non-commodified clusters of the voluntary sector and the social economy that provided visions of opportunity and progress unsullied by the market" (146); second, that resilience is not just externally induced but internally produced as "a middle ground between victim and vanguard, when social actors cannot alter circumstances but still show agency, self-organization and adeptness in coping and adaptation" (147); and third, that resilience, by sustaining survival in the way Katz outlined, can act as the precursor to resistance and potential transformation (e.g., when people find ways to "stay put" in the face of displacement threats).

Roger Keil (2014) has argued that "the politics of resilience ... is not fatalist: it suggests, by contrast, that new forms of community cohesion, working together, local empowerment, and ecological intimacy can not only prepare cities for the worst of the twenty-first-century environment and economy, but also make urban life better." Keil is more concerned with *taming* the concept of resilience, rescuing it from its neoliberalizing tendencies and toward seeing it as a "core necessity of life in a post-carbon, post-industrial, and perhaps post-capitalist society where free, urbanized communities and individuals seek work, shelter, mobility, health, clean environments and social justice." Similar to DeVerteuil and Golubchikov's third thesis and aligned with a Lefebvrian vision of urban politics, Keil has contended:

> Putting our cities on a path to resilience is a prerequisite for the possibilities urban society has to offer. If we fail at being resilient to the shocks that await us, we will not be able to leave the realm of necessity, and will not be able to enter the realm of possibility. Being resilient is both a material, socio-ecological necessity and a precondition for a perpetual "cry and demand" for a democratization and liberation of urban society. It is both substance and process which we cannot do without.

He concluded by advocating a "resilience fix" centered around "the safe-guarding of the necessary conditions for that life through forward looking and planning." Similarly, Zac Taylor and Alex Schafran (2016, 142) have argued that, while "resilience can only be redeemed in so far as it is critically engaged with the everyday [undefined] and actually existing urban politics and processes," it is possible to "view a redeemed resilience as both a tool and a practice, as a means of both imagining and building better futures."

Attempts to reclaim resilience in order to imagine and build better futures should not be trivialized or dismissed, not least because urban resilience (and resilience thinking more broadly) has been (and continues to be) embraced by progressive institutions, community organizations, grassroots struggles, and oppositional campaigns. Given material hardships, it is not difficult to see why developing resilience in contexts of entrenched and ongoing oppression is both practiced and encouraged.

Figure 2. "Stop Calling Me Resilient." Boundary Way, Belfast, Northern Ireland, June 2017. © Allan Leonard @MrUlster used by license.

However, this is in itself a revealing trend. As Danny MacKinnon and Kate Derickson (2012, 266) explain, the "fundamental problem with the mobilizing discourse of resilience is that it places the onus squarely on local actors and communities to further adapt to the logics and implications of global capitalism and climate change." Perhaps the most powerful and certainly the most renowned critical response to this problem came from Tracie Washington, president of the Louisiana Justice Institute. She reacted to policy officials' characterizations of victims of Hurricane Katrina and the BP oil spill in the Gulf of Mexico as "resilient" with words that were quickly distributed around the city on posters, and that subsequently went global, perhaps most dramatically reused in a loyalist neighborhood of west Belfast, near the Shankill Road (see figure 2).

Mackinnon and Derickson (2012, 266) call the shifting of responsibility to individuals an "apolitical ecology" that "entails the subordination and

corralling of the social within the framework of socio-ecological systems."
In this sense, the spread of resilience can be seen as central to the creeping
physical "scientization" of approaches to urban questions that I discussed
in the opening chapter. Henrik Ernstson expressed this idea eloquently:

> There is also this gesture of being in possession of an "objective" platform,
> an abstract position, from which to analyse anything—from cities, persons,
> cells, you have it—which can be disturbingly immune to take in difference,
> particularity and contingency (or history) seriously. Indeed, almost any-
> thing can be translated into the abstract theorising of systems language of
> which resilience theory is but one genre. There are few ways (if any) by
> which empirical case studies can kick back and reshape the overarching
> framework since this framework always hovers "'up there," colonising any
> place it is brought to operate onto. (2014)

Resilience, to Glasgow and Cape Town planners and policy elites,
implies bracing yourself for economic and environmental catastrophes,
and everything will be fine in the end, as cities will "survive and thrive." It
is not a strategy that leads us to question the structural and institutional
conditions that are forcing people to be resilient in the first place. Kristina
Diprose has offered a particularly strong critique of the resilience logic
and discourse:

> It is time to rid ourselves of resilience: to renounce responsibility for the
> economic crisis; to stop scapegoating people who are struggling; to refuse to
> submit to stress; to recognise healthy limits and do everything possible to
> sustain them. . . . Political reform and grassroots resistance can only work
> towards recovery if we work for the weak as well as the strong; if we promote
> a culture in which people do not just survive, but thrive. . . . Imagine if the
> time and effort invested in future-proofing ourselves was instead given to
> fully occupying the present, and to more determinedly realising the change
> we want to see. (2015, 54–55)

Mark Neocleous takes this further when commenting on the 2013 launch
of an academic journal called *Resilience*, whose editors issued a call for
papers for a special issue entitled "Resistance or Resilience?":

> But aside from raising the obvious question—why not start a journal called
> *Resistance* and devote just one special issue to resilience?—the call seems to

miss the central point: resilience is by definition *against resistance*. Resilience wants acquiescence, not resistance. Not a passive acquiescence, for sure, in fact quite the opposite. But it does demand that we use our actions to accommodate ourselves to capital and the state, and the secure future of both, rather than to resist them. (2013, 7)

To return to how I opened this chapter, imagine if those behind Glasgow's resilience strategy had asked participants, 'Would you rather 'bounce back' from hard times, or resist and eliminate hard times?' In this sense resilience serves as a sharp instrument for those wielding symbolic power in the shaping of urban agnotology, producing ignorance about the larger economic and social structures that impose shocks and stresses, and therefore is a term that "has left little room for scholars to engage language that is broadly legible to activists" (Ranganathan and Bratman 2021, 121). As those authors point out, resilience discourses must be sidelined in order to make way for a range of humanist, feminist, Black, Brown, and Indigenous knowledges concerned with climate justice in an abolitionist framework, a point that chimes with an earlier intervention by Kate Derickson (2016) in her call for an "interim politics of resourcefulness" drawing insights from folk and Indigenous knowledges among historically marginalized groups.

These interventions are important because neoliberal urbanism has proven to be extraordinarily resilient, and the most resilient community of all appears to be that of a cartel of politicians and financial executives, aided by think tanks and philanthrocapitalist foundations, who have bounced back from a crisis they created with even more doses of inequality. When policy elites talk, without any sense of dramatic irony, about how "resilient" people are in places where they want to implement grand strategies to make them even more resilient, perhaps what they really mean is that people have revolutionary impulses, and they want to tame them by promoting survival strategies over organizing strategies. As political ecologist Alf Hornborg put it: "We needed a revolution. We got resilience" (quoted in Ernstson 2014).

3 Gentrification beyond False Choice Urbanism

> [I]t was suggested that revitalization was rarely an
> appropriate term for gentrification, but we can see now
> that in one sense it is appropriate. Gentrification is part of a
> larger redevelopment process dedicated to the revitalization
> of the profit rate. In the process, many downtowns are being
> converted into bourgeois playgrounds replete with quaint
> markets, restored townhouses, boutique rows, yachting
> marinas, and Hyatt Regencies. These very visual alterations
> to the urban landscape are not at all an accidental side-
> effect of temporary economic disequilibrium but are as
> rooted in the structure of capitalist society as was the advent
> of suburbanization.
>
> Neil Smith (1982, 151–52)

The architect and urban planner Andres Duany is widely seen as the father
and guru of "New Urbanism," an American urban design and planning
cult that has gone global. New Urbanists are vehemently anti-sprawl and
anti-modernist and typically demonstrate near-evangelical belief in the
construction of high-density, mixed-use, mixed-tenure settlements with a
neotraditional vernacular, well served by public transport and pedestrian
friendly (integrated by a network of accessible streets, sidewalks, cycle
paths, and public spaces). All of these features, if you can afford to buy
into them, are supposed to nurture a profound sense of community that
will lead to harmonious, livable, and sustainable "urban villages."

In 2001, Duany wrote an essay for *American Enterprise Magazine*, published by the American Enterprise Institute, a right-wing think tank, entitled "Three Cheers for Gentrification." An obnoxious and declamatory rant directed at "the squawking of old neighborhood bosses who can't bear the self-reliance of the incoming middle-class, and can't accept the dilution of their political base," it contains caricatures, trivializations, and myths that are too numerous to dissect in full. Yet one passage in particular serves as a useful point of departure for this chapter:

> "Affordable" housing isn't always what cities need more of. Some do, but many need just the opposite. For every San Francisco or Manhattan where real estate has become uniformly too expensive, there are many more cities like Detroit, Trenton, Syracuse, Milwaukee, Houston, and Philadelphia that could use all the gentrification they can get. The last thing these places ought to be pursuing is more cheap housing. Gentrification is usually good news, for there is nothing more unhealthy for a city than a monoculture of poverty. . . . Gentrification rebalances a concentration of poverty by providing the tax base, rub-off work ethic, and political effectiveness of a middle class, and in the process improves the quality of life for all of a community's residents. It is the rising tide that lifts all boats." (Duany 2001, 39)

If we cut through the provocative tone of these sentences, not to mention the patronizing trickle-down logic, Duany is wedded to a perspective that is very common among many observers of gentrification (whether journalists, policy officials, planners, architects and urban designers, or mainstream urban social scientists). In a piece published in 2006, I called this perspective the *false choice* between gentrification (a form of reinvestment) and a "concentration of poverty" (disinvestment) (Slater 2006), drawing on these powerful words by James DeFilippis:

> Since the emergence of gentrification, it has become untenable to argue that reinvestment is a desirable end in-and-of-itself for low-income people and residents of disinvested areas. Instead, rightfully conceived, reinvestment needs to be understood through the lens of questions such as: What kind of investment? For whom? Controlled by whom? These processes have left residents of low-income neighbourhoods in a situation where, since they exert little control over either investment capital or their homes, they are facing the 'choices' of either continued disinvestment and decline in the quality of the homes they live in, or reinvestment that results in their

displacement. The importance of gentrification, therefore, is that it clearly demonstrates that low-income people, and the neighbourhoods they live in, suffer not from a lack of capital but from a lack of power and control over even the most basic components of life—that is, the places called home. (2004, 89)

DeFilippis's eloquence leads to the question of *how* low-income people can gain power and control over their homes, which he addresses via an analysis of collective ownership initiatives such as community land trusts, mutual housing associations, and limited-equity housing cooperatives in the United States. Yet since DeFilippis's book was published, the false choice perspective has been advanced time and time again. I have lost count of the number of high-profile statements on gentrification in the last two decades that have succumbed to a tired formula: weigh up the supposed pros and cons of gentrification amid attempts at levity, throw in a few half-baked worries about threats to "diversity" and housing afford-ability, and conclude that gentrification is actually "good on balance" because it represents reinvestment (facelift and uplift) that somehow stops neighborhoods from "dying."

Take, for example, a piece in *New York Magazine* in February 2014 enti-tled "Is Gentrification All Bad?" (Davidson 2014). After opening up with the ambiguous remark that "a nice neighborhood should be not a luxury but an urban right" (what makes a neighborhood "nice" is inherently a class question), the author presents a brief history of the neighborhood of Bedford-Stuyvesant in Brooklyn, once an emblem of disinvestment and racial segregation but now (like most parts of Brooklyn) a place of out-landish real estate prices, and remarks that "gentrification happens not because a few developers or politicians foist it on an unwilling city but because it's a medicine most people want to take. The trick is to minimize the harmful side effects." The piece concludes with the following:

> An ideological split [in the 1960s] divided those who wrote cities off as unliveable relics from those who believed they must be saved. Today a simi-lar gulf separates those who fear an excess of prosperity from those who worry about the return of blight. Economic flows can be reversed with stun-ning speed: gentrification can nudge a neighborhood up the slope; decline can roll it off a cliff. Somewhere along that trajectory of change is a sweet

spot, a mixed and humming street that is not quite settled or sanitized, where Old Guard and new arrivals coexist in equilibrium. The game is to make it last.

"Mixed and humming" hides what is effectively a fatalistic conclusion, but one very common in writing that reduces gentrification to a moral question (good versus bad) rather than a *political* one.[1] In sum, the *New York Magazine* article argued that gentrification is here to stay, we have to live with it, it just needs some policy fine-tuning to stabilize or "manage" it and soften the blows it inflicts, and the urbanists' holy grail is some kind of middle ground between "up the slope" and precipitous "decline."

In order to situate gentrification in a sturdier analytic register, this chapter blasts open this tenacious and constrictive dualism of "prosperity" (gentrification) *or* "blight" (disinvestment) by showing how the two are *fundamentally intertwined* in a wider process of capitalist urbanization and uneven development that creates profit and class privilege for some while stripping many of the human need of shelter. No viable alternatives will be found unless we ask why there are neighborhoods of astounding affluence and of grinding poverty, why there are "new arrivals" and an "Old Guard," why there are renovations and evictions concurrently; in short, why there is inequality in the first place.

Despite many attempts to sugarcoat it and celebrate it, *gentri*fication, both as term and process, has always been about how housing opportunities of middle-class people are expanded while those of working-class people are restricted. When we jettison the journalistic embrace of "hipsters," question the political relevance of the enormous literature on the gamut of individual preferences and lifestyles of middle-class gentrifiers, and consider instead who and what makes urban land profitable for (re)development, then questions such as urbanization *for whom*, *against whom*, and *who decides* come to the forefront—and false choice urbanism is exposed as a red herring.[2] Anchoring my arguments in this chapter are the important theorizations of the late geographer Neil Smith, which are important not only for understanding why gentrification occurs, how it unfolds, and whom it affects, but also for understanding and learning from the many strategies of resistance to gentrification.

THROUGH RUTH'S LOOKING GLASS

In 1951, Ruth Glass took up a post as director of social research at University College London. Her sustained intellectual and critical engagement with the postwar upheavals that resulted in the formation of the British welfare state led her to immersion in the writings of Marx and Engels and encouraged her gradual switch from urban planning to urban sociology. The links between housing and class struggle in London (particularly in Islington, where she lived) became her long-term research interest, and concerns about the accelerating rehabilitation of Victorian lodging houses, tenurial transformation from renting to owning, steady property price increases, and the displacement of working-class occupiers by middle-class incomers led her to coin the term *gentrification* in 1964 (Glass 1964). By the time Glass passed away in 1990, gentrification had not only generated a large international literature; it had become a word around which class struggles and urban social movements (fighting for the rights of those at the bottom of the urban class structure in a variety of contexts) could mobilize and gain visibility and political momentum. This remains the case today, and that large literature has now morphed into an immense body of scholarship, one so large that it makes concise summaries, syntheses, and critique a considerable challenge.

As Glass intended, *gentrification* simply yet very powerfully captures the class inequalities and injustices created by capitalist urban land markets and policies. The rising housing expense burden for low-income and working-class households, and the personal catastrophes of displacement, eviction, and homelessness, are symptoms of a set of institutional arrangements (private property rights and a "free" market) that favor the creation of urban environments to serve the needs of capital accumulation at the expense of the social needs of home, community, and family. Gentrification commonly occurs in urban areas where prior disinvestment in the urban infrastructure creates opportunities for profitable redevelopment, where the needs and concerns of business and policy elites are met at the expense of urban residents affected by work instability, unemployment, and stigmatization.

For almost as long as gentrification has been studied, there has been considerable disagreement over how to define it; in short, whether gentrification should refer only to the residential rehabilitation described by Glass or to a much larger-scale production of urban space for middle-class consumers, involving inter alia "new-build" developments on vacant land (Davidson and Lees 2005). There are some who worry about the stretching of the term and insist that we go no further than the fine details of Glass's original definition, as it will lose all meaning if we do (Boddy 2007; Maloutas 2011). But as Neil Smith and Peter Williams wrote over thirty years ago:

> If we look back at the attempted definitions of gentrification, it should be clear that we are concerned with a process much broader than merely residential rehabilitation. . . . [A]s the process has continued, it has become increasingly apparent that residential rehabilitation is only one facet . . . of a more profound economic, social, and spatial restructuring. In reality, residential gentrification is integrally linked to the redevelopment of urban waterfronts for recreational and other functions, the decline of remaining inner-city manufacturing facilities, the rise of hotel and convention complexes and central-city office developments, as well as the emergence of modern 'trendy' retail and restaurant districts. . . . Gentrification is a visible spatial component of this social transformation. A highly dynamic process, it is not amenable to overly restrictive definitions. (1986, 3)

In terms of sheer geographical scale, we are dealing with a quite different urban phenomenon from what was observed in the 1960s, and also from when Smith and Williams wrote the words just quoted (Lees, Shin, and Lopez-Morales, 2015). Where Glass does remain important and relevant is less in the empirical details of 1960s Islington and more in her critical perspective on class transformation and deep commitment to social justice. In our book *Gentrification*, Loretta Lees, Elvin Wyly, and I (Lees, Slater, and Wyly 2008, xv) defined gentrification as "the transformation of a working class or vacant area of the central city into middle class residential and/or commercial use." I still think this is an acceptable definition, but on reflection I would note two things. First, gentrification is not just something that occurs in the central city (it can certainly occur in suburban, exurban, and rural locations), and second—more importantly—while it always involves a degree of class transformation, it is very often about much more than that. Take, for instance, a recent definition provided by Causa Justa/Just Cause (2018, 8), an organization based in the Bay Area of California working for better housing for marginalized people: "A profit-driven racial and class reconfiguration of urban, working-class and communities of colour that have suffered from a history of disinvestment and abandonment."

There are indeed hundreds of examples in the academic literature of gentrification as a process of class *and* racial reconfiguration. The precise character of this reconfiguration depends on local histories and geographies. One recent and remarkable contribution to this literature has been provided by Ida Danewid, who analyzed the Grenfell Tower disaster of 2017 as part of a much wider global city cartography of imperial and racial violence, in which "the 'making' of global cities often goes hand in hand with racialized policies and practices designed to 'clean up the streets' through revitalisation programmes and plans to displace actually existing inhabitants" (2020, 291). Drawing on the literature on racial capitalism, Danewid argues that race is not simply an effect of discriminatory landlords, lenders, and employers, but rather a constituent logic of capital:

> While gentrification, of course, looks different in different cities, it is typically underpinned by a set of racialized assumptions about who belongs in certain spaces and who does not. This racial logic ultimately helps explain why Grenfell residents' years of complaints about safety were ignored and why many residents have still to be properly housed more than two years after the fire. In the eyes of urban elites, Grenfell was disposable and expendable ... standing in the way of gentrification and urban regeneration schemes. (299-300)

Furthermore, Danewid reminds us that modern forms of urban planning such as segregation, "slum" administration, and clearance were first experimented with in colonial and settler cities before they were implemented back in the imperial metropoles, and this practice has simply continued in the colonizing ethos of contemporary housing regeneration and renewal schemes in cities like London. Therefore, for Danewid, gentrification "takes place through the creation of raced space" (302) and is less about a "new" urban colonialism (Atkinson and Bridge 2005) than about a continuation of the old one.

The importance of defining gentrification beyond just class can also be seen in the literature on the relationship between gender and gentrification. As Bahar Sakizlioğlu (2018, 205) points out, "gentrification alters the ways in which places are gendered and in doing so it reflects and affects the way gender is constructed and experienced." For this reason, it is rather remarkable that the literature on gender and gentrification is small when considered in relation to the numerous other ways in which the process has been analyzed. This is problematic on multiple fronts, but perhaps mostly because, as Winifred Curran (2018) has demonstrated, when a majority of public sector workers, public housing residents, and the social services–dependent elderly are female, the impact of gentrification disproportionately affects women. It is well documented in particular that evictions and displacement caused by gentrification disproportionately threaten women's social commitments, livelihoods, and place attachments. The challenges gentrification causes for elderly people, low-income people, people of color, people with disabilities, and queer people are all mediated by gender. As Curran also demonstrates, it is no coincidence (given that women tend to suffer most from gentrification) that some of the most effective antigentrification movements have been led by and fought by women. Across the United States, Matthew Desmond (2016) has observed and explained that evictions disproportionately affect low-income women of color, which points to the importance of emerging intersectional approaches that examine how "different axes of oppression cut across each other and are expressed and negotiated through the process of gentrification" (Sakizlioğlu 2018, 219). The point here is that while the coinage of gentrification may have been solely about class transformation, and while class transformation is happening wherever there is gentrification, the process is by no means *reducible* to just one dimension of social differentiation. Furthermore, as discussed in the next section, dimensions of social differentiation—intersecting or not— are crucial to the devalorization and revalorization of urban land.

FROM FALSE CHOICE AGNOTOLOGY TO THE CIRCULATION OF CAPITAL: THE ENDURING RELEVANCE OF THE RENT GAP THEORY

A quarter of a century ago the academic literature on the process had collapsed into a deeply tedious debate over production-side versus consumption-side explanations. Both explanations had emerged in reaction to the obfuscations of 1970s neoclassical economists' take on gentrification as a natural, inevitable market adjustment process, as something to be celebrated as part of an apparent middle-class return to the central city from suburbia (Lipton 1977; Wheaton 1977; Kern 1981; LeRoy and Sonstelie 1983; Schill and Nathan 1983). Those explaining gentrification from a consumption perspective reacted to simplistic neoclassical accounts of demographic changes and lifestyle preferences by illustrating how changes in the industrial and occupational structure of advanced capitalist cities, occurring as they did at a time of significant social and cultural upheaval (post-1968), produced an expanding pool of middle-class gentrifiers with a disposition toward central-city living and an associated rejection of suburbia for the blandness and monotony it symbolized (Ley 1996; Hamnett 1991; Butler 1997).[3]

Scholars prioritizing a production perspective rejected the neoclassical view that gentrification was an expression of the changed consumption choices among certain sections of the middle class and instead emphasized the role of capital and its institutional agents (public and private) in creating gentrifiable spaces (Smith 1979; Clark 1987; Engels 1994; Hammel 1999). Far too many papers were published taking one side or the other vis-à-vis which explanation was more convincing, and far too many papers were published summarizing the debates. It became exasperating, so much so that many scholars moved on to different topics. There is frankly no point in reopening those debates; while they occurred, people were being displaced by gentrification.

I consider Neil Smith's rent gap theory to be the most useful available, not only to explain the political economy of gentrification but also to respond to the rampant agnotology that circulates about gentrification's supposed benefits. The theory helps explain how propitious political-economic conditions are created for the extraction of profit from urban land markets and, far from being economistic or deterministic (as it is frequently critiqued or dismissed), it is a crucial theory to understand as part of a critical and/or resistant response to gentrification and as a critique of the logic undergirding the process. It is necessary to clarify the theory, as misunderstandings, errors of interpretation, and sometimes lazy critiques still circulate widely and distort not only the debate over the theory but also the field of gentrification studies more generally.

Neoclassical economics continues to play a powerful ideological role in societies today and in many instances is the undergirding logic driving urban policy, so it is important to understand the particular battle for ideas in which Smith immersed himself early on in his career. Remarkably, the empirical study that led to the generation of the rent gap theory was an undergraduate dissertation in geography he completed at the University of St. Andrews, Scotland, in 1977. Smith had spent a year as an exchange student in Philadelphia, where he had become captivated by the profound changes visited upon the neighborhood of Society Hill. Having first noticed gentrification in 1972 on Rose Street in Edinburgh, when a trendy new bar called The Galloping Major distinguished itself from neighboring pubs by serving "quite appetizing lunches adorned with salad" (Smith 1996, xviii), he felt that existing neoclassical urban land use models and predictions regarding the miserable fate of central cities were inadequate in terms of explaining the gentrification he had seen in Edinburgh and Philadelphia.

Smith was very skeptical of neoclassical models and predictions because of the *consumer sovereignty* paradigm undergirding them, which held that the rational choices of individual consumers of land and housing determined the morphology of cities. Middle-class consumer demand for space, the neoclassical argument went, explained suburbanization, a process seen by many inside and outside academia to be the only future for all urban places. But the empirical reality of Society Hill—gentrification— seemed to call that paradigm into question. Smith could not accept that consumers were suddenly demanding en masse the opposite to what had been predicted and "choosing" to gentrify central city areas instead. In Society Hill he unearthed data showing that a majority of middle-class people had never left for Philadelphia's suburbs because *space was being produced for them* via state-sponsored private sector development. This created handsome profits for developers at the expense of working-class people who were displaced from central city space. His undergraduate dissertation was distilled and published in *Antipode* in 1978 (Smith 1978) and was refined further in the *Journal of the American Planning Association* (Smith 1979), where the rent gap theory was first articulated.

A starting point for Smith was that, in capitalist property markets, the decisive "consumer preference" (with characteristic mischief he adopted the neoclassical language) is "the preference for profit, or, more accurately, a sound financial investment" (1979, 540). As disinvestment in a particular district intensifies, as had happened in Society Hill, it creates lucrative profit opportunities for developers, investors, homebuyers, and local government. If we wanted to understand the much-lauded American "urban renaissance" of the 1970s, the argument and title of the rent gap essay went, it was much more important to track the movement of capital rather than the movement of people (the latter movement was the exclusive focus of the "back to the city" rhetoric of the time and of the scholarship on it).

Crucial to Smith's argument was the ever-fluctuating phenomenon of *ground rent*: the charge that landlords are able to demand (via private property rights) for the right to use land and its appurtenances (the buildings placed on it and the resources embedded within it), usually received as a stream of payments from tenants but also via any asset appreciation captured at resale. Landlords in poorer central city neighborhoods are often holding investments in buildings that represented what economists and urban planners call the "highest and best use" over a century ago; spending money to maintain these assets as low-cost rental units becomes ever more difficult to justify with each passing year, since the investments will be difficult to recover from low-income tenants. It becomes rational and logical for landlords to "milk" the property, extracting rent from the tenants yet spending the absolute minimum to maintain the structure. With the passage of time, the deferred maintenance becomes apparent: people with the money to do so will leave a neighborhood, and financial institutions "redline" the neighborhood as too risky for lending. Physical decline accelerates, and moderate-income residents and businesses moving away are replaced by successively poorer tenants who simply cannot access housing anywhere else.

In late 1920s Chicago, Homer Hoyt had identified a "valley in the landvalue curve between the Loop and outer residential areas . . . [which] indicates the location of these sections where the buildings are mostly forty years old and where the residents rank lowest in rent-paying ability" (Hoyt 1933, 356–58). For Smith (1979), this capital depreciation in the inner city meant that there is likely to be an increasing divergence between *capitalized ground rent* (the actual quantity of ground rent that is appropriated by the landowner, given the present land use) and *potential ground rent*

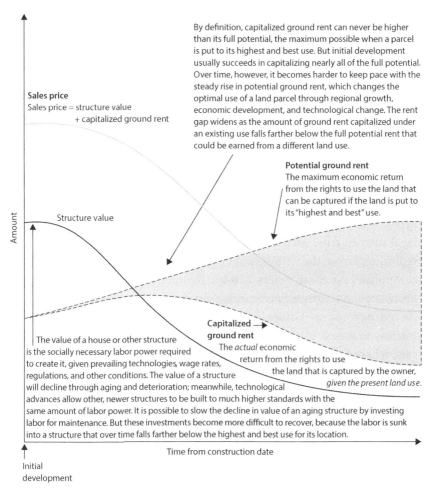

By definition, capitalized ground rent can never be higher than its full potential, the maximum possible when a parcel is put to its highest and best use. But initial development usually succeeds in capitalizing nearly all of the full potential. Over time, however, it becomes harder to keep pace with the steady rise in potential ground rent, which changes the optimal use of a land parcel through regional growth, economic development, and technological change. The rent gap widens as the amount of ground rent capitalized under an existing use falls farther below the full potential rent that could be earned from a different land use.

Sales price
Sales price = structure value
          + capitalized ground rent

Potential ground rent
The maximum economic return from the rights to use the land that can be captured if the land is put to its "highest and best" use.

Structure value

Amount

Capitalized ground rent

The value of a house or other structure is the socially necessary labor power required to create it, given prevailing technologies, wage rates, regulations, and other conditions. The value of a structure will decline through aging and deterioration; meanwhile, technological advances allow other, newer structures to be built to much higher standards with the same amount of labor power. It is possible to slow the decline in value of an aging structure by investing labor for maintenance. But these investments become more difficult to recover, because the labor is sunk into a structure that over time falls farther below the highest and best use for its location.

The *actual* economic return from the rights to use the land that is captured by the owner, *given the present land use.*

Time from construction date

Initial development

Figure 3. Neil Smith's rent gap theory, redrawn by Elvin Wyly. *Source:* Lees, Slater, and Wyly (2008, 52).

(the maximum that could be appropriated under the land's "highest and best use"). So, Hoyt's land value valley, radically analyzed and reconceptualized, "can now be understood in large part as the rent gap" (see figure 3):

> Gentrification occurs when the gap is wide enough that developers can purchase shells cheaply, can pay the builders' costs and profit for rehabilitation, can pay interest on mortgage and construction loans, and can then sell the

end product for a sale price that leaves a satisfactory return to the developer. The entire ground rent, or a large portion of it, is now capitalized: the neighbourhood has been "recycled" and begins a new cycle of use. (Hoyt, 545)

The elegance of the rent gap theory lies not just in what Ley (1996, 42), one of Smith's more astute interlocutors, has referred to as its "ingenious simplicity," but in its critical edge and political impulse. The flight of capital away from certain areas of the city—depreciation and disinvestment—has devastating implications for people living at the bottom of the urban class structure. The "shells" referred to by Hoyt do not simply "appear" as part of some naturally occurring neighborhood "decay"; they are actively produced by clearing out existing residents via all manner of tactics and legal instruments, such as landlord harassment, massive rent increases, redlining, arson, the withdrawal of public services, and eminent domain/ compulsory purchase orders. Closing the rent gap requires, crucially, *separating people currently obtaining use values from the present land use providing those use values* in order to capitalize the land to the perceived highest and best use. The rent gap thus highlights specific class interests, where the quest for profit takes precedence over the human need of shelter.

The rent gap theory has been the subject of intense debate for nearly forty years. But those debates, often shot through with intractable ideological confrontations and petty bickering, became rather frustrating for many, leading to many cursory, dismissive summaries. It is unnecessary here to recite and summarize in any great detail the rent gap debates. Far more helpful is to consider what can be learned from considering, as a body of scholarship, the most valuable lessons from studies that have grasped the importance of the political thrust of the rent gap from the outset and have understood its theoretical premises in order to conduct detailed empirical tests. Given the intense empirical grafting involved—there are no readily available variables to measure capitalized and potential ground rent, so scholars have to dig into planning archives and land records going back several decades in order to construct their own proxy indicators—few thorough empirical studies exist. Those that do, however, considered as a collective, are all valuable as part of a wider scholarly effort to understand and resist gentrification, wherever and under whatever conditions it is happening. From all those studies, and from Neil Smith's original writings, four things above all become clear about the rent gap theory.

1) The rent gap theory is not narrowly economistic, but a theory of the state's role in creating the economic conditions for gentrification.

Perhaps the most frequent charges leveled at the rent gap theory are that it is pure economic determinism (Hamnett 1991); that it "overlooks regulatory contexts which may well discipline capital's freedom of expression" (Ley 1996, 42); and that it has no place for a consideration of the role of "extra-economic force," to use the language of arguments made by Asher Ghertner (2014, 2015). To be sure, rent gaps are produced by economic agents and actors (landlords, bankers, developers, realtors), and the theory was formulated as part of a broader critique of uneven development under capitalism, but the role of the state in the theory is far from laissez-faire or absent; rather, it is one of *active facilitator*, as Smith had found in Society Hill: "The state had both a *political* role in realizing Society Hill, and an *economic* role in helping to produce this new urban space" (1979, 28). It has been demonstrated multiple times in contexts where gentrification is occurring (particularly in recent years as gentrification—though never used in name by policy officials—has become a strategic urban development vision in many contexts) that the role of the state in producing rent gaps is *direct* and *pivotal*, to the point where rent gaps simply would not exist without the state (e.g., Uitermark, Duyvendak, and Kleinhans 2007; Glynn 2008; Hodkinson 2012; Kallin and Slater 2014; Paton 2010; Mendes 2018). As Hamish Kallin (2018, 45) has pointed out in a study of a failed state-driven gentrification strategy in the Edinburgh district of Granton, "if claims to difference are grounded in the notion that extra-economic force is alien to gentrification in 'the West', then these are weak claims to difference." It is also worth noting that Neil Smith's undergraduate dissertation even carried the subtitle, "State Involvement in Society Hill, Philadelphia."

Matthias Bernt (2016, 641–42) complains about the "essentially universalizing undercurrent which is at the core of the rent-gap theory" and argues that "downplaying non-economic instances is deeply embedded within the reductionist conceptual architecture of the rent gap theory and

integrating different institutional, social, cultural and political constella-
tions has remained an enduring problem." In my view, such charges are
diversions in an epoch of aggressive state-led accumulation strategies and
the ever-sophisticated mutation of neoliberal urbanism (Brenner, Peck,
and Theodore 2010). Perhaps these charges keep appearing because the
original rent gap paper was rather muted on the role of the state, as its
author's main purpose was to critique the consumer sovereignty assumptions undergirding neoclassical land use models (even though the piece of
empirical research that informed the theory had the state as core to the
explanation of how gentrification was unfolding). But the point remains:
conclusions should not be drawn about the rent gap theory unless one
takes the trouble to read the original studies closely.

*2) The rent gap theory helps us understand the circulation of interest-
bearing capital in urban land markets, together with speculative landed
developer interests.*

After a visit to inner Detroit, to east Glasgow, to Vancouver's Downtown
Eastside, or to the "shrinking cities" of Eastern Europe, it is easy to understand why purveyors of false choice urbanism are so numerous. But they
are left analytically stranded when rent gap theory is brought to bear on
their "gentrification is better than the alternative" discourse. The valorization of capital in cities (its investment in search of surplus value or profit)
is necessarily matched by its devalorization (as the investor receives
returns on the investment only piecemeal when capital is "fixed" in the
landscape). However, new development must proceed if accumulation is
to occur, so the steady devalorization of capital creates longer-term possibilities for a new phase of valorization. The devalorization of capital
invested in the central city leads to a situation in which the ground rent
capitalized under current land uses is substantially lower than the ground
rent that could *potentially* be capitalized if the land uses were to change.
When redevelopment and rehabilitation become profitable prospects,
capital begins to flow back into the central city, and then substantial fortunes can be made.

However, it is worth noting that Smith pointed out that

it is also possible to conceive of a situation in which, rather than the capitalized ground rent being pushed down through devalorization, the potential ground rent is suddenly pushed higher, opening up a rent gap in a different manner. This might be the case, for example, when there is rapid and sustained inflation, or where strict regulation of a land market keeps potential ground rent low, but is then repealed. (1996, 68)

Dissecting these words in a study of the privatization and financialization of a rent-regulated multifamily housing complex in Manhattan, Ben Teresa (2019, 1401) has pointed out, "We no longer have to only *conceive* of such a situation, but we can *observe* this process in motion." He demonstrates that privatization involves "the reorganization of state power from managing social goods to ensuring the private profitability of those assets" and that financialization (the integration of finance and real estate markets) "introduces new actors and practices that reorder the scale for establishing potential rent and increase expectations about profitability and risk" (1405). The intensity and magnitude of capital flows in New York City are such that sustained disinvestment is no longer a precondition for gentrification. Along these lines, David Wachsmuth and Alexander Weisler (2018, 1152) examined the explosion of Airbnb rentals in New York City and argued that "across certain neighborhood types (primarily still-gentrifying areas and now-affluent, formerly gentrifying areas), the new, technologically-enabled possibility of short-term rentals systematically raises potential ground rents - and thus creates rent gaps even where there has been little or no devalorization of existing housing." Short-term rentals have massively widened the scope for land and real estate speculation—and the scope for displacement.

What does all this mean for how we understand and use the rent gap theory? Writing in the immediate aftermath of the 2008 financial crisis, David Harvey (2010, 180) remarked that speculative landed developer interests are "a singular principle power that has yet to be accorded its proper place in our understanding of not only the historical geography of capitalism but also the general evolution of capitalist class power." He continued: "Investments in rents on land, property, mines and raw materials thereby becomes an attractive proposition for all capitalists. Speculation in these values becomes rife. The production of capitalism's geography is propelled onwards by the need to realise speculative gains on these assets" (181).

In many capitalist economies, due to the decades-long shrinkage of the manufacturing sector, capital has switched from its primary circuit of industrial production to its secondary circuit of accumulation, urban land, and real estate markets, which runs parallel to the primary circuit. But the secondary has supplanted the primary in terms of its overall importance, often accounting for over 40 percent of all economic activity (Merrifield 2014). As an illustration, 76 percent of all bank loans in Britain go into property (and 64% of that into residential mortgages), and 87 percent of all household debt is tied up in mortgages. To address the crisis of continuous compound growth under long cycles of accumulation, capital has to devalue the existing capital fixed to the land, among other things, to reinvent investment opportunities for the absorption of a surplus (Harvey 2014; Christophers 2018).

At times of crisis, speculation in land that is being devalued becomes rife. In Britain for example, the institutional arrangements behind the distribution of housing incentivize rampant land speculation: the urban housing market in the United Kingdom (London especially) has become a place for very rich people—especially investors from overseas—to park their money at an annual rate of return of around 10 percent (Lansley and Mack 2015). Speculation means that more and more capital is being invested in search of rents and interest and future gains, rather than being invested in productive activity, a trend toward a rentier form of capitalism: a parasitic economy characterized by the marked escalation of *extracted unearned income*. Rentiers make staggering fortunes simply from ownership of assets or resources that all of us need. They have everything to gain from the global circulation of interest-bearing capital in urban land markets and from the municipal absorption of surplus capital via all kinds of debt-financed urbanization projects.

The relevance of the rent gap theory to the growth of speculative landed developer interests is that, as originally intended, it helps to "redirect our theoretical focus toward the sphere of circulation . . . [where] we can trace the power of finance capital over the urbanization process, and the patterning of urban space according to patterns of profitable investment" (Smith 1979, 24). The function of rent under a capitalist mode of production is to underpin investment and reinvestment opportunity. Land value is not created from owning land; it is created from collective social investments in land, which landowners then extract as unearned income via private property rights. Exploiting the rent gap requires the *expropriation of socially created use values*: a form of structural violence visited upon working-class people in contexts that are usually described as "regenerating" or "revitalizing." Instead of building shelter for people in need, the capitalist system encourages rentiers to see who can best use their land-banking skills to anticipate the next housing bubble and survive the last one. In relation to false choice urbanism, the critically important point to grasp is that investment and disinvestment do not represent some sort of moral conundrum, with the former somehow, on balance, being better than the latter. Nor does reinvestment represent some sort of magical remedy for those who have lived through and endured decades of disinvestment. Gentrification and "decline'; *embourgoisement* and "concentrated poverty"; regeneration and decay: these are not opposites, alternatives, or choices, but rather *tensions* and *contradictions* in the overall system of capital circulation. Rent gaps do not just appear out of nowhere; they represent certain social (class) interests, where the quest for profit takes precedence over the need for shelter. It's worth noting how Smith closed his 1979 rent gap paper:

> Gentrification and other kinds of urban renaissance could be the leading edge of a larger restructuring of urban space. According to one scenario this restructuring would be accomplished according to the needs of capital. . . . According to a second scenario, the needs of capital would be systematically dismantled, to be displaced by the social, economic and cultural needs of people as the principle according to which the restructuring of space occurs. (546)

3) Rent gaps are produced via the activation of territorial stigma.

A signal contribution of the rent gap theory was to show that, first, the individual, personal, rational preferences in the housing market much cherished by neoclassical economists, and second, the "new middle-class" dispositions toward a vibrant central city (and associated rejections of bland, patriarchal suburbia) that intrigued liberal-humanist and feminist geographers, are all tightly bound up with larger, collective social relations and investments (core to the rent gap concept is that ground rent is *produced by the labor power invested in land*, and that consumer preferences are not "exogenous" to the structures of land, property, credit, and housing). Contrary to, for example, the interventions of distinguished science writers drawing upon one dubious source (Ball 2014), consumer preferences and tastes visible in gentrifying neighborhoods are not naturally occurring phenomena; they are deliberately made by agents seeking to extract profit from urban land, usually in relation to a set of negative images about what places could become, or how they might remain, if they did not experience an upward economic trajectory.

A frequent charge against the rent gap theory is that it fails to predict which neighborhoods will gentrify and which will not (missing completely the fact that it was never designed as a predictive model). But there is an unresolved analytic puzzle: Why does it appear to be the case that gentrification rarely seems to occur first in the most severely disinvested parts of a city or a region—where the potential for substantial profit is at its greatest—but proceeds instead in devalorized, working-class tracts that are certainly disinvested but by no means the poorest or offering the maximum profit to developers? Dan Hammel (1999, 1290) helpfully offered a clue: "Inner city areas have many sites with a potential for development that could return high levels of rent. That development never occurs, however, because the perception of an impoverished neighbourhood prevents large amounts of capital being applied to the land."

The challenge remains enticing: to consider the disparity between potential and capitalized ground rent in the context of how urban dwellers at the bottom of the class structure are discredited and devalued *because of the places with which they are associated*. As we will see in chapter 6, the negative manner in which certain parts of cities are portrayed (by journalists, politicians, and think tanks especially) has become critically important to policies geared toward their future. A mushrooming body of work points to a direct relationship between territorial stigmatization and the process of gentrification (Gray and Mooney 2011; Slater and Anderson 2012; Kallin and Slater 2014; August 2014; Lees 2014; Thorn and Holgersson 2016), in which neighborhood "taint" becomes a target and rationale for "fixing" an area via its reincorporation into the secondary circuit of accumulation (Wacquant 2008b). But sometimes the perception Hammel outlines is so negative and entrenched that it acts as a symbolic barrier or diversion to the circulation of capital. As territorial stigmatization intensifies, there are major consequences for urban land markets and therefore implications for rent gap theory. Using the example of the "regeneration" of Craigmillar, Edinburgh, Kallin (2017) has posited a *reputational gap* to explain the role that territorial stigma plays in the process of state-led gentrification. He argues, "The rent gap model can be increasingly useful even in instances where no market (re)valorization of the land occurs, precisely because state policy is so fixated on the possibility that it *could* (and, of course, that it *should*) occur" (103).

Analyzing interviews with those responsible for the delivery of a regeneration project on land that was once a large social housing estate, Kallin explains that their relentless articulation of the "potential" in the "new" Craigmillar relied on their simultaneous and equally relentless denigration of the "old" Craigmillar. This reputational gap is by no means a rival model or an amendment to the rent gap theory itself, but rather a way of showing how "territorial stigmatization functions . . . as part of the gentrification process not just as the justification for intervention, but as a necessary component of that intervention" (114). For Kallin it is the state-led opening of a reputational gap that facilitates the state-led closure of a rent gap.

4) The rent gap theory can help explain gentrification beyond the Global North.

Up to the mid-2000s, there were hardly any studies of gentrification beyond the usual suspects (Lees, Shin, and Lopez-Morales 2015, 2016). Almost everything scholars knew about the process, and the rich body of theory developed to understand it, came from (predominantly large) cities of the Global North. But the scale and pace of urban development (and the extent of displacement) beyond the North have led to fascinating recent empirical and theoretical interventions and changed the landscape of gentrification research in ways that are highly instructive for urban scholars, regardless of where they are located. For example, Marieke Krijnen (2018a, 1042) reminds us that the rent gap theory is especially helpful when seeking to "understand how areas become susceptible to renewed capital investment, i.e. what happens *before* gentrification occurs" and addresses this question in the context of Beirut, Lebanon. Not only does she trace the local and national laws and regulations pertaining to construction, rent, urban planning, and heritage protection that created rent gaps (a common research approach), but she also demonstrates that "forces not commonly discussed in rent gap theory, such as informality, illegality, exceptionalism, conflict and forced displacement, create rent gaps as well, through enlarging potential ground rents by allowing developers to build (more) where this was legally not allowed, and through forced population movements leading to sudden shifts in actual and potential ground rent" (1043). Theoretically, Krijnen demonstrates that calls to make urban theory more cosmopolitan and comparative (e.g., Robinson 2006, 2011) need not necessarily involve jettisoning existing theories formulated in the North and formulating new theories at ground level, but rather extending existing theories methodologically and conceptually to account for particular political, economic, and institutional contexts.

Judy Whitehead and Nitim More (2007) examined the massive changes visited upon the central mills districts of Mumbai in the context of the 1980s informalization and decentralization (to the suburbs) of the textile industry in that city. Aided by an NGO organization actively supporting the "relocation" of slum dwellers from those districts to the outskirts of Mumbai, mill owners and multinational developers seeking opportunities for commercial real estate realized that the (actively disinvested) land upon which the mills once worked was not at its highest and best use, and to gain maximum profit from the land they pushed successfully for changes to development regulations (which had stipulated that only one-third of the mill lands could be used for real estate development). The result was an exclusive apartment and shopping mall development in a city where over 70 percent of residents officially live in "slum" conditions. True to the original formulation of the rent gap thesis, the role of the state was far from laissez-faire:

> The state government has changed to become an organisation attracting off-shore and domestic investment to the island city, while service provision becomes secondary. It has been reshaped to enable, facilitate and promote international flows of financial, real estate and productive capital, and the

logic of its policies can be read off almost directly through calculations of rent gaps emerging at various spots in the city. (Whitehead and More, 2434)

The propitious role of the state in creating the disparity between capitalized and potential ground rent has also been illustrated by Ernesto López-Morales (2010, 2011), in two striking papers on gentrification by ground rent dispossession in Santiago, Chile. After the return to democracy in Chile in 1990 (following seventeen years of military dictatorship), various state policies were designed with a view to attracting professional middle classes into deeply disinvested parts of central Santiago, with varying degrees of success. From the 2000s onward, however, a second phase of much larger-scale, state-sponsored entrepreneurial redevelopment has been taking place on formerly industrial sites and on small owner-occupied plots in traditionally working-class peri-central areas known locally as *poblaciones*, all of which exhibit wide rent gaps in the context of a city that has positioned itself as one of the economic powerhouses of Latin America. López-Morales traced and mapped the policy-driven production and accumulation of potential ground rent in Santiago alongside the land devaluation produced by strict national building codes and the underimplementation of previous state upgrading programs. Just as in the Mumbai case, the state was critically important in the opening and closing of rent gaps, as well as in creating the conditions for national and foreign speculation in urban land markets, because "the way developers can acquire and accumulate large portions of inhabited land is by buying, at relatively low prices, from inner city owner-occupiers, and they often hold it vacant while passively waiting (or actively lobbying) to get building regulations loosened" (López-Morales 2010, 147).

Another deployment of the rent gap thesis is in a remarkable analysis by Melissa Wright (2014) of the gentrification of the *centro historico* of Ciudad Juarez on the Mexico-United States border in the wake of the carnage and devastation caused there by a transcontinental drug war (2006–2012) instigated by both countries' governments. Wright found rent gap theory to be highly applicable to explain a situation whereby "in order to rescue the *centro* and augment its economic value, the city first needed to be economically and socially destroyed. The formerly vibrant downtown, in short, needed to be killed before it could be rescued" (2).

Wright weds feminist and Marxist approaches to accumulation by dispossession to explain a class struggle between, on the one hand, ruling elites intent on a strategy of denigrating the lives and spaces of working-class women and their children living in the *centro* in order to expand the rent gap and ultimately "clean up" the area and "reestablish" it as a place for upstanding families, and on the other, activists drawing public attention to the exploitation (in maquiladora factories and in sex work) of working poor women, and especially to *feminicidio* (the killing of women with impunity):

> Activists used the language of feminicidio to launch a counter-offensive against the political and business elites who minimized the violence by declaring that the victims were not worth remembering. In so doing, they challenged the story that equated women's disappearance from public space, either through their deaths or through municipal social cleansing projects, with value. And, as such, they disabled a key technology for widening the rent gap between the places known for poor women and the places known for their disappearance. (9)

While gentrification plans were disrupted by activists for some time, this did not last, for those same policy and business elites then targeted young men caught up in the violence of the drug war:

> Rather than refer to the male youth population that dominates the body count as the resident population of the city's poor working-class families, the mayor referred to them as "venomous vermin" who had descended upon the city. . . . Such depictions . . . sought to whitewash the public memory of these young people who were being gunned down on the very streets that had raised them. (11)

This official "politics of forgetting" is now working to close the rent gap and extract profits from massively devalorized spaces.

In these contexts beyond the North at least, the rent gap theory was helpful in explaining gentrification. This really seems to bother some urbanists working with postcolonial theory, not least Ghertner (2015), who argues that the term *gentrification* has been imposed by scholars on places where it doesn't fit, or where it makes little sense to struggles occurring at ground level; that it doesn't recognize the diversity of activities taking place where "public land ownership, common property, mixed tenure, or informality" (552) endure; that it is "agnostic on the question of extra-economic force" (553) (a highly questionable claim, as I explained previously); that Western gentrification scholars "see like capitalists" (553) in their assumption that private land tenure/capitalist urbanization is everywhere; and that those scholars are not alert to forms of displacement that are driven by processes other than gentrification (such as the violent evictions taking place over privatization of nonprivate land tenures).[4]

Although it is very important to ask theoretical questions about the pertinence of certain concepts and whether they are helpful or not in dissecting urban processes beyond where they were formed, the fact that the rent gap theory was developed from research in the United States in the 1970s is not by itself a valid reason to dismiss it, ignore it, or indeed to unlearn it, in very different contexts, four decades later. The challenge is to take it seriously, and if it turns out not to be useful vis-à-vis a certain geographical context or struggle, then it should not be used.

But at least from the research that is available, and still emerging, it seems to be the case that rent gap theory has a lot to teach us about gentrification in contexts beyond the North, and is far from "less than adequate in much of the world" (Ghertner 2015, 554). In their recent book, *Planetary Gentrification*, Lees, Shin, and Lopez-Morales (2016), argue that the term *gentrification* has not been stretched too far, but rather is unfolding on a planetary scale, even if changing conditions and local circumstances matter enormously. Even where the processes are not called gentrification locally, or where there is no equivalent term, class-driven urban redevelopment is an embedded process in multiple Southern and Eastern contexts. Finally, their synthesis of available research evidence points to the growing importance of secondary circuits of accumulation and the planetary shift to rentier extraction and what might be termed the *robbery* of value, rather than the production of value. Asset pursuit and asset stripping, via land grabbing and evictions, is a hallmark of contemporary urbanization and shows little sign of retreating on a planetary scale. It is not "seeing like a capitalist" (Ghertner's accusation) to consider rent gap theory in radically different contexts, nor is it an act of intellectual imperialism to do so, as long as one theory does not shut out the possibility of developing new theories that may teach us even more or using theories from the South to explain phenomena in the North (Lemanski 2014; Wyly 2015).

RESISTING 'CHRISTOPHER COLUMBUS SYNDROME'

In this chapter I have shown how the rent gap theory, understood in the political and analytical spirit in which it was originally delivered, can serve not only as a convincing explanation of what creates the conditions necessary for gentrification to occur, but also as a powerful response to claims that gentrification is to be applauded and promoted because it is somehow better than the imagined alternative of urban "decline." Such a response is important, as unfortunately false choice urbanism is still very much alive, and judging by the numerous journalistic reactions to a 2019 study sponsored (and well publicized) by the Federal Reserve Bank of Philadelphia (Brummet and Reed 2019), it is doing very well. Briefly, that study used longitudinal US Census microdata to study the effects of gentrification on the educational achievement and household status of (loosely defined) "original residents" of low-income, central-city neighborhoods in the one hundred largest metropolitan areas. The authors interpreted the data to argue that "many original residents, including the most disadvantaged, are able to remain in gentrifying neighborhoods and share in any neighborhood improvements" and that "low-income neighborhoods that gentrify appear to improve along a number of dimensions known to be correlated with opportunity" (24). Concerns about the displacement of low-income people, they subsequently concluded, are overblown.

This line of argument has been made before. In the first decade of the twenty-first century, three quantitative studies of gentrification and displacement in US contexts became very high profile: by Jacob Vigdor (2002) in Boston, by Lance Freeman and Frank Braconi (2004) in New York City, and a national study by three urban economists (McKinnish, Walsh, and White, 2008). These studies analyzed data on household mobility drawn from various government housing databases and found that low-income and lesser-educated households exit gentrifying neighborhoods at significantly lower rates than comparable households in non-gentrifying neighborhoods. The conclusion of each study was, first, that critiques of gentrification are misplaced, for large-scale displacement is not happening, and second, that gentrification has a positive side that should be encouraged by urban policy as it brings better services and amenities to neighborhoods affected for so long by disinvestment.[5] Newman and Wyly explained the impact of those studies:

> The new evidence on gentrification and displacement . . . has rapidly jumped out of the obscure scholarly cloister to influence policy debates that have been ripped out of context . . . [and] used to dismiss concerns about a wide range of market-oriented urban policies of privatisation, home-ownership, "social mix" and dispersal strategies designed to break up the concentrated poverty that has been taken as the shorthand explanation for all that ails the disinvested inner city. If displacement is not a problem, many are saying, then regeneration (or whatever else the process is called) is fine too. Perhaps it will even give some poor people the benefits of a middle-class neighbourhood without requiring them to move to a middle-class community." (2006, 25)

This is where a robust conceptualization of displacement becomes essential. In a series of studies, Peter Marcuse (1985a, 1985b, 1986) built upon and extended the earlier work of George Grier and Eunice Grier (1978) and Richard LeGates and Chester Hartman (1981) to identify four types of displacement:

- *Direct last-resident displacement*. This can be physical (e.g., when landlords cut off the heat in a building, forcing the occupants to move out) or economic (e.g., a rent increase).
- *Direct chain displacement*. This looks beyond standard "last resident" counting to include previous households that "may have been forced to move at an earlier stage in the physical decline of the building or an earlier rent increase."
- *Exclusionary displacement*. This refers to those residents who cannot access housing because it has been gentrified/abandoned:

  > When one household vacates a housing unit voluntarily and that unit is then gentrified or abandoned so that another similar household is prevented from moving in, the number of units available to the second household in that housing market is reduced. The second household, therefore, is excluded from living where it would otherwise have lived. (Marcuse 1985a, 206)

- *Displacement pressure*. This refers to the dispossession suffered by poor and working-class families during the transformation of the neighborhoods where they live:

> When a family sees the neighbourhood around it changing dramatically, when their friends are leaving the neighbourhood, when the stores they patronise are liquidating and new stores for other clientele are taking their places, and when changes in public facilities, in transportation patterns, and in support services all clearly are making the area less and less livable, then the pressure of displacement already is severe. Its actuality is only a matter of time. Families living under these circumstances may move as soon as they can, rather than wait for the inevitable; nonetheless they are displaced. (Marcuse 1985a, 207)

Although this categorization of displacement is anchored in an analysis of New York City's housing market in the 1980s, the huge literature on gentrification since the 1980s provides ample evidence that these insights are applicable elsewhere. For instance, among many studies, exclusionary displacement and displacement pressure have been documented not only more recently in New York City (Stabrowski 2014; Valli 2015), but also in Los Angeles (DeVerteuil 2011), Istanbul (Sakizlioğlu 2014), Melbourne (Shaw and Hagemans 2015), and Shenzhen (Liu et al. 2017), as well as in multiple Latin American contexts (Janoschka and Sequera 2016; López-Morales 2016). Marcuse (1985a, 208) was arguing for a panoramic view of displacement wherever there is gentrification: "The full impact of displacement must include consideration of all four forms. . . . It must include displacement from economic changes, physical changes, neighbourhood changes, and individual unit changes." He was acutely sensitive to the difficulties in measuring gentrification-induced displacement, yet he was pointing out that it is essential to have *conceptual clarity before research on displacement begins, and before any conclusions can be drawn*.

The "gentrification isn't much of a problem" literature, as well as being devoid of careful conceptualization, completely and conveniently ignores a substantial theoretical and empirical international literature on the trauma of displacement experienced by established residents. The agnotology at work is best evidenced by Brummet and Reed's (2019, 1) claim that "understanding how gentrification actually occurs and whether it harms or benefits original residents" is something on which "there is little comprehensive evidence." Theirs is precisely the kind of injection of doubt where there is little doubt that feeds right-wing commentators on the prowl for any kind of academic (always quantitative) "evidence" to support their belief that gentrification is the desirable and only conceivable remedy for "concentrated poverty." For example, the *Financial Times* reported Brummet and Reed's study under the heading, "Gentrification 'Benefits Local Residents', Research Finds"; *The Philadelphia Inquirer* as "Effects of Gentrification on Longtime Residents Are Not as Negative as Typically Perceived"; *City Lab* as "The Hidden Winners in Neighborhood Gentrification"; and *City Journal* as "Gentrification for Social Justice?"

The cumulative effect of the frequent rescripting of gentrification as a collective urban good is what the film director Spike Lee, in a speech at the Pratt Institute in New York City in 2014, dubbed "Christopher Columbus Syndrome." This occurs when newcomers to a neighborhood, and those who facilitate and celebrate their arrival, think they have "discovered" a new place:

> Then comes the motherfuckin' Christopher Columbus Syndrome. You can't discover this! We been here. You just can't come and bogart. There were brothers playing motherfuckin' African drums in Mount Morris Park [in Harlem] for 40 years and now they can't do it anymore because the new inhabitants said the drums are loud. My father's a great jazz musician. He bought a house in nineteen-motherfuckin'-sixty-eight, and the motherfuckin' people moved in last year and called the cops on my father. He's not—he doesn't even play electric bass! It's acoustic! We bought the motherfuckin' house in nineteen-sixty-motherfuckin'-eight and now you call the cops? In 2013? Get the fuck outta here! Nah. You can't do that. You can't just come in the neighborhood and start bogarting and say, like you're motherfuckin' Columbus and kill off the Native Americans. Or what they do in Brazil, what they did to the Indigenous people. You have to come with respect. There's a code. There's people. (Quoted in Michael and Bramley 2014)

The main symptom of Christopher Columbus Syndrome is a lack of reflection on why it takes *gentrification* to improve the schools, policing, and public services, when low-income communities of color have been crying out for these improvements for decades. The Columbian encounter was uneven development by genocide and false treaty: accumulation by colonial dispossession. Today it's the world urban system of cities competing for investors and creative-class gentry on the new urban frontier. It has always been in the border areas that "a killing could be made, so to speak, with so little risk of simultaneously being scalped" (Smith 1996, 209).

This leads to the question of resistance to gentrification. A crucial tactic in this respect is to expose policy and planning hypocrisy at every opportunity. When politicians and planners speak of their desires to create "mixed-income communities" in poor areas (almost always cover for a gentrification strategy), there is much to be learned from what happened in New Orleans in 2006, when members of the Survivor Village tent city outside the St. Bernard public housing project set a new benchmark for challenging politicians with their own rhetoric. The public housing project had been subject to minimal damage by Hurricane Katrina in 2005, but for months they were not allowed back into their homes in the context of politicians using the disaster to push through plans to demolish public housing in favor of building "mixed-income housing." The activists marched uptown, along one of the most affluent residential thoroughfares in the city, St. Charles Avenue, holding a huge banner that said "Make This Neighborhood Mixed Income" (see figure 4).

Along these lines, it is also essential to call into question at every opportunity the insulting terms *regeneration* and *revitalization*. To target for "regeneration" a place and its people is to imply that they must be *degenerate*, and "revitalizing" a place suggests that it is full of *devitalized* individuals, or people *not vital* to a city.

It would take a (much-needed) whole book to analyze the varied struggles against gentrification that have taken place in different cities at different times and to dissect the links between those struggles, the lessons learned, and the gains made. As gentrification has become a leading edge of the neoliberal imagination in countless contexts, "resistance to neoliberal urbanism necessarily means resistance to gentrification" (Benach and Albet 2018, 290), so it is important to note that what might not be specifically an anti*gentrification* strategy may have important consequences in the fight for affordable housing and protecting people from eviction. As Mayer (2013) explains, antigentrification struggles are just one element of the variegated, fragmented field of urban social movements that deal with a very diverse set of practices such as squatting, autonomous social centers, and commoning campaigns. A superb starting point for identifying and analyzing the myriad ways in which gentrification is resisted is an essay by Sandra Annunziata and Clara Rivas-Alonso (2018), which offers

Figure 4. Survivor Village residents march along St. Charles Avenue, New Orleans, June 2006. Credit unknown. *Source:* This image appeared on the New Orleans Indymedia web page for many years before the site was taken down in 2021. Every effort was made to track down the photographer, and it is used here in good faith.

a classification of antigentrification practices; I have simplified and condensed the points made in the essay in table 1.[6]

As these authors argue, "difficulties arise when individual everyday actions that allow dwellers to stay put, or to find other options in the face of brutal evictions, are not considered part of traditional forms of organized resistance" (409). Therefore, they call for an approach to understanding resistance that takes account of the broad spectrum of political practices from the institutional, structural, and collective action to microscale actions and interactions in neighborhoods, streets, and households.

Especially effective in contexts where gentrification is occurring have been campaigns for policy action beyond the urban scale, such as living wage campaigns. The high cost of housing in so many nations is consigning

Table 1 Annunziata and Rivas-Alonso's (2018) Classification of Antigentrification Practices

Type of Resistance	Examples
Prevention, institution-based measures	Publicly subsidized housing programs; tenant protections, rent control, and regulations; urban development without evictions; building conversion regulations: anti-privatization struggles; single-room occupancy hotels; street vendors' resistance; community land trusts; vacancy control, confiscation/acquisition of abandoned property; anti-speculation ordinances; land value tax/extraction policies; defense of traditional retail markets
Mitigation and legal bricolage: delay, negotiation, compensation	Zoning regulations; anti-eviction practices; displacement free zones; legal actions and struggles; tenant tactics of negotiation; court cases against master plans; compensation following condo conversations; grassroots movements; legal controls over urban renewal policy; environmental legal struggles
Building alternatives: community planning, squats, occupations, protests, and urban commons	Community organization, grassroots movements, and alternative planning; anti-gentrification protests; political housing squats; reproduction of the commons; informal occupation and land squatting; armed conflict
Enhancing visibility, counternarratives, building awareness, and strategic mobilization of identities	Counternarratives to mainstream urban governance; alternative cultural and social centers; mutual support for threatened groups; informal networks of support; "invisible" forms of resistance (collective and individual)

SOURCE: Author's adaptation, with kind permission from Clara Rivas-Alonso.

the poor to great financial strain, so the work of living wage activists is absolutely crucial to the right to housing. Policy interventions and even some social movements are too often "area based," when the differences that could be made at the level of the welfare state and labor market are substantial. Unfortunately, attacks on welfare states are happening in multiple contexts because these remnants of a Keynesian-Fordist political economy are viewed by the political classes as dangerous "impediments to the advancement of financialisation" (Observatorio Metropolitano 2013, 20). To continue the relentless pace of expanding global accumulation, more and more of those human needs that have not been commodified in previous rounds of financialization have been monitored and monetized. Pensions, health care, education, and especially housing have become much more aggressively appropriated, colonized, and financialized (Aalbers 2016; Rolnik 2019). Antigentrification struggles should be—and usually are—part of broader struggles to protect the legacies of the welfare state against predatory attacks by this generation's vulture capitalists. As important as it is to explain the dirty process of gentrification, supported by accounts of destroyed lives, evictions, homelessness, loss of jobs, loss of community, loss of place, and so on, it is just as important to monitor and understand how gentrification has been resisted, and with what outcomes.

4 Displacement, Rent Control, and Housing Justice

Moving people involuntarily from their homes or neighbourhoods is wrong. Regardless of whether it results from government or private market action, forced displacement is characteristically a case of people without the economic and political power to resist being pushed out by people with greater resources and power, people who think they have a 'better' use for a certain building, piece of land, or neighborhood. The pushers benefit. The pushees do not.

Hartman, Keating, and LeGates (1982, 4–5; emphasis in original)

Having mapped out what I consider to be a helpful analytic framework for gentrification research, in terms of both understanding the process (via the rent gap theory) and contesting the agnotology surrounding the process, I now focus on the most harmful effect of the process (displacement from urban space) and the production of ignorance vis-à-vis one of the more effective policies to address it: rent control. Evictions and displacement (and especially the threat of them) are a frequent occurrence for people living at the bottom of the class structure in cities throughout the world, to the point of being near-routine events in contexts where housing markets have the least regulation (Hartman and Robinson 2003; Newman and Wyly 2006; Porter 2009; Harvey 2010; Clark 2011; Desmond 2012; Anguelovski 2015). Furthermore, rare are the instances in which displacement results in either a neutral or beneficial outcome for the displaced household; common to the majority of qualitative accounts of dislocation are disruption, humiliation, bitterness, pain, and grief (e.g., Fried 1966; Marris 1986; Porteous and Smith 2001; Fullilove 2004; Dumbledon 2006; Keene and Ruel 2013; Zhang 2016). It is therefore important not only to identify the causes of displacement, but also to recognise its many forms; to understand what it does to communities; and to agitate for the institutional, legal, and political economic changes necessary to protect those most vulnerable to it.

One of these changes is rent control. For a long time an effective tool for preventing evictions and displacement, it has also led to some of the most heated debates across a variety of disciplines and professions concerned with urban and housing issues. The mainstream view is that rent controls—in any form, in any context—will eventually hurt those on whose behalf they are supposedly introduced (people struggling to find somewhere affordable to live). Like so much agnotology, however, this view is riddled with vested interests and grounded in contempt for state regulation and veneration of the supposed efficiency of the "free" market. Once we take the trouble to look closely at different kinds of rent control and, more broadly, at what leads to high housing costs, then it is possible—as I attempt in this chapter—to shift the analytical and political focus toward the urgent question of housing justice.

It is important at this juncture to clarify that not all displacement is caused by gentrification and that even the term *displacement* might not adequately capture what is happening in low-income communities of color in multiple societies. For example, Ananya Roy (2017, 8) has argued that "the concept of gentrification is not sufficient to explain the forms of displacement—the sheer disappearance of African-Americans—that are now underway in cities such as Los Angeles." Roy prefers the concept of "racial banishment" to diagnose the forms of dispossession underway in the context of the articulation of state and market vis-à-vis housing precarity in already segregated US cities. Likewise, both Louis Moreno (2014) and Raquel Rolnik (2019) see gentrification-induced displacement as just one aspect of a much grander-scale financial expropriation happening in many cities, summarized by Philip Lawton (2020, 272) as "the current reworking of urban space through the intersections of social class, race and shifting forms of financial arrangements in combination with longer term spatial domination." There are fascinating and ongoing conceptual debates about displacement, but as I think most participants in those debates would agree, the intellectual and political energies expended by taking part in conceptual struggles must be matched (if not exceeded) by those expended by scholarship aligned with struggles for housing justice. This is particularly important given the influence of scholarship that, for all its merits, does not align itself as such.

EVICTED AND THE HOUSING VOUCHER PROBLEM

In the history of urban and housing studies, there are few books that have garnered as much attention, received as much praise (within and well beyond academia), and won as many prestigious awards as Matthew Desmond's (2016) *Evicted: Poverty and Profit in the American City*. It is not difficult to understand why; it is a poignant ethnographic study of what was for too long (among people not affected nor on the front lines of resistance) a "hidden housing problem" (Hartman and Robinson 2003; Purser 2016). Desmond has certainly raised wider awareness of the brutal socioeconomic and emotional realities of evictions (not to mention their appallingly expansive and expanding scale), and perhaps more importantly, how evictions disproportionately impact women of color.

Evicted reports on dislocation from a mobile home park and a poor African American neighborhood in Milwaukee, Wisconsin, with a close-up focus on landlord-tenant relations. Desmond then blended his qualitative data with quantitative analysis of Milwaukee court records of evictions in order to situate his study within a legal and policy context. It is a compelling read, with powerful evidence of how unaffordable and insecure housing amplifies, aggravates, and in some cases *produces* a range of social problems: unemployment, hunger, malnutrition, psychosocial stress, addiction, educational failure, and crime. However, my own reaction to Desmond's book is that, while it certainly deserves its place among the landmark ethnographic studies of social suffering and constitutes a tremendous contribution to knowledge on multiple fronts, it has a desperately disappointing ending. This is because of his principal policy recommendation, which issues from an analysis that never had sight of actors beyond landlords and tenants: namely, state agencies, developers, the construction industry, and financial institutions.

Given the subtitle of the book, and Desmond's focus on how the exploitation of low-income tenants is umbilically connected to the profits of landlords, one might expect some conclusions that would tackle frontally the structural and institutional arrangements behind the grotesquely high cost of rental housing in the United States vis-à-vis widening class and racial inequality, stagnant wages, and rising employment insecurity. As he builds toward his conclusion, Desmond chastises sociologists of urban marginality and poverty in the United States for barely using the word *exploitation* in their analyses. This was extremely refreshing, and as a reader I was excited to see where the analysis was heading. Then, in the concluding chapter, Desmond argues that exploitation and evictions could be reduced massively if there were a universal rollout of a housing voucher scheme to allow more tenants access to the private rental sector via subsidies:

> There are two freedoms at odds with each other: the freedom to profit from rents and the freedom to live in a safe and affordable home. There is a way we can rebalance these two freedoms: by significantly expanding our housing voucher program so that all low-income families could benefit from it. (308)

Unfortunately Desmond does not consider the systemic problems that create such a massive imbalance of "freedoms," nor does he consider that the latter freedom is a universal human need, whereas the former freedom is very far from that. He elaborates on what this voucher program would entail:

> Every family below a certain income level would be eligible for a housing voucher. They could use that voucher to live anywhere they wanted, just as families can use food stamps to buy groceries virtually anywhere, as long as their housing was neither too expensive, big and luxurious nor too shabby and run-down. . . . Program administrators could develop fine-grained analyses, borrowing from algorithms and other tools commonly used in the private market, to prevent landlords from charging too much and families from selecting more housing than they need. The family would dedicate 30 percent of their income to housing costs with the voucher paying the rest. (308)

Desmond insists that this program will only work if current and widespread landlord discrimination against voucher holders is outlawed (making landlord participation mandatory), if rents only rise at the rate of inflation, and if a voucher scheme is flexible enough to allow landlords a modest rate of return: "If we are going to house most low-income families in the private rental market, then that market must remain profitable" (311). Desmond is adamant that large-scale public housing construction is not the answer to housing problems in the United States (he calls public housing projects "failures" without even considering the systematic disinvestment and neglect that have caused so many problems, not to mention all the well-documented mythology surrounding public housing). Perhaps more concerning is Desmond's endorsement of Housing Benefit in the UK as some kind of template for best practice in housing policy:

> Universal housing programs have been successfully implemented all over the developed world. In countries that have such programs, every single family with an income below a certain level who meets basic program requirements has a right to housing assistance. Great Britain's Housing Benefit is available to so many households that a journalist recently reporting on the program asked, "Perhaps it is easier to say who does not get it?" "Indeed," came the answer. This benefit, transferred directly to landlords in most cases, ensures that paying rent does not plunge a family into poverty. (309)

Coming from the pen of a shrewd scholar of urban poverty and housing precarity, this passage is unfortunate. To be sure, Housing Benefit has been absolutely crucial to millions of households in Britain in order for them to pay rent and stay put. However, Desmond makes two huge oversights in holding it up as an example of best practice. The first is that Housing Benefit has been under attack by successive Conservative governments since 2010, first in the form of caps to payments made depending on how many bedrooms are in the property (the infamous "bedroom tax"), and more recently via its current incorporation into the disastrous Universal Credit system (all welfare payments delivered to claimants in one monthly total), ridden with delays, payment reductions, and punitive eligibility checks that have been catastrophic for low-income people across the United Kingdom. When Desmond wrote his book, he really should have known that these attacks were underway. The second, more serious oversight is that housing subsidies like the British scheme do very little to address the high cost of rental housing; they simply offload the problem of landlord greed onto the taxpayer, doing nothing to halt landlord-tenant exploitation.

Housing Benefit in Britain was introduced in 1988 with the objective of subsidizing the cost of rental accommodation for tenants in the social-rented and private-rented housing sectors. A means-tested benefit, it was administered by councils (local state authorities) and paid directly to landlords in order to allow vulnerable people such as pensioners, low-wage workers, the unemployed, single parents, and the disabled to make rent. Entitlement was calculated by comparing current household needs and resources with household rent payments (Hamnett 2010). The reason that Housing Benefit became so widespread in the United Kingdom has nothing to do with benevolence or social justice, and everything to do with assault on the idea and provision of decommodified housing that was ignited by Margaret Thatcher via her Right to Buy legislation. Right to Buy offered council tenants the opportunity to purchase their homes from the state at very low cost. Over the past forty years, three million publicly owned homes have been sold off under the scheme (Hodkinson 2019). There are many declamatory debates on Right to Buy, but they tend to silence the fact that it actually failed as a privatization strategy if we consider the costs to the state and ultimately, to taxpayers. Some 42 percent of all those who exercised Right to Buy then sold on to private landlords, who rented their assets to tenants at much higher rents than those charged by councils, which required those tenants to apply for Housing Benefit from the state in order to pay rent. Given significant long-term increases in the cost of rental housing, the Housing Benefit bill rose dramatically to over £35 billion a year. Thatcher's flagship policy, therefore, actually ended up costing the taxpayer far, far more in housing subsidies than it ever did in the provision and maintenance of council homes. The main long-term effect of Right to Buy was to rob subsequent generations of affordable housing, diverting them into the landlord bonanza that is the taxpayer-supported private-rented sector. Housing Benefit in Britain was all about sustaining landlord-tenant exploitation, the very process Desmond won a Pulitzer Prize for highlighting so vividly. It is an own-goal for Desmond to use Housing Benefit as a model for how to end exploitation.

In a particularly astute critique of Desmond's policy proposals, Joseph Ramsey explains the problems very clearly:

Unlike rent control, or the publicly financed construction of nonprofit housing, the vouchers Desmond champions do not challenge the financial interests of real estate owners. . . . Most immediately, pumping public money into the private housing market does nothing to bring down rapidly increasing rents. . . . Furthermore, Desmond's proposed vouchers would funnel billions in taxpayer dollars right back into the pockets of landlords, a class whose interests remain—as Desmond reminds us—"fundamentally opposed" to those of renters. This plan does not just postpone the fight for public housing or rent control, it strengthens those forces committed to making sure such proposals never happen." (2016)

In a critical engagement with Desmond's methodology, Michael Burawoy (2017, 280) makes a similar observation when he notes that if vouchers do not exist alongside rent control, they simply feed the exploitation Desmond denounces and "become a subsidy for landlords as well as tenants" whereby "exploitation becomes super-exploitation." For Burawoy, housing vouchers "do not solve the underlying problem, namely the lack of affordable housing, which is causing astronomical rents for dilapidated dwellings" and this is because Desmond "does not move beyond the field site to the political and economic field that shapes it—the operation of the housing market and the role of the municipality, banks, and developers." (281). As Susanne Soederberg (2018) reminds us, evictions are "a global capitalist phenomenon."

Since publishing *Eviction*, Desmond has funneled his energies into setting up the Eviction Lab at Princeton University to address the frustration he felt at the lack of data on evictions on the national scale, and ultimately to allow online users to monitor eviction trends by neighborhood and state. This is, again, very valuable work. Data are collected in two ways, by approaching community organizations that have been engaging in eviction defense and data collection/analysis for some time, and by approaching private sector big data firms if the first approach does not yield sufficient data. Given the delicacies and sensitivities surrounding eviction data, the second method is highly questionable, as a team of activists and academics have explained:

We don't want to create data sets that can be potentially used by the real estate industry against tenants and tenant organizing. Rather than working with community groups to address our concerns so they could use the statewide data we had already collected, the *Eviction Lab* team stopped talking to us and chose to purchase California eviction data covering the same areas for $100,000 from American Information Research Services, a group that lists on its website "tenant screening" as a service they offer. Companies such as this profit from selling its eviction database to assist landlords in not renting to "high-risk" tenants, who are often low-income people of color. (Aiello et al. 2018)

These authors expressed serious concerns about where the Eviction Lab sits in relation to Desmond's call for exploitation to be at the core of housing poverty research. They also noted that Desmond "failed to engage with them as peers" and "failed to recognize and support the ongoing organizing, political struggles, and deep local-level work that his data project purportedly seeks to assist," before also criticizing his universal voucher proposal as one that "does nothing to disrupt the profitability and exploitation in the landlord-tenant relationship."

To be sure, Desmond is clear that a universal voucher program is "but one potential policy recommendation" and calls for many more to come, recognizing the importance of local contexts. But his book never comes close to questioning the commodification of housing and its role in our economic and social system, and never considers policies aligned to the interests of people living in poverty that have fundamentally challenged the causes of their exploitation by landlords. In promoting his book in talks given in the United States and beyond, Desmond has cautioned against rent control, telling audiences he has seen too many studies demonstrating that it doesn't work. In doing so, he simply repeats the simplistic messages and ideological warnings of most mainstream economists and the profiteering interests they serve. As Ramsey (2016) asks, "How can Desmond's powerful account of contemporary tenants end with a call to enact policies preferred by their exploiters?"

THE HARD-CORE AGNOTOLOGY OF RENT CONTROL

The previous section advanced an admittedly pointed critique of an otherwise excellent and valuable piece of scholarship. To substantiate this critique, I now take closer look at the rent control question and the agnotology surrounding it. The mainstream view—that rent controls anywhere are always harmful, even to those they are introduced to protect—offers a fascinating yet disturbing example of the triumph of ideology and propaganda over evidence. There is a striking disconnect between, on the one hand, the way that economists across the conservative-liberal political spectrum speak about rent control, and on the other, the material consequences for tenants and the work of campaigns run by (often tenant-led) organizations that advocate for them. This disconnect is not a new development, but it has strengthened in recent years as calls and social movements for rent control have increased in the context of the global crisis of housing affordability.

The Institute of Economic Affairs (IEA) is a free-market think tank and a pivotal institution in the birth of neoliberal ideology in the United Kingdom. It was founded in 1957 by Anthony Fisher, a former military pilot, wealthy chicken farmer, and personal friend of Friedrich Hayek, and it went on to have a massive influence in the rise of Margaret Thatcher and informed many of her most significant policies. In 1972 the IEA published an assault against state intervention in housing markets entitled *Verdict on Rent Control*, including essays by none other than Hayek himself and numerous other giants of neoclassical economics, including Milton Friedman (Hayek et al. 1972). Many of the contributors to the pamphlet were part of the original Mont Pelerin Society, the birthplace of the neoliberal creed. In the introduction, the reader is left in no doubt as to the tenor of what follows: "These essays should serve as a warning to economists, sociologists and social workers who think that the best way of helping people with low incomes is to equip them with cheap housing at rents fixed by government, a 'solution' that exacts a savage price to be paid by future generations" (ix).

Ever since this "verdict" was issued, the IEA has been quick to jump on any proposal for rent control in the United Kingdom. To take a recent example, against the 2015 general election backdrop of the Labour Party proposing an upper limit on rent increases within tenancies in the private rented sector, the IEA published a report entitled *The Flaws in Rent Ceilings* (Bourne 2014). A declamatory crusade against all forms of rent regulation anywhere, the report began by stating that there is a "rare consensus" among economists that rent control "leads to a fall in the quantity of rental property available and a reduction in the quality of the existing

stock" (10). The source of this "consensus" is in fact a 1990 American Economic Association survey of nearly two thousand mainstream economists
(Alston, Kearl, and Vaughan 1992), probably the most striking example of
a small survey (of a skewed sample) with a very large footprint in the history of housing economics.

The IEA report argued that "under rent control there is less incentive
for families to reduce their accommodation demands, therefore exacer-
bating the shortage of properties for others" (Bourne 2014, 16). The tone
of the document reached a crescendo a few pages later with the assertion
that "the truth would appear to be that tenants are unwilling to pay for
increased security" (25), leading to the conclusion that any "extra security"
for tenants "comes at the expense of reduced economic efficiency" (35).
Instead of rent regulation, the report calls for another round of deregulation in the form of "planning liberalisation," which is described as a "welfare enhancing policy" (36) that would lead to the construction of new
housing on land currently shielded from development by government zoning. For the IEA, the housing crisis is a basic economic conundrum—too
much demand and not enough supply—and its solution is thus to increase
supply by stopping all government interference in the competitive housing market, which (true to neoclassical beliefs) must be allowed to operate free of cumbersome restrictions to provide incentives for producers
and consumers to optimize their behavior and push the market toward
equilibrium (so that there are no shortages of housing), while yielding the
maximum amount of utility for the maximum number of people.

The IEA immediately went about the task of circulating sound bites from
the report as widely as possible. Its "solution" certainly caught the attention of newspapers and commentators supporting a conservative agenda,
one illustration being a feature in the *Daily Telegraph* under the headline,
"Think-Tank Criticises 'Pointless' Labour Rent Cap Scheme" (September 6,
2014). It also caught the attention of the editors of *Channel 4 News*, a
widely respected national television news program, who invited the author
of the report to discuss the issue of rent control alongside Jasmine Stone,
an activist from the FOCUS E15 movement in London (which campaigns
against the regeneration and demolition of social housing estates) (Bourne
and Stone 2014). Even after Stone described her and her neighbors' experiences of struggling to make rent due to various profiteering schemes,

Ryan Bourne maintained that the "fundamental reason" for very high rents was not "greedy landlords." According to Bourne, the "real" reason is that "over years and years we haven't built new homes and have restricted supply artificially through greenbelts and other planning restrictions."[1] When Stone answered positively the interviewer's question of whether she would like to see rent controls introduced in London, Bourne immediately retorted that she was wrong because "economists agree" that such "crude" controls are "absolutely disastrous." It did not appear to matter at all to Bourne that Stone was speaking from the experience of poverty, housing precarity, and repeated evictions. Among conservative economists like him, there is much symbolic power to be gained by generating images of hardworking or even sympathetic landlords who have been forced by socialists and activists to reduce rents against their economic freedoms.

It is not just economists on the right who argue against rent control (Jenkins 2009). In 1965, the Nobel Prize–winning Swedish welfare economist Gunnar Myrdal said, "Rent control has in certain Western countries constituted, maybe, the worst example of poor planning by governments lacking courage and vision" (1965, 12). In possibly the most famous tirade against rent control of all time, the long-term chair of the Nobel Prize in Economics committee, Assar Lindbeck, remarked, "Rent control appears to be the most efficient technique presently known to destroy a city— except for bombing" (1971, 39). This exaggeration and exercise of symbolic power has in multiple international contexts repeatedly shut off any useful debate about rent control before it even gets started and has led to numerous imitations, such as Craig Gurian's (2003, 343) remark that rent control in New York City had done "as much damage to the city's housing market as an atomic bomb would." The terms mainstream economists use to condemn rent control are always the strongest possible, such as Peter Salins's (1999, 59) much-quoted remark that rent control is "the granddaddy and arch-villain of New York's regulatory ensemble." In 2000, the liberal economist Paul Krugman argued in his *New York Times* column that years of rent control in San Francisco had led to a diseased housing market:

> Surely it is worth knowing that the pathologies of San Francisco's housing market are right out of the economics textbook, that they are exactly what supply-and-demand analysis predicts. But people literally don't want to

know. So now you know why economists are useless: when they actually do understand something, people don't want to hear about it.

Liberal economists who argue against rent control claim that it always drives up rents for other tenants who are unprotected by it (I look into the details of this argument in due course). Yet tellingly, *this argument is always framed against rent control, not against unregulated landlords.* Many of these economists are very well known and very well read public intellectuals. When they condemn rent control, their audiences listen to them and believe them.

Underpinning all arguments against rent control, conservative and liberal, is the ongoing battle over the commodity nature of housing and its role in our economic, social, and urban system. Just hearing those words—*rent control*—is deeply unsettling to anyone who cannot cope with the idea of price controls, to anyone who believes in "free" and competitive market economies, the sanctity of private property rights, and the idea that nobody should be prevented from making as much money as they can from housing. I have been in quite a few professional and social settings where mentioning rent control generates the same kind of reaction as insulting someone. The near-hysterical reactions of the mostly right-wing economists to rent control are quite fascinating if seen in a wider context. In most countries there are laws protecting the rights of shareholders and protecting investors from the consequences when they invest in companies that do awful, illegal things and even kill people. Mainstream economists don't often talk about those laws. But when rent control is put forward as a law protecting the rights of people to have somewhere to live, those same economists go completely berserk.[2]

Strong negative reactions to rent control are not purely ideological. They are also driven by the fact that very few economists ever get past the destructive consequences of what are today referred to as *first-generation* rent controls: a complete long-term freeze on nominal rents, significantly below the market level. European countries imposed these during World War I, but they really took off as a policy in multiple international contexts (including North America) during or just after World War II, in order to cope with the massive relocations of labor during that time and to ensure affordable housing for returning military personnel. In European contexts, housing reconstruction after World War II was slow due to extensive damage and especially war-ravaged economies, so rent controls remained in place, often with little adjustment from wartime levels of rent.

It has also been argued that "many governments maintained those controls as a façade to hide the lack of an effective housing programme" (Gilbert 2003, 109). The consequences for many urban housing markets were very damaging: landlords had chronically insufficient income for necessary maintenance expenditure, which led to large-scale physical decay and abandonment; there were serious mismatches between housing units and tenants and therefore reductions in availability to the point of saturation; and rent freezes encouraged highly exploitative residual, informal, and illegal markets in housing provision. Sonia Arbaci (2019) has perhaps most painstakingly documented these processes from (roughly) the late 1940s to the mid-1980s in southern European contexts of Spain, Italy, Greece, and, especially, Portugal (as we shall see shortly, Arbaci has also documented the damaging effects when rent controls are abolished). Evidence of the deleterious effects of first-generation rent controls is substantial far beyond Europe and North America, such as in India (Ramaswamy and Chakravarti 1997), Mexico (Romero 1990), Egypt (Soliman 2002), and South Africa (Morris 1997). When economists across the conservative-liberal spectrum condemn rent controls, it is first-generation rent freezes they have in mind. Among the left, very few, if any, scholars or housing justice activists are calling for them.

Second-generation rent controls are considerably different, much more varied, and still remarkably underresearched. Richard Arnott offered a clear definition:

> They entail a complex set of regulations governing not only allowable rent increases, but also conversion, maintenance and landlord-tenant relations. [They] commonly permit automatic percentage rent increases related to the rate of inflation. They also often contain provisions for other rent increases: cost pass-through provisions which permit landlords to apply for rent increases above the automatic rent increase, if justified by cost increases; hardship provisions, which allow discretionary increases to assure that landlords do not have cash-flow problems; and rate-of-return provisions, which permit discretionary rent increases to ensure landlords a 'fair' or 'reasonable' rate of return. . . . Such rent regulation often contains provisions

which accord tenants improved security of tenure . . . and it often includes
restrictions to prevent cutbacks in maintenance, and on the conversion of
controlled rental housing to owner-occupied housing. (1995, 102)

In short, second-generation rent controls protect tenants from excessive
rent increases by creating a set of conditions for any increases (usually
depending on housing quality), while ensuring that landlords will always
receive a reasonable return on their investments (Lind 2001). They are
so varied that it is difficult to generalize about them, and so different
from their predecessors that Arnott argues, quite rightly, "they should be
evaluated largely independently of the experience with first-generation
rent controls" (1995, 201) This evaluation work is extremely difficult to
do, however, because of the need to disentangle the effects of rent controls
from numerous other policies that shape local housing markets, such as
the state of the local and macroeconomy, government housing and taxa-
tion policies, welfare regimes, land values and land ownership, and real
estate transactions (Jenkins 2009). Arnott (2003) later identified *third-
generation* rent controls, in which rent increases are controlled within a
tenancy but are unrestricted between tenancies, but as these are often
connected to strategies of free-market-oriented deregulation it seems far-
fetched to call them rent controls.

At this juncture, as there is compelling evidence from multiple contexts
that "the control of rent restricts economic eviction . . . and make noneco-
nomic eviction [e.g., through renovation or conversion] more difficult"
(Arnott 2003, 108), it seems more than a little necessary to expose and
dissect rent control agnotology. The production of ignorance about rent
control and how to counter that ignorance would be a topic worthy of a
book in its own right. In what follows, I narrow it down to three myths
that I see as the most prevalent whenever rent controls are mentioned:
that they will threaten the *quality, supply,* and *efficiency* of a housing sector anywhere at any time.[3]

The quality myth goes as follows: rent controls would have deleterious consequences for the overall standard of rental units on the market.
The specter of first-generation rent controls dominates this argument:
if landlords cannot charge tenants the rent they would like to charge in
order to make a profit, they will have insufficient funds for expenditure on

property maintenance (Albon and Stafford 1990; Ho 1992; Glaeser 2002; Turner and Malpezzi 2003). As mentioned previously, this was indeed the case vis-à-vis a total freeze on rents in multiple international contexts in the three decades following the end of World War II. But today the most obvious flaw with such an argument is that housing quality within the private rental market in so many contexts is *already* atrocious. In the United Kingdom, it is the absolute worst of all tenures, with the most sophisticated surveys of poverty showing that one in three tenants in the sector live in structurally inadequate housing (Lansley and Mack 2015). This is confirmed by the UK government's own recent reports: almost one-third of privately rented accommodation—millions of units—fails to meet the government's standards for decent homes (UK Parliament 2016).

Furthermore, in the decades before post–World War I state intervention in housing (when the vast majority of the UK population was privately renting), standards were *far* worse. The historical record of laissez-faire liberalism in housing standards was simply terrible, with slum conditions and overcrowding commonplace in British cities, where chronic poverty would siphon wealth upward through rent (Rodger 1989). Those arguing that rent controls of any kind will always and everywhere worsen housing quality cannot have it both ways; whenever there has been little or no regulation, rental housing quality has been truly appalling. For example, Glasgow in 1900 was as close to the conditions of a "perfect" free market in housing as a neoclassical economist could possibly desire: no public housing, no regulated standards of accommodation, a lack of monopoly in the hands of any single owner, and virtually no protection whatsoever of tenants' rights. But rents were high and conditions were dismal, with slumlords cramming tenants into stairwells, courtyards, and alleys, denying them access to light, water, or dignity (McCrone and Elliot 1989). Any consideration of the quality of a housing sector must have the question of safety at its core. Stuart Hodkinson (2019) has recently exposed vividly— and explained convincingly—the consequences of steady and long-term deregulation and privatization of housing in the United Kingdom, where landlords cut corners wherever they can to maximize profits, with dangerous implications for tenants. Only regulation, effectively enforced, can uphold housing quality and safety standards. It is misleading to claim that introducing even "soft," second-generation rent regulation would make that quality and safety problem even worse. This is abundantly clear in the case of the Netherlands, where the amount landlords are allowed to increase rent on an annual basis is conditional upon the standard of the property they are leasing. The result is a rental housing stock in much better shape than in countries that have no rent control (Olsen 1988; Anas 1997; Kutty 1996).

The second myth is the most dominant and concerns the question of supply. Again via appeals to the experience of first-generation rent controls, the argument goes that, if any rent controls were introduced, there would be no incentive for anyone to become a landlord, existing landlords would withdraw their properties from the market, and developers would not build any new rental housing (Heffley 1998; Hackner and Nyberg 2000; Glaeser 2002; McFarlane 2003). The result, therefore, would be a restriction in the supply of new housing for rent, which would lead to any existing housing crisis getting worse (with prices going up further due to demand dwarfing supply). This is the supply-and-demand cocoon of neoclassical economics writ large, and dubious logic on several levels. The logic implies that *any* curtailing of the profits to be made from a sector will simply stop people investing in it. This is akin to believing that the minimum wage means companies stop employing people, that sales tax means nobody sells anything anymore, and that fuel tax means nobody drives. It is an argument based on the belief that people will only seek to make money in conditions of totally unhampered profitability: a fantasy of a perfectly competitive market in which landlords compete to produce homogeneous housing units, where there are no externalities, where every actor possesses perfect information. But if landlords are told that they cannot, by law, charge a tenant whatever they like without meeting certain conditions, it is highly unlikely they are all suddenly going to sell up and get out of the sector, and there is no robust evidence from anywhere to demonstrate that this happens. For instance, research by Loïc Bonneval (2019) on sixty-four buildings under rent control in central Lyon, France, found no evidence that the profitability of real estate was affected by rent control over a period of fifty years.

The evidence on rent regulation reducing new housing construction is also weak or nonexistent. For example, David P. Sims (2007) and David H. Autor, Christopher J. Palmer, and Parag A. Pathak (2014) looked at the abolition of rent control in Massachusetts in the 1990s and found it had little effect on the construction of new housing (and by contrast, they found that rents increased considerably when controls were ended). The same is true for San Francisco (Diamond, McQuade and Qian 2019). Ben Teresa (2019) has explained how the gradual relaxation of rent stabilization laws, if not their abolition, in New York City has enabled private equity firms and asset managers to exploit increases in potential rents and engage in value extraction practices (leading to vast profits) from regulated housing stock.

But if we assume for one moment that the supply myth is in fact the reality, then the solution to any resulting decline in available rental stock is very simple: build more affordable housing. In tight rental markets (where developers and landlords have market power), rent controls can actually *increase* supply. If developers cannot generate extra profit through rent increases, this creates strong incentives to build more affordable units on a large scale, or for landlords to subdivide larger rental units. Evidence from New Jersey does indeed suggest this to be the case (Gilderbloom and Ye 2007; Ambrosius et al. 2015). A splendid intervention in the rent control debate came from economist Joshua W. Mason (2019), when he testified before the Jersey City council on rent control:

> "[W]hat rent control is limiting are the rent increases that are not the result of anything the landlord has done—the rent increases that result from the increased desirability of a particular area, or of a broader regional shortage of housing relative to demand. There is no reason that limiting these windfall gains should affect the supply of housing. . . . In a setting where the supply of new housing is already limited by other factors—whether land-use policy or the capacity of existing infrastructure or sheer physical limits on construction—rent regulation will have little or no additional effect on housing supply. Instead, it will simply reduce the monopoly profits enjoyed by owners of existing housing.

In her magnum opus on segregation processes in Southern European cities, Arbaci (2019) has demonstrated that ending entrenched first-generation rent controls in cities in Italy, Spain, Portugal, and Greece did not open the floodgates for the supply of adequate and affordable housing. By contrast, it "facilitated processes of embourgeoisement, gentrification, deproletarianisation and other forms of expansion by middle-class homeowners, often associated with forced evictions and the displacement of low-income and other vulnerable tenants (e.g. non-Western foreign groups)" (254). In addition, deregulation and corresponding liberalization of the market meant that, in all the cities she studied, "rents escalated not just in the upgraded districts but in the whole municipal area, thus outpricing lower middle- and low-income tenants—both natives and foreigners—from most municipal districts" (254)

Third is the efficiency myth. For many economists, something is inefficient if it "artificially" interferes with the "natural" operation of the price mechanism of the market. Rent controls are repeatedly condemned as forms of price fixing that will have deleterious consequences in terms of distorting market values and encouraging the problem of sitting tenants who will (a) block outsiders to the rental property market from gaining a foothold in it; (b) affect the functioning of a dynamic labor market, as they will refuse to move house to take any offer of employment elsewhere (as they would have to give up their low-cost rental housing if they did); and (c) occupy housing that is larger than they apparently require, limiting the availability of accommodation to larger households (Arnott and Igarashi 2000; Munch and Svarer 2002; Basu and Emerson 2003; Glaeser and Luttmer 2003; Krol and Svorny 2005). The problems with these appeals to rent controls being inefficient are, first, the assumption that low-income consumers not only have a choice about needing to be housed but also have the freedom to "rationally choose" where they want to live, without any kind of structural constraints on their lives, and second, the way inefficiency is skewed toward the interests of economists' models and, ultimately, landlords. Mason has noted:

> When a landlord gets an income because they are lucky enough to own land in an area where demand is growing and new supply is limited, or an income from an older building that has already fully paid back its construction costs, these are rents in the economic sense. They come from a kind of monopoly, not from contributing real resources to production of housing. And one thing that almost all economists agree on is that removing economic rents does not have costs in terms of reduced output or efficiency. (2019)

The lesson here is that if we consider housing as a question of social justice, a human need, then inefficiency arguments are to be treated with the utmost caution. David Madden and Peter Marcuse (2016, 49) capture

this concisely: "One person's inefficiency is another person's home. . . .
From the perspective of a tenant facing displacement from their long-
time home, it is the system of commodified residential development that
is inefficient, not to mention cruel and destructive." There is a world of
difference—different worlds—between tenured economists working in
elite universities or well-funded think tanks and the lives of tenants struggling to feed their families on very low incomes or even having to make
the choice between paying rent or eating. Real efficiency is surely not
achieved when rental housing costs have reached at least 50 percent of
household income; when households have hardly any money to spend on
other necessities; when the effects of housing insecurity place pressure on
other sectors such as health-care provision; and, in the case of the United
Kingdom, when the state hemorrhages £35 billion a year on payments to
private sector landlords through Universal Credit housing costs.

Underpinning the three-pronged agnotology of rent control is a long
and seemingly unending debate on what leads to high housing costs. For
neoclassical economists, conservative think tanks, developers, and anyone
in some way connected to the housing industry, the high cost of housing is due to a simple imbalance vis-à-vis supply and demand: too many
people and too few homes. In this register, the remedy for the imbalance
is equally simple: remove any barriers that prevent developers building as
much housing as possible. For example, not long ago the neoclassical economist Ed Glaeser (2013) famously used a *New York Times* op-ed to call for
complete deregulation: "The best way to make cities more affordable is to
unleash the cranes. To do so, end the dizzying array of land use regulations
in most cities that increase cost." Such thinking is not only riddled with
vested interests (see Peck 2016 on Glaeser's approach), it is empirically
misleading. Danny Dorling (2016) has helpfully explained why:

> Housing prices are not determined by supply and demand because you do
> not have a choice about needing to be housed. Allow an unregulated market
> to develop when social housing is also being cut and there is no choice not to
> buy what is on offer, other than sleeping on the streets. Prices will go sky-
> high. . . .We now have more housing than we have ever had before, per person
> and per family. We just share it out more unfairly than we have ever done
> before. If housing prices were about supply and demand then our surplus of
> bedrooms would result in falling prices, but this is not a free market. You are

not free to buy a flat that has been left empty in London to appreciate in value by its owner. They do not want to sell, or sometimes even rent it out, and you almost certainly would not have the money even if they did.

In his book-length treatment on housing, Dorling (2014, 231) argues that rent control is needed to bring down rents; to deter the landlords most interested in making a profit and most intent on offering a bad service; and to bring down housing prices, "resulting in more people buying when they need[. . .] to and fewer looking to rent unless they want[. . .] to." In addition, as Brett Christophers (2018) has demonstrated with reference to the United Kingdom, supply and demand analyses are wholly inadequate in explaining the problems of affordable housing because of the significant matters of land value and, especially, land ownership. Land value now constitutes nearly three-quarters of the cost of a house in the United Kingdom. Approximately 70 percent of the land is owned by 0.66 percent of the population. Just six thousand or so landowners—large institutions, aristocrats, and the royal family—own about forty million acres, or two-thirds of the United Kingdom. Cramming the population into a small percentage of the land—and hoarding/speculating on urban land that is available—creates an artificial land shortage that pushes up land values (land now constitutes 51% of the United Kingdom's entire net worth, almost double the percentage in Germany). This makes house prices astronomically high and ever more divorced from stagnant wages.

As Friedrich Engels presciently observed long ago, the housing question is deeply embedded in the structures of capitalism. A large and vibrant critical literature on the financialization of housing—the integration of financial and real estate markets—offers a more convincing explanation than supply and demand of why urban housing has become so expensive in multiple societies (e.g., García-Lamarca and Kaika 2016; Aalbers 2016; Fields 2017; Rolnik 2019). Unlike for the housing vouchers proposed by Desmond, there is very substantial evidence that rent control brings down rents and, when acting in tandem with other progressive policies that are geared toward tenants and the use values of homes and land (not the exchange values preferred by landlords and the housing industry), it makes a serious dent in the high cost of housing more broadly.

TOWARD "A CORNERSTONE FOR HOUSING JUSTICE"

The phrase "the rent is too damn high" is so familiar these days that it is unusual to find an urban context where it is not uttered verbatim or in some linguistic variant. At the time of writing, rent control has become a crucial battleground in struggles for housing justice in many cities across the globe, having been off the political and community organizing agenda for a long time. In 2019 the Berlin city government took action to stop soaring housing costs and rampant gentrification when it approved a five-year (2020–2025) freeze on rents, following which there will be rent increases limited to 1.3 percent per year, in line with inflation. This comes in the context of a forthcoming referendum on whether the government should expropriate nearly 250,000 private apartments in the city rented out by "mega-landlords" (corporations with 3,000 apartments or more).

In the United States, Oregon enacted a statewide law in February 2019 that will result in no household seeing a rent increase of more than 7 percent per year (plus the annual change in the consumer price index). In Florida, Colorado, Illinois, and Nevada, state legislators have recently introduced bills to lift bans against rent control. In the summer of 2019, the state of New York expanded rent control from 1 million to 2.4 million housing units. In California, despite the 2018 defeat of Proposition 10—which would have enabled the comprehensive statewide expansion of rent control—the Tenant Protection Act was enacted in January 2020, a law that makes it illegal for any residential landlord in the state to raise rents more than 5 percent plus the local rate of inflation in one year. This law is designed to prevent the most egregious rent hikes and also contains an end to evictions without just cause. Also in 2019, a collaborative report produced by PolicyLink, the Centre for Popular Democracy and the Right to the City Alliance, entitled *Our Homes, Our Future: How Rent Control Can Build Healthy, Stable Communities*, pulled together a remarkable range of qualitative and quantitative evidence from across the United States to present a compelling case for nationwide rent controls (of the second-generation variety). Four points in particular were made: that controls increase housing stability and affordability for current tenants (serving especially to stabilize communities affected by the ravages of gentrification); that they are unrivaled in their speed and scale; that they are cost effective relative to other housing policies; and that they protect low-income households that are disproportionately seniors, people of color, women with young children, and the sick and disabled. It is difficult to imagine a more convincing call for rent control as "a cornerstone of housing justice" (PolicyLink, 40), not least because the report relied first and foremost on the expertise of people working with tenant organizations at ground level to promote rent control programs where tenants play a central role in their design and implementation.

In Scotland, the Living Rent campaign was formed in the aftermath of the Scottish independence referendum in 2014 (Saunders, Samuels, and Statham 2018). Its initial leadership was comprised entirely of students in their twenties, a cohort hit particularly hard by high rental housing costs. Living Rent set out to accomplish a very simple mission: to bring back the words *rent control* to the political debate, where it had been erased for so long. The campaign began by reaching out to existing organizations, particularly labor unions and student unions, and to the general public, notably through a large number of weekend street stalls and online activism. Living Rent also organized marches and public protests to deliver completed petitions, and a major campaigning intention was to push the ruling Scottish National Party (SNP) to be more progressive about housing issues. Within six months of beginning its campaigning, Living Rent had affiliations with organizations representing more than a million people in Scotland, from trade unions and student associations to women's organizations, faith and youth groups, and more. It was able to articulate the intersection of housing precarity with other social problems: how housing affects many different marginalized groups in particularly acute ways. These organizations backed the campaign because rent control, quite simply, resonated with them all as a commonsense solution to an increasingly pressing problem: the high cost of housing dominating people's lives.

Living Rent organizes and campaigns

- for initial rents to be set against a "points" system to reflect the quality of the property (using rent regulation in the Netherlands as a model);
- for rent increases to be part of a rent affordability index to ensure increases do not push tenants into hardship;

- for a move toward indefinite tenancies as the default, away from short-term contracts;
- for all tenants to be entitled to a hardship defense in relation to evictions; and
- for the creation of a Scottish Rent Commission, to oversee these recommendations and to serve as a center of expertise for the Scottish private rental sector.

The organization's achievements so far are impressive, given over three decades of the rampant neoliberalization of housing in Scotland and the United Kingdom more broadly. Under pressure, the Scottish government announced the end of the right of landlords to reclaim their properties from tenants without any reason. Achieving this security of tenure was a huge victory, as indeed is just getting the question of rent control on the political agenda in Scotland. Living Rent continues to campaign for rent controls that link rent levels to the quality and safety of a home, to make the campaign more grassroots (including more direct action), and to build a tenants' union to shift the power balance away from landlords and toward the question of the human need for shelter.

Rent controls work best when they are paired with tenant security measures (such as just cause evictions) and are implemented without any loopholes or any free-for-all when units under control become vacant for any reason (what is termed "vacancy decontrol"). The abovementioned evidence-based testimony by Mason concluded with what I think is a helpful set of "design principles" for what contemporary, progressive rent controls could look like in the United States:

1. Rent control needs to be combined with other measures to create more affordable housing. The main goals of rent regulation are to protect renters' legitimate interest in remaining in their homes; to advance the social interest in stable, mixed-income neighborhoods; and to curb the market power of landlords. Other measures, including subsidies and incentives, reforms to land-use rules, and public investment in social housing, are needed to increase the supply of affordable housing. These two approaches should be seen as complements.

2. There are good reasons that most existing rent control focuses on rent increases rather than the absolute level of rents. Rent control structured this way allows new housing to claim the market rent,

giving the developer a chance to recover the costs of construction. Rent increases many years after the building is finished are more likely to reflect changes in the value of the location rather than the costs of production. From the point of view of allowing existing tenants to remain in their homes, it also makes sense to focus on increases, rather than the absolute level of rents.

3. Since rent regulation is aimed at the monopoly rents claimed by landlords, it should allow for reasonable rent increases to reflect increased costs of maintaining a building. At the same time, there is a danger that landlords will engage in unneeded improvements if this allows them to raise rents more than they would otherwise be allowed to. A natural way to balance this is to adjust the allowable rent increase each year based on some measure of average costs or a broader price index.

4. For rent control to be effective, tenants also need to be protected from the threat of eviction or other pressure from landlords. To give renters genuine security in their homes, they need an automatic right to renew their leases, unless the landlord can demonstrate nonpayment of rent or other good cause.

5. Rent control is more likely to have perverse effects when the controls are incomplete. When rent regulations do reduce the supply of affordable rental housing, this is typically because they have loopholes allowing landlords to escape them. In particular, vacancy decontrol or allowing larger rent increases on vacancy significantly reduces the impact of rent control and may encourage landlords to push out existing tenants. There is also some evidence that landlords seek to avoid rent regulation by converting rental units into units for sale. To avoid these kinds of unintended consequences, rent regulations should be as comprehensive as possible, and options to remove units from the regulated market need to be closed off wherever possible.[4]

In other contexts, these suggestions may need adjusting vis-à-vis institutional and historical circumstances, but as a set of principles to protect tenants from evictions, they are a most excellent point of departure for housing justice. Perhaps the key lesson is that rent control is *just one policy among many* that can and should be implemented in order to reframe the debate around housing away from assets and profit and investments to community, family, home, and shelter. Furthermore, the history of rent strikes teaches us that when landlords, the housing industry, and profit-driven state legislation refuse to concede any ground, tenants always fight back, and they often win (Hua 2018; Gray 2018). The production of ignorance about rent control will continue—there are enormously powerful vested interests behind it—but so will the struggles for adequate and affordable housing. Tenants massively outnumber landlords.

5 Neighborhood Effects
as Tautological Urbanism

LAVENDER HILL

Celebrity urbanists like Richard Florida, Thomas L. Friedman, and David Brooks often seem to begin their books and newspaper columns with anecdotes they learn from taxi drivers who take them from the airport to their five-star hotels to deliver lucrative paid speeches to corporate crowds. Such "quote-the-cabbie" punditry, as Liz Cox Barrett (2004) calls it, can be excruciating. (Barrett encapsulates the "Thomas L. Friedman manual of reporting" as "Everything I needed to know about outsourcing I learned from Harish, who drove me to my Mumbai hotel.") For instance, Florida's much-trumpeted book *The New Urban Crisis* (2017) begins with its author recounting what his taxi driver told him on the way in from the airport about all the empty luxury flats in London, which apparently endorses his theory that the crisis is about wide inequality and high house prices, which would be instantly solved if only they could both be reduced a little by city mayors everywhere. In short, these authors harvest the 'word from the street' from their taxi drivers and incorporate the drivers' wit and wisdom into an otherwise going nowhere "'explanation'" of urban problems that they are passing by in their taxis. But in September 2018

I experienced a different kind of taxi revelation, from a very different kind of perspective.

I was living in Cape Town, South Africa, on a short fellowship at the University of Cape Town. I did not have access to a vehicle and found Uber to be by far the fastest and safest way to get around a city with a totally inadequate and often dangerous public transportation system (since 2015, suburban train carriages in the city have been subject to frequent fire attacks, the motivations for which are still the subject of intense debate at the time of writing). It is well known that Uber is a rapacious and exploitative multinational corporation built on pure speculation, based on digital economies of individualization and big data surveillance (see chapter 1), with a near-complete absence of workers' rights, but it does offer a welcome opportunity for many poor people (mostly men, mostly recent immigrants) to earn money. One evening I took an Uber ride from the university back to the place where I was staying. It was driven by a young man aged twenty-four, who was raised in a Cape Town neighborhood called Lavender Hill. The things he told me about his life in that place, which I detail shortly, can only be understood with reference to what the system of apartheid (1948–94) did to Cape Town.

Lavender Hill, like most neighborhoods on the Cape Flats (a vast, sandy, windswept plain between the Cape Peninsula and the Hottentot-Holland mountains), exists because of the Group Areas Act (1950), the most damaging instrument of segregationist social engineering during the apartheid era. This was facilitated by another piece of legislation that same year, the Population Registration Act, which organized all South Africans into four rigid racial categories: Whites, Asians, Coloureds (people of mixed race), and Black Africans, in that strict hierarchy. This had dramatic effects on an individual's life chances, depending to which category an individual was assigned. As there could never be any scientific basis at all for the classification of a population with extremely diverse origins and phenotypical features, doubt was a regular occurrence. One's entire life could be determined by whatever a state employee thought was the correct classification vis-à-vis official constructions of racial appearance. For example, this was the official definition of a 'White' person in South Africa from 1948–91: "Any person who in appearance, obviously is, or who is generally accepted as a white person, other than a person who although in appearance obviously a white person, is generally accepted as a coloured person."

The Group Areas Act was effectively a strategy of ethnic cleansing of urban space. Cities were carved up into Group Areas: residential neighborhoods that were for the sole occupation of one specific racial category. Therefore, if you were classified as Coloured, Asian, or Black African, and lived in an area that became classified as a 'White Group Area', you became a 'disqualified' person and were forced to leave, as you had become an illegal occupant of your home. Those homes, and often entire neighborhoods, were then either redeveloped or razed to prepare the Group Area for White occupation. This happened on a huge scale across South Africa; in Cape Town, it was done in order to turn valuable land to more remunerative uses and to realize the apartheid vision of turning the central city, the Atlantic seaboard, and the Southern Suburbs into an 'orderly' white city, serviced by cheap non-white labor that would, under no circumstances, be allowed to live and play in that white city. In 1948 Cape Town was one of the very least racially segregated cities in sub-Saharan Africa, but all that changed in dramatic and appalling fashion under the Group Areas Act.

The 'Coloured' label used under apartheid has stuck and has long been appropriated by people of mixed race in South Africa. Coloured people in South Africa are the outcome of the mixing of white colonizers, their slaves (uprooted by the Dutch East India company from Malaysia, Indonesia, South Asia, Madagascar, and many parts of East Africa), and the indigenous San and Khoi people. Today, the degree of mixing among Coloured Capetonians is even more diverse. Regarding the apartheid instruments of the Population Registration and Group Areas Acts, John Western explained the farce of it all:

> Given the city's three and a half centuries of intercontinental trade and slavery—of the mingling of peoples—the majority of Capetonians have been neither Whites nor Blacks but "mixed race" persons designated "Cape Coloureds." Imagine trying strictly to impose a legal system of watertight, mutually exclusive "racial" categories upon a million or more persons whose appearance and culture makes them impossible to classify in such a way. How can it be done? Roughly, is one answer. Rough in the sense of approximation and rough in the sense of bruising. (1996, xvi)

Figure 5. The original Lavender Hill, District Six, Cape Town, 1970. © Rudolf Ryser.

The bruising was extreme. Beginning in the 1960s, nearly all Capetonians of mixed race were uprooted from their homes and neighborhoods and then scattered and dumped into barrack-like structures in 'Coloured townships', built quickly and cheaply on the Cape Flats. These areas, of course, were segregated from the Black African townships. The distances people were expelled varied, but it was not uncommon for people to find themselves living over thirty kilometers away from where they had previously lived, surrounded by people whom they did not know, due to the systematic policy of scattering the evicted: breaking up communities and their associations in order to preclude organized resistance.

There is no Lavender and no Hill to speak of in Lavender Hill. Just like the townships of Hanover Park and Sea Winds, it gets its name from a former street (see figure 5) in probably the most famous of all the South African urban areas destroyed by apartheid rulers: District Six.

For most of its existence, District Six was perceived, portrayed, and stigmatized by people who did not live there as a degenerate slum, a place only of vice and crime, an embarrassment to the "Mother City" of South Africa. This was mostly due to the condition of many of the buildings and the severe disinvestment in people's lives; absentee landlordism was rife, overcrowding was severe, and many people did live in entrenched poverty in dismal conditions. It is beyond dispute that District Six had severe degradation and disease, as well as gangs, crime, addiction, and prostitution. Yet there were two sides to multiethnic, multifaith District Six. It was an extraordinarily vibrant place. Deborah Hart described it as

> a paradox of warmth and variety, dirt and rubble, gaiety and sadness; of respectability and rascality; of poverty and decent comfort; of tenements shamefully neglected and homes well-cared-for and well-loved.... District Six hummed with the enterprise of its residents, boasting a bewildering assortment of stores that served the population far beyond its immediate boundaries. Mingled with the more commonplace small general stores, tailors, butchers, fruiterers, and fishmongers, were the spice and curry shops and dimly lit herbalists' stores, reflecting the diverse cultures of their owners and patrons. Informal trading flourished as hawkers set up their barrows at nearly every street corner, bartering animatedly with great exhibitionism and adding to the chaos of what was said to be a "'river of people, cars, barrows, buses, horse-drawn carts; a bustling, laughing, shouting, chatting river of people'." (1988, 610–11)

In short, there is abundant evidence that District Six was a truly remarkable community (much of this evidence is now collected and displayed by the curators of the District Six Museum, as detailed in Rassool and Prosalendis 2001). The importance of District Six to Capetonian and South African culture (especially music, food, art, and literature) cannot be overstated (Swanson and Harries 2001). However, the slum stigma attached to District Six was very convenient for white supremacists, who knew that its thriving community spirit was a threat to their Nazi-inspired beliefs in racial purity and that District Six was one vast rent gap: the potential economic value of the land (literally right next to the central business district) was very high if it could be grabbed for white occupation and gentrified. The stigma was amplified and activated by the apartheid regime, which on February 11, 1966, declared District Six a White Group Area. It is always much easier for government authorities to justify obliterating a place if they can convince everyone that it is a threat to wider public health and safety, and that people will somehow be better off if they are relocated into new housing elsewhere.

More than sixty thousand District Sixers faced forced eviction and displacement, which began in 1967 and lasted until 1984. Attempts at resistance occurred and were wide ranging (Soudien 1990), but they had to face the bureaucratic, legal, and military might of the white nationalist government. District Six was almost entirely razed, and only places of worship were spared.

Buckingham Palace: District Six, by one of the great South African scholars of color, the late Richard Rive, is an account of the fascinating characters living in a row of houses in the heart of the district before, during, and after the demolition. Rive describes the aftermath of community destruction:

> Everyone in the District died a little when it was pulled down. Many died spiritually and emotionally. Some like my mother also died physically.... Many were forced to move to small matchbox houses in large matchbox townships which with brutal and tactless irony were given names by the authorizes such as Hanover Park and Lavender Hill to remind us of the past they had taken away from us. There was one essential difference between the old places and the new ones. District Six had a soul. Its centre held together till it was torn apart. Stained and tarnished as it was, it had a soul that held together. The new matchbox conglomerates on the desolate Cape Flats had no soul. The houses were soulless units piled together to form a disparate community that lacked cohesion....
>
> They had taken our past away and left the rubble. They had demolished our spirits and left broken bricks. They had destroyed our community and left dust and memories. And they had done all this for their own selfish and arrogant reasons. They had sought to regulate our present in order to control our future. And as I stood there I was overwhelmed by the enormity of it all. And I asked aloud, "'What men have the moral or political right to take away a people's past? How will they answer on that day when they have to account for this? For the past will not be forgotten.'" The south-easter [a strong wind regularly affecting Cape Town] swept the voices of accusation and recrimination into all the houses into which the people had been driven.... And the people on the bleak Flats whisper and remember what greed and intolerance have done to them. And they tell their children and their children's children because it must never be forgotten. (1986, 126–27)

Following the forced removals of tens of thousands of people due to the color of their skin, their quality of life and their life chances deteriorated dramatically. The deeply entrenched and serious social problems that affect the neighborhoods of the Cape Flats today can be traced to the prolonged and damaging psychological distress caused by apartheid-era forced removals, to the geographical fragmentation of the identity and heritage of the communities that were bulldozed, and to decades of abandonment and disinvestment in apartheid's dumping ground (Jensen 2008; Samara

Figure 6. Lavender Hill, Cape Town, September 2018.

2011; Salo 2018). While a majority of township residents now make a life in the best way that they can in the context of profound neglect, disinvestment, and stigmatization, many of these areas are quite literally dominated by disaffected and abandoned youths who have very few economic and social alternatives available to them other than membership in brutal criminal gangs. The result is a constellation of some of the most segregated and violent urban areas in the world, with homicide rates equivalent to or surpassing those of war zones (Pinnock 2016; Walker 2018).

The young man who drove me home—the grandchild of a family displaced from District Six—told me a great deal about life and death in Lavender Hill: the false promises made by politicians, the abysmal housing conditions (see figure 6), the unemployment, the persistent neglect, and the intense stigmatization of race and place that affects everything he does. He spoke with unsettling frankness about the unbelievable violence (in particular the gendered brutality inflicted by gangs), the distressing symptoms of addiction to methamphetamine (known locally as '*tik*'), the corruption and thuggery of the police, and the prison at nearby Pollsmoor as "a better and easier life" for many young men who might otherwise die on the streets. He spoke movingly about the extraordinary courage of people living there who try to make a difference, against the odds. He left Lavender Hill as soon as he could and now lives in a far more salubrious area called Wynberg, where "housing is too expensive but it is safe." I asked him how he stayed out of trouble, and he replied, "Oh I've been in trouble! But my mother is very tough and God gave me a family." He had a wife, training to be a teacher, and two young children: "I want them to have a father, as I never knew mine." Uber was one way of earning money; his other job, packing fruit and vegetables, involved getting out of bed at 4:30 a.m. and working until 9:30 a.m. He then rested and started his Uber job after lunch, often working till late. "I don't see my family very much," he said. He spoke beautifully and eloquently about his city, the local politics, the problems that never seemed to go away, his hopes and dreams for his family and his people. His knowledge of Cape Town and its tortured history was astoundingly comprehensive.

After he had dropped me where I was staying, I sat in silence for some time, mostly trying to process what I had heard, but also saddened that such an intelligent and articulate young man—someone who lived, understood, and communicated the experience of urban poverty so profoundly—was not in a position of political or economic power. I reflected on whether there was any theoretical work available on urban inequality to help me interpret what I had just learned from him. A simple interpretation would be to put his life into a register of how *where* we live shapes our entire existence. As a geographer this register has considerable appeal; from my first day as a geography undergraduate I was told, in no uncertain terms, that places shape our lives, that geography matters. But as this chapter explains, this is by itself an inadequate analytic framework that diverts attention away from the structural, political, and institutional causes of urban inequality. The enormous neighborhood effects literature, which has recently been used to explain the violent conditions in Cape Town's townships (Pinnock 2016), tends to downplay or even ignore altogether these crucial causes.

UNSETTLING A COTTAGE INDUSTRY

Neighborhood effects stems from an understanding of society that adheres to one overarching assumption, that *where you live affects your life chances.*

It is seductively simple, and on the surface, very convincing. For example, in the Cape Town context, somebody growing up today in a grand house overlooking the Atlantic Ocean in the very affluent neighborhood of Camps Bay will have far more chances in life than somebody growing up in Lavender Hill. The striking simplicity and inherent *fait accompli* of this line of thinking in a complex world have led to a belief among mainstream urban scholars that neighborhoods matter and shape the fate of their residents (and their young residents most acutely); therefore, urban policies must be geared toward poor neighborhoods, seen not as expressions of social dysfunction but as its *incubators*. A belief in *causal* neighborhood effects has become widespread among mainstream urban scholars, policy elites, journalists, planners, and think tank researchers in multiple contexts across the Global South, North, East, and West.

Almost two decades ago, Robert Sampson and his colleagues (Sampson, Morenoff, and Gannon-Rowley 2002, 444) wryly observed that "the study of neighborhood effects, for better or worse, has become something of a cottage industry in the social sciences." Their observation was made in a thorough review of the neighborhood effects literature, where they noticed that "the mid 1990s to the year 2000 saw more than a doubling of neighborhood studies to the level of about 100 papers per year" (444). This prodigious output is not dissimilar to that of the earlier intellectual cottage industry on the "underclass" (Wacquant 1996), to which the neighborhood effects literature is closely related. A great deal of time and money has been spent by scholars in several disciplines working on neighborhood effects, and any newcomer to the literature is struck immediately by not only its sheer size—"hundreds more" studies appeared in the decade after the abovementioned review (Sampson 2012, 46)—but also the tautology regularly demonstrated by exponents of the genre and the near-total dominance of statistical approaches (including the soporific use of the word *controlling* for a range of individual and place characteristics in respect of trying to identify such effects).

In cities of the Global North, the "where you live affects your live chances" view has shaped flagship urban and housing policies to a significant extent, most famously in the case of the federal Moving to Opportunity (MTO) experiment in the United States from 1994 to 1998. MTO randomly allocated housing vouchers to poor families from poor neighborhoods in five cities to induce their movement into low-poverty neighborhoods. Families living in "concentrated poverty" (40 percent or greater) in those cities were deemed eligible to apply for vouchers, and those that did were randomly assigned to one of three groups: the experimental (who were assisted in a move to a neighborhood with a poverty rate of less than 10 percent, almost always suburban in the United States), the comparison (who received a Section 8 voucher—a rent subsidy—with no restrictions on where they could move, but with few options available in tight housing markets), and the control (who stayed in public housing). This was an experiment premised on the assumption that *neighborhoods cause poverty*, so the response was to assist families in moving to neighborhoods with better schools, low crime rates, more jobs, positive role models, and so on. Despite the proclamation of the Brookings Institution's Bruce Katz that MTO was a "'home run' in social science research" due to its clean experimental design (quoted in Goering 2003), the outcomes of MTO have been modest, to put it mildly. Five sets of outcomes were studied: mental health, physical health, adult economic "self-sufficiency," education, and "risky behavior" (the language is revealing and is discussed later on). "Null effects have been reported for a number of outcomes" (Sampson 2012, 263), adverse effects on the "delinquency" (one of the "risky behaviors") and physical health of adolescent males, and positive effects on adult mental health and the education and health of young women (Briggs, Popkin, and Goering 2010, 223–37). Despite the mixed outcomes reported, urban scholars in the United States have consistently trumpeted the "significant positive effects" of the experiment, notably in the wake of Hurricane Katrina in 2005 (Imbroscio 2008).

There is, however, an absolutely fundamental *structural* question that is rarely tabled at gatherings of those concerned with neighborhood effects *Why do people live where they do in cities*? If *where* any given individual lives affects their life chances as deeply as neighborhood effects proponents believe, it seems crucial to understand *why* that individual is living there in the first place. A related question is: *Why is there so much difference between the richest and poorest neighborhoods*? It has long been the case in most cities of the world that there are neighborhoods of astounding affluence and persistent poverty, often side by side. Life chances will of course be very different for residents of those very different neighborhoods, but stating the obvious and "controlling" for various externalities (especially popular among statistically oriented urban sociologists) does not explain why such urban inequality exists. The driver from Lavender Hill (unwittingly) invited me to think in more detail not only about the chances of where you are born and raised, but how these uneven life chances are politically determined, by historical legacies of colonial oppression and racial domination, by uneven geographical development, and by massive inequalities in public service delivery and welfare provision across a metropolis (deliberate state neglect of certain neighborhoods concurrent with strong state support for others).

Therefore, examining the structural factors that give rise to differential life chances and the inequalities they produce across a city requires an inversion of the neighborhood effects thesis to "your life chances affect where you live," and closer inspection of how differential life chances are expressed in the urban landscape. In what follows I argue that in societies living under a capitalist mode of production, a theory of capitalist urbanization provides an appropriate understanding of the problems inherent in letting the market (buttressed by the state) be the force that determines the cost of land and housing, and correspondingly, the major determinant of where people live. The environmental determinism practiced by many neighborhood effects scholars stands on very shaky ground when placed in the context of well over a century of theoretical advances in respect of how differential life chances are created in cities. In this respect it is helpful to elucidate the analytical tradition from which the Marxist critique of capitalist urbanization emerged in the mid- to late twentieth century, to which I now turn. The symptomatic silence over Marxist analyses among mainstream urban and housing scholars necessitates the task of recounting what can be learned from such analyses, particularly vis-à-vis neighborhood effects.

LOCATIONAL SEESAWS

The field of urban studies was arguably born in the 1920s in Chicago as a consequence of the prolific writings of Robert Park and his colleagues based at the University of Chicago's sociology department. There was little place for structural reasoning amid all their land use models, ethnographic accounts of Chicago life, appeals to natural science metaphors, and interpretations of the city as social laboratory. By the 1960s, urban studies had crystallized into a hegemonic blend of the social and spatial theories of the Chicago School, infused with the methods and assumptions of neoclassical economics. Morphological analyses, with, suspiciously, "half the city submerged under Lake Michigan" (Smith 1992, 110), portrayed the suburbanization of middle-class and wealthy households as *the* driving force of urban growth, suburban expansion, and overall metropolitan housing market change. Among the numerous legacies of the Chicago School, arguably the most enduring was the idea that the urban environment tends toward equilibrium much as an organism does, with individuals and groups sorting themselves into "natural areas" that constituted a city symbiotically balanced between cooperation and conflict (Metzger 2000). This logic—an attempt to account for why certain population categories lived in certain districts of the city—laid the foundation for ideas of *spatial equilibrium* and economic competition that were used to develop neoclassical models of urban land markets in the late 1950s and early 1960s (Alonso 1964; Muth 1969). These models explained suburbanization in terms of an overriding *consumer preference* for space, combined with differences in the ability of high- and low-income households to engage in locational trade-offs between access to centralized employment and the cheaper land prices available on the lower-density urban periphery. The neoclassical models seemed to account for the spatial paradox of the US city: middle-class and wealthy households living on cheap suburban land, poor and working-class households forced to crowd into dense apartment blocks on expensive, centrally located, inner-city land.

In the course of creating elegant land use models, however, the neoclassical urbanists had built everything on the dubious foundation of *consumer sovereignty*. Viewed through neoclassical analytic lenses, the form and function of the city is always and everywhere attributable to the result of *choices* made by individual consumers about land and housing. The argument goes that each consumer rationally chooses among available options in order to maximize their "utility," subject to the constraints of their available resources, and institutions then compete against each other to serve the needs of these utility-maximizing consumers. In respect of neighborhoods and housing, the resulting market will produce the spatial trade-offs between space and accessibility that structure different residential patterns. All that remains to complete the calculus are the "optimal" political-economic conditions for the operation of such a competitive market; if it is allowed to operate free of any constrictive regulations enforced by the state, the incentives for both producers and consumers to make rational and economically sound decisions will push the urban environment toward an equilibrium while yielding the maximum amount of utility for the maximum number of people.

Neoclassical theories have come to dominate urban theory and especially urban policy (Lees, Slater, and Wyly 2008, 46), and they constitute the analytic foundation of numerous proponents of neighborhood effects, who leave political-economic structures unquestioned just as they assume that people living where they do is a matter of individual choices made under resource constraints. But the very conceptual simplicity of neoclassical urban thought leaves it wide open to criticism. If we are interested in resource constraints, how do those constraints come about? A more urgent task is to consider the *limits* on individual choice, the *boundaries* set by ever-present inequalities of wealth and power. What about the limited choices available to the poor and working classes?[1] In short, there is much more to the question of neighborhood change than descriptive accounts of who moves in and who moves out. These questions were at the forefront of a radical shift in how we understand cities that began in the early 1970s and continue to shape a critical imagination, wherein concerns for a more socially just spatial arrangement of urban places under a different mode of production drive intellectual inquiry. Much of the literature reflecting such concerns has bypassed the research agendas of those locked within the neighborhood effects paradigm.

In 1969, David Harvey decamped from his first teaching post in Bristol, England, and arrived in Baltimore, Maryland, a city with districts hit hard by grotesque racial injustices, systematic disinvestment, and rioting in the wake of the assassination of Martin Luther King Jr. The previous year he had submitted the manuscript of *Explanation in Geography* (a landmark text in the quantitative/positivist geographical tradition), and he felt politically irresponsible:

> I turned in the manuscript in the summer of 1968 with near revolutions going on in Paris, Berlin, Mexico City, Bangkok, Chicago and San Francisco.

I had hardly noticed what was happening. I felt sort of idiotic. It seemed absurd to be writing when the world was collapsing in chaos around me and cities were going up in flames. (Harvey 2002, 167)

To understand the origins of inequality and injustice in the city in which he now resided, Harvey quickly became the leading force of a new analytic framework that returned to the roots of contemporary neoclassical theory: the classical political economy debates between Smith, Ricardo, Malthus, and Marx. Harvey's (1973) *Social Justice and the City* was the manifesto of this new urban studies, and his critique of the dominant neoclassical explanation of inner-city decline and ghetto formation is crucial for any analytic interrogation of neighborhood effects. He took aim at the models of urban structure that William Alonso (1964) and Richard F. Muth (1969) had built using the principles of agricultural land-use patterns that had been devised by a Prussian landowner, Johann Heinrich von Thünen (1793–1850):

> After an analytic presentation of the theory, Muth seeks to evaluate the empirical relevance of the theory by testing it against the existing structure of residential land use in Chicago. His tests indicate that the theory is broadly correct, with, however, certain deviations explicable by such things as racial discrimination in the housing market. We may thus infer that the theory is a true theory. This truth, arrived at by classical positivist means, can be used to help us identify the problem. What for Muth was a successful test of a social theory becomes an indicator of what the problem is. *The theory predicts that poor groups must, of necessity, live where they can least afford to live.*
>
> Our objective is to eliminate ghettos. Therefore, the only valid policy . . . is to eliminate the conditions which give rise to the truth of the theory. In other words, we wish the von Thünen theory of the urban land market to become not true. *The simplest approach here is to eliminate those mechanisms which serve to generate the theory. The mechanism in this case is very simple—competitive bidding for the use of the land.* (Harvey 1973, 137; emphasis added)

This critique is acutely relevant today, when neoclassical assumptions have been revitalized and appropriated by the political triumphs of neoliberalism, when cities "have become the incubators for many of the major political and ideological strategies through which the dominance of neoliberalism is being maintained" (Brenner and Theodore 2002, 375–76).

Municipal administrations now tend to act less as regulators of markets to protect marginalized residents and more as *entrepreneurial* agents of market processes and capital accumulation (Harvey 1989; Peck 2005; Weber 2010), resulting in spectacular wealth inequalities within and between cities.

Together with Neil Smith, Harvey added a geographical, spatial dimension to something that had fascinated Marx: the powerful contradictions of capital investment and accumulation. Investments are required to create the places that must exist in order for profits to be made: offices, factories, shops, homes, and all the rest of the infrastructure that constitutes a city. Yet once these investments are committed to a certain place, capital cannot be quickly or easily shifted to newer, more profitable opportunities elsewhere. This is because capitalists are always forced to choose between investing to maintain the viability of previous capital commitments (or exploiting new opportunities) and neglecting or abandoning the old. Therefore capital investment is always animated by a geographical tension: between the need to *equalize* conditions and seek out new markets in new places and the need for *differentiation* (and particularly a division of labor that is matched to various places' comparative advantage). The result is a dynamic "seesaw" of investment and disinvestment over time and across space, in an ongoing process of uneven geographical development (Smith 1982, 1984; Harvey 1973, 1982). Capitalism is always creating new places, new environments designed for profit and accumulation, in the process devalorizing previous investments and landscapes:

> The logic behind uneven development is that the development of one area creates barriers to further development, thus leading to underdevelopment, and that the underdevelopment of that area creates opportunities for a new phase of development. Geographically this leads to the possibility of what we might call a "locational seesaw": the successive development, underdevelopment, and redevelopment of given areas as capital jumps from one place to another, then back again, both creating and destroying its own opportunities for development. (Smith 1982, 151)

As discussed in chapter 3, the flight of capital away from certain areas of the city—depreciation and disinvestment—has devastating implications for people living at the base of the seesaw, the bottom of the urban class structure. The lack of maintenance expenditure leads to tough housing conditions for poor residents, amid myriad other consequences of capital disinvestment such as high unemployment, poor schools, inadequate retail services, dismal health outcomes, and so on. Crucially, and in sharp contrast to much popular and intellectual perception, such areas usually see social networks and community ties within them *strengthen* as a coping mechanism for the withdrawal of capital. Residents living in disinvested parts of cities fall back on what they know and what they have: each other.

What is the relevance of the theory of uneven development to a critique of neighborhood effects? Recall the paradigm: that where you live affects your life chances. Applied to poor people, this implies that the influences of what surrounds them have caused their poverty: negative role models and miscreants mired in a culture of concentrated poverty that stops people rising up and finding a better life and escaping their neighborhoods. So, in any society where class inequality is present, or is diffracted through an ethnoracial prism (or through any other aspect of sociocultural differentiation), residential turnover leading to entrenched disinvestment almost invariably unleashes an all-encompassing, discriminatory, and stigmatizing argument: that the clustering of a poor population category is *causing* neighborhood decline. Yet it is structural factors that cause neighborhood disinvestment and truncate the life chances of the poor, who become trapped where they are due to the exclusive nature of a city's highly competitive housing market. Contrary to the neoclassical paradigm, there is nothing remotely natural about such a situation. The clear injustice is that the owners of capital tend to see spectacular wealth gains at the expense of those residing in neighborhoods robbed (often quite literally) of adequate investment. When the seesaw tips again and investment does arrive, it is seldom geared to the interests of the poor; on the contrary, tenants are evicted and displaced as rent gaps (see chapter 3) are exploited and gentrification begins.

Capitalist land and housing markets, in short, favor the creation of urban environments to serve the interests of profit:

> Capitalist development has therefore to negotiate a knife-edge path between preserving the exchange values of past capital investments in the built environment and destroying the value of these investments in order to open up

fresh room for accumulation. Under capitalism there is, then, a perpetual struggle in which capital builds a physical landscape appropriate to its own condition at a particular moment in time, only to have to destroy it, usually in the course of a crises, at a subsequent point in time. (Harvey 1978, 124)

Harvey was quick to show that the urban process under capitalism was far more than a matter of capital flows: it was about class inequality, the formation of an exploited and alienated urban working class and "the violence which the capitalist form of accumulation inevitably inflicts upon it" (124), and the possibilities the contradictions of capitalism create for resistance by the working class (class struggle). On that final point, Friedrich Engels (1845) long ago noted that the intensity of working-class clustering and oppression in particular districts of industrial Manchester meant that "the spatial configuration of the city only accelerated the nurturing of class consciousness" (Hunt 2009, 109), something which is rarely, if ever, mentioned among scholars of neighborhood effects on the lookout for social pathologies.

STRUCTURAL DEFICIENCIES

Having summarized the analytic tradition of Marxist theory toward addressing the urbanization question and offered a glimpse of the lessons it offers in respect of understanding why people live where they do, I turn now to some of the conclusions and arguments of proponents of the neighborhood effects thesis, particularly a consideration of the *political* implications of such scholarship. Due to the sheer size of the literature, I can only offer some examples of scholarship that reflect the popular view that where you live affects your life chances at precisely the same time that it ignores the structural and institutional causes of urban inequality.[2] In doing so it becomes pertinent to draw upon some of the lonely yet crucial critiques that have been advanced in recent years to call the neighborhood effects paradigm into question and, in particular, to elucidate its troubling political import.

As David Manley, Maarten van Ham, and Joe Doherty (2011) explain, the initial stimulus to engage with neighborhood effects was provided by

William J. Wilson (1987, 1991) in his influential attempts to wrench the term *underclass* away from conservative researchers and give it an economic and spatial foundation, one faithful to the initial coinage of the term by Gunnar Myrdal in the 1960s. Wilson was particularly persistent with the research question of entrenched unemployment in neighborhoods exhibiting high poverty; he attributed "joblessness" (to use his preferred term) not only to the refusal of employers to hire residents from certain neighborhoods with a negative reputation, but also to the very *concentration* of residents experiencing long-term unemployment, which led to "negative social dispositions, limited aspirations, and casual work habits" (Wilson 1991, quoted in Manley, van Ham, and Doherty 2011, 153). Wilson's arguments influenced a generation of liberal scholars interested in far more than simply the labor market outcomes of "concentrated poverty," as Manley and colleagues summarize: "Explanations of neighbourhood effects . . . include role model effects and peer group influences, social and physical disconnection from job-finding networks, a culture of poverty leading to dysfunctional values, discrimination by employers and other gatekeepers, access to low quality public services, and high exposure to criminal behaviour" (153).

For the liberal proponents of the thesis, then, it is the *neighborhood* that is the problem to be addressed by policy, over and above the personal characteristics of its residents (the exclusive focus of conservative scholars). Harold Bauder captures these thematics succinctly:

> The idea of neighbourhood effects suggests that *the demographic context of poor neighbourhoods* instills "dysfunctional" norms, values and behaviours into individuals and triggers a cycle of social pathology and poverty that few residents escape. . . . [It] implies that the residents of the so-called ghettos, barrios and slums are ultimately responsible for their own social and economic situation. (2002, 85)

Neighborhood effects, perhaps by definition, is a register that has little concern over what happens *outside* the very neighborhoods under scrutiny. Take, for instance, the conclusions of a regression analysis of school dropout rates among Australian teenagers from various socioeconomic categories (Overman 2002). After stating that "living in an area where the immediate neighbourhood has low socioeconomic status has a negative effect on dropout propensities" (128), the author offers the following policy recommendation: "Government policies placing small clusters of low SES [socioeconomic status] families in better [*sic*] neighbourhoods may have little significant impact on dropout rates. 'Forced' mixing through government housing programmes may need to ensure that low SES families are well dispersed throughout more affluent neighbourhoods, rather than concentrated in 'sink' estates" (128).

This article is completely silent on the general quality of the education system, the relevance of the school curriculum to the hopes and dreams of young people, the availability of inspiring teachers, the educational opportunities beyond school corridors (such as in apprenticeships and mentoring schemes), the possibility that leaving school early to find work might be an economic necessity (part of a household survival strategy), or the fact that teenagers may have to sacrifice their studies to help care for a frail relative. These issues are ignored in favor of recommending that the Australian government disperse poor teenagers and their families as widely as possible, because when clustered together, they feed off each other in a shameful school dropout culture. Were these conclusions not dressed up in scientific language and legitimized by tables of parameter values, they would be highly controversial.

Poor educational attainment does not result from concentrations of poverty in neighborhoods but needs to be considered as an offshoot of the unequal provision of public goods and unequal treatment by the state of the different areas. The degree of inequality between neighborhoods with bad schools and good schools is *not a property of the neighborhood, but a property of the school system.* However, Overman's analysis offers considerable ammunition for an embrace of the neighborhood effects thesis: concentrations of poverty in "low status' neighborhoods in Australia apparently harm life chances, so reducing those concentrations by scattering poor young Australians among richer young Australians (prospective educational role models, presumably) apparently will solve the problem.

Another example comes from a study of "neighborhood income mix" in respect of the earnings of adults in Sweden. Deploying regression analysis of government data on income, education, labor market, and population, George Galster and colleagues comment that their results are consistent with the view that, for males who are not fully employed, low-income neighbors provide negative role models and middle-income (but not high-income) neighbors provide access to networks with valuable employment-related information. For those already fully employed, high-income neighbors probably are valuable because they provide access to networks with information about opportunities for more lucrative employment. (2008, 868)

Most troubling of all about these words is that *not a single Swede of any income category was interviewed* for the study. Therefore, the authors could not possibly offer detailed analytical insights about social networks vis-à-vis employment opportunities in different urban districts of Sweden (it is not a social networks analysis). Their conclusions also contradict ethnographic inquiries that offer strong evidence that one thing common to the experience of living in a poor neighborhood anywhere is precisely the "valuable employment-related information" that is passed around as a collective economic survival strategy (Newman 2001; Venkatesh 2006). Furthermore, rather than serve as role models for those worse off, middle-income neighbors are in fact far more likely to socialize and share information *among themselves*, as has been documented in countless sociological analyses of the middle classes (e.g., Butler and Robson 2003; Bacque et al. 2015). In addition, to men who are "not fully employed," low-income neighbors offer solidarity, empathy, informal social care, community, and kinship. They may not lead the way to full employment, but that does not make them "negative role models."

In addition, aside from the underclass caricatures invoked by that language, it speaks volumes about the neighborhood effects literature that few scholars ever ask what turns someone into a destructive influence on someone else's life. What leads someone to impress on others the view that everyone is against them, that there is no hope in their neighborhood, so they might as well give up on education and the formal economy and join a gang and immerse themselves in a world of drugs, crime, and violence? The answers can be found in terrains that are rarely controlled for: a hostile entry-level labor market, the lack of a living wage or basic income, the absolute indignity of living in a stigmatized territory, the expansion of the penal fist of the state, and the compassion fatigue displayed by civic institutions; the tragedy is that there are simply so many structural factors that condemn people to poverty and social suffering (Bourgois 2003; Wacquant 2008b).

The assumptions of that article are matched in a study of whether neighborhoods matter in the "transition from welfare to work" in the Dutch city of Rotterdam (van der Klaauw and van Ours 2003). Before any data are presented and analyzed, here is what the authors assume, and what guides their empirical inquiry:

> On the one hand in a neighbourhood with high unemployment, there might be less (informal) information about jobs available, i.e. social networks in these neighbourhoods are less valuable when searching for a job. On the other hand, the attitude towards joblessness and the social norms concerning work may differ between low and high unemployment neighbourhoods. (961)

The language is more than a little problematic: "less valuable," "attitude towards joblessness," and "social norms." Another regression analysis later, here is are the principal finding and the recommended policy package:

> Our empirical results show that the neighbourhood affects the individual transition rates from welfare to work of young Dutch welfare recipients. These transition rates are lower if the unemployment rate within the neigh-bourhood is higher. . . . From a policy point of view this implies that when it comes to youth unemployment policy special attention should be given to young welfare recipients in high unemployment neighborhoods. . . . [I]f high unemployment rates have a negative effect on individual transition rates from welfare to work because they cause a negative attitude towards work then a policy of strict monitoring is useful. (984)

The structural factors that give rise to a toughening entry-level labor market for young people in Rotterdam are disregarded. In addition, the "strict monitoring" recommended is particularly worrisome; effectively the authors are suggesting that the Dutch authorities need to travel down the US welfare-to-work program path, regardless of its widely docu-mented devastation of poor communities across the United States. The title of their essay suggests as much, as does their comment that "in most literature on neighbourhood effects in the US results similar to ours are found" (982).

Considered together, the essays I have discussed here provide a snap-shot of the neighborhood effects genre, in which authors are as quick to make sweeping assertions about communities into which they rarely (if ever) set foot as they are to ignore the political implications of their scholarship. Bauder has advanced a powerful critique:

> The direct causality implied by neighbourhood effects models presents a simple and "straight-forward" explanation for the social and economic marginality of inner-city residents, which entices through its use of quantitative methods and its claim to be objective and value-free. Yet . . . this literature makes ideological assumptions that remain unacknowledged by many researchers. One of these assumptions is that suburban middle-class lifestyles are normal, and inner-city, minority lifestyles are pathological. (2002, 89)

A note on methodology becomes necessary here. It is unwise to cast aside the political potential of quantitative exploration, especially when considered in creative tension with qualitative accounts (Sheppard 2001; Wyly 2011). But there is a serious analytic booby trap that afflicts those working with regression techniques (which is the modus operandi of the neighborhood effects literature). Regressions appear to show that it is not just that poor people live in poor neighborhoods, but that the neighborhood effects *exceed* what would be predicted by poverty alone. But even if that were true, dispersing the poor to wealthier places, as is so often advocated, would only eliminate that incremental difference (the concentration effect), without addressing the institutional and structural arrangements driving poverty. The incremental "after controlling for" logic and discourse, then, seems deeply misguided. It is underpinned by a *ceteris paribus* argument that is necessarily false: statistically controlling for characteristics of entrants into different neighborhoods *does not make these individuals equal*, because we know that the processes of allocation through space are not random and are highly *un*equal. As two astute practitioners of the quantitative craft researching housing foreclosures in the United States warned: "When we control for everything, we lose control" (Wyly and Ponder 2011, 560).

Sampson (2012) has attempted to transcend these difficulties in his impressive magnum opus on neighborhood effects in Chicago, but his reluctance to engage with the institutional apparatus of capitalist urbanization renders incomplete his insistence on viewing "individual selection" into different neighborhoods as something "embedded in a process of structural sorting" (378). Throughout his book, Sampson insists that "selection bias" (the term used by quantitative analysts to describe the effect of people grouping themselves together based on common characteristics) is itself a neighborhood effect, as "neighbourhoods choose people and information flows" rather than the other way around, as well as that "there is an ongoing social structure that is continually operating and within which any individual and family makes decisions" (377). This is a useful intervention into a debate dominated by those who argue that the effects we attribute to poor neighborhoods are caused by the characteristics of families and individuals living in them, but Sampson holds fast to the view that neighborhoods cause and/or amplify poverty and inequality, at the expense of a consideration of the economic and political structures responsible for differential life chances. Sampson has responded to critiques of his book that he needs to incorporate a more structural perspective, especially vis-à-vis the persistence of structural racism in American society, but maintains that "neighbourhood contexts are important determinants of the quantity and quality of human behavior in their own right, and . . . play an important in mediating both macro and micro processes" (2018, 7).

The lack of attention to wider structures is not just an occupational hazard of the quantitative analyst. Those who spend time in poor communities can also fall into the trap of becoming so immersed in their research context that they fail to consider in significant depth the broader institutional political economy that would shed light on their findings. For instance, in a Chicago study of racial differences in neighborhood social networks, Mario Luis Small claims that his "findings are most consistent with the work of [William J.] Wilson" after arguing that

> the consistency of the neighborhood poverty effect across different types of outcomes makes it difficult to rule out a neighborhood effect. . . . At a minimum, it is certainly the case that individuals with identical observed characteristics face alarmingly higher rates of social isolation if they live in high poverty neighborhoods than if they live in low poverty neighborhoods. (2007, 339)

But is social isolation in a high-poverty neighborhood a neighborhood effect, or something much deeper? In an exhaustive review of area-based policies in advanced capitalist societies, Roger Andersson and Sako Musterd (2005, 386) remarked that "we should keep in mind that problems *in* the neighbourhood are seldom problems *of* the neighbourhood ... an area focus cannot by itself tackle the broader structural problems, such as unemployment, that underlie the problems of small areas."

In a similar vein, Loïc Wacquant (2008b, 284) argues that neighborhood effects convey a "falsely depoliticized vision of urban inequality" and are best understood as *the effects of the state inscribed into urban space*: "In reality they track the extent to which the state works or fails to equalize basic life conditions and strategies across places." Mario Luis Small, Erin Jacobs, and Rebecca P. Masengill (2008, 408) attempt to protect themselves from such a criticism when they state that their study of organizational ties (specifically, childcare provision) in New York City neighborhoods "points to the importance of reconsidering the state and the non-profit sector, especially under the current political economy." Yet in their study we actually learn very little about the historical path to the state's renouncement (on various scales) of its regulatory and protective functions, which have placed major pressures on the providers of social care for the population living at the bottom of the class structure in that city.

NEIGHBORHOODS DON'T "DO" ANYTHING

Robert Sampson, Jeffrey D. Morenoff, and Thomas Gannon-Rowley (2002, 444) did not see the "cottage industry" of neighborhood effects research as a problem; more troubling to them was that "this recent spurt in quantity has not been equally matched in quality; much hard work remains to be done." In the decade that followed these remarks, the cottage industry did not relent at all. In European neighborhood effects circles especially, where research funding seems plentiful but evidence of such effects is rather limited, it has become de rigueur to conclude research papers by insisting that we need more and more and more research to see if neighborhood effects exist. We are witnessing tautological urbanism: the main voices in the literature keep on saying the same things in different publications, and *substantial funds are made available by government agencies in order for scholars to keep on researching something they keep finding to be not very important.* Perhaps this is unsurprising as, beyond the standard fare of the measurement and controlling debates, the literature appears to serve primarily as ideological justification for the policy hubris of creating mixed-income communities via poverty "deconcentration." Neighborhoods *become the problem* rather than expressions of structural problems to be addressed.

There are rich pickings available for those who hold fast to the view that neighborhoods cause poverty. In October 2018 the *New York Times* ran a major piece entitled "How Neighborhoods Shape Children for Life," with the subtitle, "Some Places Lift Children out of Poverty: Others Trap Them There." It was based on the work of Opportunity Insights, a grouping of urban economists at Harvard and Brown Universities led by Raj Chetty, who constructed *The Opportunity Atlas*, a publicly available set of maps displaying children's outcomes in adulthood by Census tract using anonymized longitudinal data covering twenty million Americans who are in their mid-thirties today (Chetty et al. 2018a). This is without question a valuable database that can be used and interpreted in various ways, but the sheer importance the large research team gave to neighborhoods at the expense of any structural, political, or institutional determinants of urban inequality was striking (indeed, the entire project was driven by the question, "Which neighbourhoods in America offer children the best chances of climbing the income ladder?" (Chetty et al. 2018b, 1). Even more striking was their identification of a list of "opportunity bargains," or neighborhoods that "produce good outcomes for children without high rents" (3), which they feel low-income families should be able to access with MTO-style housing vouchers. At no point in the lengthy research paper is there any consideration of why disadvantaged children live where they do, why rents are high, or why there is extreme neighborhood inequality in the first place. The *New York Times* reporters could hardly contain their excitement:

> This work, years in the making, seeks to bring the abstract promise of big data to the real lives of children. Across the country, city officials and philanthropists who have dreamed of such a map are planning how to use it. They're hoping it can help crack open a problem, the persistence of

neighborhood disadvantage, that has been resistant to government interventions and good intentions for years. (Badger and Bui 2018)

Across the Atlantic, health geographers in Scotland have been funded by
government agencies for many years to explore "how where you live affects
your health" and spend considerable time researching marginalized people's
exposure to tobacco and alcohol products in poor neighborhoods (Pearce et
al. 2016; Moon et al. 2018; Shortt et al. 2018; Clemens et al. 2020). They
explore the high density of tobacco and alcohol retailers in Scotland's most
deprived neighborhoods and argue that teenagers in the poorest areas are
the most likely to encounter tobacco and alcohol products in nearby shops
or on their journey to school (much more so than their peers in more affluent parts of the country). But instead of analyzing the structural and institutional causes of neighborhood inequalities, they target the neighborhood
environment for the teenagers' exposure to unhealthy products and argue
that addressing the local supply of those products should be a policy priority.
Given the existence and persistence of enormous health disparities that
map onto enormously disparate neighborhoods, a research agenda guided
by a political economy approach would arrive at the different conclusion
that addressing the causes of those disparities should be the next priority
for policy makers (as opposed to recommending what products local stores
in poor neighborhoods can and cannot sell). The "place effects on health"
canon has become a triumph of the "where over the why of inequality," as
Mika Hyötyläinen (2019) put it so succinctly, despite repeated pleas to pay
close attention to political economy of place (Smith and Easterlow 2005;
Jokela 2014; Shrecker and Bambra 2015).

In a recent review of the neighborhood effects literature, specifically of
empirical studies that examine the relationship between residential contexts and individual outcomes, Patrick Sharkey and Jacob W. Faber (2014)
urge researchers to move away from the question of whether neighborhoods matter and move toward the questions of "when, where, why, and
for whom do residential contexts matter" (562). At first sight a refreshing
approach, guided by their insistence that "no single definition of the neighbourhood and no specific operationalization of this concept are sufficient
to capture the ways that residential contexts affect the lives of individuals

within them," it rather disappointingly morphs into a plea to engage obsessively with local contexts, or with "the salient social processes that operate within individuals' residential settings, and the consequences for the individual" (572). Their concluding echo of Sampson's call for researchers to "relentlessly focus on context" (2013, 4) therefore sits very uncomfortably with their call "for progress in theorizing, measuring, describing, and analyzing the operation of systems that generate inequality in individuals' residential environments" (573).

Life chances are shaped not by the neighborhood you live in, but by what social class, color, gender, or sexuality you are; what you can afford to eat; what medical care you can access; what education your parents can afford; and so on. To claim that where you live affects your life chances is to reverse social and historical causation, for where you live is a symptom of what position you (and generations of your family before you) have in the class, ethnic, gender, and sexuality structures of society and the material consequences of that position. To return to the remarkable taxi driver I met in Cape Town, Lavender Hill didn't "do" anything; politicians did things to his grandparents, forcing them and their neighbors out of their vibrant community and scattering them into inadequate housing in neglected spaces of racial oppression. Subsequent politicians failed his parents, and the economic apartheid in South Africa today continues to fail him and other young people who live in such environments, while rewarding the children and grandchildren of those who were never banished from anywhere in Cape Town due to the color of their skin. This historical injustice is compounded by the fact that blaming neighborhoods like Lavender Hill for the problems within them serves to divert attention from the abysmal "violence from above" (Wacquant 2008b) that they have suffered for so long.

As Harold Bauder reminds us, "Researchers should be particularly critical of neighbourhood effects because the concept lends itself as a political tool to blame inner-city communities for their own marginality . . . [and] provides scientific legitimacy to neighbourhood stereotypes among employers, educators and institutional staff, and justifies slum-clearance and acculturation policies" (2002, 90). It is also important to reflect upon why there is such a deficit of research on extremely rich neighborhoods, and correspondingly, of policies aimed at dispersing the rich when their concentration may have played a part in grievous collective disasters such as the 2008 financial crisis. This requires close attention to why the social standing of the poorest neighborhoods is so low, which is the focus of the next chapter.

6 The Production and Activation of Territorial Stigma

The cottage industry of neighborhood effects research outlined in the previous chapter has played a significant role in the phenomenon that is the focus of this chapter, *territorial stigmatization*: how people are discredited, devalued, and poorly treated because of the places with which they are associated. Before delving into the mushrooming literature on this theme, a brief illustration of the enormous disconnect between neighborhood reputations and realities is offered to explain why it matters to be alert to the ways in which stigma is (re)produced and to the implications of neighborhood taint.

The Downtown Eastside of Vancouver, Canada, is the historic heart of the city, right next to the central business district, with a very diverse but predominantly low-income population strongly connected to Vancouver's Indigenous or First Nations populations. Comprising the poorest urban census tracts in Canada, it is also a crucial area of affordable housing in one of the most expensive cities in the world, and for decades it has been right at the heart of antigentrification activism in the city. It has a remarkable network of neighborhood organizations and a civic energy unmatched in the city. Unfortunately the Downtown Eastside is widely known—not just nationally but internationally—for all the wrong reasons. It faces many challenges, including entrenched poverty, homelessness, prostitution, unemployment, mental illness (especially drug and alcohol addiction), and crime. It has a reputation as "Canada's worst neighbourhood" (see Sommers and Blomley 2002) and, despite its proximity to the central business district, people go to great lengths to avoid it. Hastings Street in particular, the main thoroughfare, gained the stigmatizing label "skid row" many years ago. That generic North American term for a degraded space originates from the Pacific Northwest timber industry, where loggers in Seattle and Vancouver used to skid logs down a road to timber mills. Hastings Street is the first recorded derogatory application of the term; countless other skid rows have been labeled in cities across North America, references to skidding down into despair (Allen 1995).

The literature on the Downtown Eastside is substantial and beyond the scope of this discussion. My focus is on a policing experiment that took place there in early 2015. In the wake of an escalation in robberies of wheelchair-using people in Vancouver—two-thirds of them in the Downtown Eastside (the area of central Vancouver in which disabled people are most likely to live)—Vancouver Police staff sergeant Mark Horsley found himself at the center of a new scheme to try to find those responsible. He got himself an electric-powered wheelchair, grew some facial hair, didn't wash for a week, and wheeled into the neighborhood, undercover. The objective was to pretend to be disabled and brain injured from a motorcycle accident, then bait the criminals by flashing cash and valuables. "My boss tied a pork chop around my neck and threw me into a shark tank," Horsley recalled. "We wanted a serious assault or a robbery," he said. "That's all we were after" (quoted in Hutchinson 2015).

The operation didn't go quite as planned. Instead, local people approached with offers of sympathy, hope, and encouragement, as well as friendly cautions. They made unsolicited donations: food, clothing, and a total of $24 in spare change. In five days of undercover work, with loot hanging from a waist pack for all to see and perhaps snatch, and after more than three hundred encounters with passersby, Horsley did not make a single arrest. Passersby insisted on dropping coins into his lap, without Horsley ever asking for change. Two people bought him pizza. Others just stopped and chatted, passed the time, exchanged pleasantries. On one occasion, a man came along and crouched over Horsley. He reached in, as if making for Horsley's waist pack. Here it was: a heinous crime in progress, with the perpetrator about to be caught. The man's fingers touched the waist pack . . . and the prospective criminal zipped it shut. He asked Horsley to please be more careful with his belongings. Several more times, Horsley was approached and told to take care, even by people Horsley recognized as having a criminal past.

When the operation ended, Horsley admitted to huge disappointment, as a great deal of planning had gone into it. Before deployment, police analysts had studied the Downtown Eastside and determined five specific locations—"high-value target areas"—where he ought to station himself. Horsley also had patrolled the neighborhood himself, watching how local wheelchair users conducted themselves. He spent hours in the borrowed wheelchair practicing his moves inside police headquarters and practicing his altered speech. After the experiment, Horsley concluded that robbing the disabled is below the "ethical standards" of local residents, "as they know the community will not stand for it." Disturbingly, the Vancouver Police Department denied that the operation was a flop. It refused to admit that its stereotypes were wrong, that it had maligned the neighborhood, and that its expectations had been foiled. Word will spread, it noted, and henceforth, a thief might think twice the next time he sees a vulnerable-looking person in a wheelchair, because that person might be a police officer. Vancouver's police chief simply said, "I wish we would have collared one of those predators, but I guess we are twenty four dollars ahead of when we started" (quoted in Hutchinson 2015).

ANALYZING A 'BLEMISH OF PLACE': THEORETICAL GUIDANCE

The Vancouver example I have just provided is a useful illustration of why the concept of symbolic power matters in the analysis of urban inequalities. The generic modes of analysis in mainstream *and* critical urban studies tend to shortchange the symbolic dimension of urban processes and therefore preclude the possibility that one way to understand urban inequalities is via intense scrutiny of the "symbolic defamation" of particular urban places (Wacquant 2007, 2008b). For centuries—and certainly since the mid-nineteenth century with the confluence of urbanization, industrialization, and upper-class fears—particular quarters, districts, and locales have suffered from negative reputations, so it is rather surprising that, until recently, the urban studies literature paid rather limited attention to the symbolic defamation of places in comparison to the array of stigmatized circumstances addressed by scholars at both the individual and collective levels.

Sociologists, geographers, psychologists, and anthropologists have developed a substantial body of scholarship on the stigma attached to those experiencing, inter alia, unemployment; poverty; social assistance; homelessness; mental illness; racial, gender, and sexuality discrimination; HIV/AIDS; and single parenthood. This has not been matched by a sustained focus on the burdens carried by residents of *places* widely perceived as "urban purgatories" (Wacquant 2008b) to be shunned and feared. The disgrace of residing in a notorious place can become affixed to personal identity and may prove to become—true to the Greek meaning and history of *stigma*—an indelible mark during encounters with outsiders. It is only in recent years that a growing body of scholarship has emerged revealing that urban dwellers at the bottom of the class structure are discredited and devalued not simply because of their poverty, class position, ethnoracial origin, or religious affiliation, but also because of the *places* with which they are associated.

It is perhaps unsurprising that some parts of cities suffer from negative reputations: they are typically working-class districts that have been subject to long-term and systematic disinvestment, where unemployment tends to be higher; the presence of the welfare state is clearer than in other parts of the city (e.g., with inordinate densities of social housing), levels of recent immigration are high or rising; and street crime, vice, physical abandonment, and dereliction are prevalent. The concept of territorial stigmatization was forged by the urban sociologist Loïc Wacquant in several publications that have generated significant attention among urban analysts across a range of social science disciplines (e.g., Wacquant 2007, 2008b, 2009, 2010). Based on his comparison of the structure, function, and trajectory of the remnants of the Black ghetto of Chicago's South Side with a working-class peripheral housing estate in La Courneuve, Paris, he documented and then analyzed the crystallization of what he termed a "blemish of place" (2007, 67): the profound sense of neighborhood taint emerging on both sides of the Atlantic. It is instructive to read Wacquant's account of his research experiences:

> The high-level civil servants whom I interviewed [in Paris] all spoke of the deteriorating working-class districts of the urban periphery with anguish and disgust in their voices. Everything in their tone, their vocabulary, their postures and gestures expressed regret at being in charge of a mission and a population degraded and therefore degrading. Then I found the same feeling of disgust and indignity at the very bottom of the urban ladder, among the residents of the *Quatre Mille* housing project in the Parisian industrial periphery and among Black Americans trapped in Chicago's hyperghetto. (2009, 116–17)

In the French case, stigmatization had reached such heights that those high-level civil servants "considered receiving an assignment in one of the officially designated 'sensitive neighbourhoods' a personal black mark and an impediment to their career advancement" (Wacquant, Slater, and Pereira 2014, 1272).[1]

These qualitative encounters required an analytic register, and Wacquant thus sought theoretical guidance from the work of Erving Goffman and Pierre Bourdieu. In his famous sociological study of stigma, Goffman (1963, 14–15) argued that individuals become "discredited" and then "disqualified" from society in three respects: "abominations of the body" (e.g., disability); "blemishes of individual character" (imprisonment, addiction, unemployment, etc.); and "tribal stigma of race, nation and religion." In all three, he posited a relational view, whereby an individual possesses "an undesired differentness from what we had anticipated. We and those who do not depart negatively from the particular expectations at issue I shall call the *normals*" (14–15).[2]

To Goffman's dissection of stigma, Wacquant married Bourdieu's theory of symbolic power, which is of course a conceptual anchor for this book. Bourdieu was always interested in symbolic struggles between different classes, and particularly the ways in which agents, authorities, and institutions attempt to impose the definition of the social world best suited to their own interests, where symbols become instruments of knowledge and communication in the production of consensus on the *meaning* of the social world. Notably, Bourdieu's theory was also relational, for symbolic power "is defined in and through a given relation between those who exercise power and those who submit to it" (Bourdieu 1991, 170).

Wacquant (2007) added *place* both to Goffman's three categories of social discredit and to Bourdieu's observation that symbolic power is the "power of constructing reality" (or the power of making representations stick and come true). The result is that these two theorists lead us closer to understanding urban marginality *from above and below*:

> Bourdieu works from above, following the flow of efficient representations from symbolic authorities such as state, science, church, the law, and journalism, down to their repercussions upon institutional operations, social practices, and the self; Goffman works from below, tracing the effects of procedures of sense-making and techniques of "management of spoiled identity" across encounters and their aggregations into organizations. They can thus be wedded to advance our grasp of the ways in which noxious representations of space are produced, diffused, and harnessed in the field of power, by bureaucratic and commercial agencies, as well as in everyday life in ways that alter social identity, strategy, and structure. (Wacquant, Slater, and Pereira 2014, 1272–73).

Wacquant (2008b, 169) claimed that territorial stigmatization is "arguably the single most protrusive feature of the lived experience of those trapped in these sulphurous zones," and two key aspects of his conceptualization of territorial stigmatization bear stressing at this juncture. First, he argues there are some areas of disrepute in many societies that have become nationally infamous and denigrated: a vamped-up circuit of symbolic production has emerged, quite different from earlier portrayals of destitution and delinquency that smeared the working-class quarters of the industrial city.[3] Now, it is not only policy elites and upper-class voyeurs who recoil at, mock, or slam a small set of notorious urban districts; it is also the citizenry at large (many of whom have never visited them), and sometimes even the residents of those districts themselves.

Second, territorial stigmatization is not reducible to the "spoiled identities" of, for example, poverty, ethnoracial origin, working-class position, unemployment, and so on, even if it may be closely tied to them in certain contexts. Wacquant argues that we are seeing a phenomenon of spatial disgrace that has become so powerful that it is partially autonomized from other forms of stigmatization, exerting its own very real and deleterious effects. It is a considerable analytical challenge to disentangle the effects of territorial stigmatization from myriad other ways in which those residing in lower-class districts of cities are disqualified and stained. Much of this challenge stems from the intense racialization of residents of tainted neighborhoods of relegation, which are so often portrayed in homogenizing sociospatial terms (e.g., Black or immigrant or Muslim "ghetto"), when their demographic composition and cultural characteristics are in fact extremely diverse (I explore this in further detail in chapter 7). Nonetheless, the challenge is vital for knowledge and understanding, not to mention for remedial action in the form of appropriate social policies and effective community activism.

In recent years there has been increasing research momentum around the concept of territorial stigmatization, partly spurred by Wacquant's writings but particularly in response to various policy and legal developments that appear to rely on the activation and (re)production of stigmatizing images and discourses attached to spaces of relegation. An exemplar in this respect is Esther Sullivan's (2018, 25) riveting diagnosis of the "mutually constitutive relationship between the perception of place and the regulation of place" vis-à-vis mobile home parks in the United States, which are frequently threatened with closure via invocations of putting the land to "highest and best use" and thus disposing of the "trailer trash" believed to occupy that land. There are severe consequences of stigmatization for maligned people living in maligned places.

The sense of social indignity that has come to enshroud certain urban districts in increasingly unequal cities has major implications for residents, not only in terms of remaining in those districts, but also in terms of employment prospects, educational attainment, and the receipt of social assistance. The difficulties of searching for employment, succeeding educationally, and dealing with public agencies (the police, the courts, and street-level bureaucracies such as state unemployment and welfare offices) can be exacerbated when residents of stigmatized areas mention where they live (Sernhede 2011; McKenzie 2012). There are examples in the literature of employers, educators, and public officials modifying their conduct and procedures once addresses are revealed. Lisa McKenzie discussed the treatment of a young single mother by local state officials in St. Ann's, a stigmatized housing estate in Nottingham, England:[4]

> She felt an acute stigma, particularly whenever she went to any of the ben-efit agencies . . . [and] told me that when she gave her address to any of the "officials" there was often a silence as they mentally processed her single-parent status, the ethnicity of her children, and then her address in St. Ann's: *"I know what they're thinking you can see it ticking over in their brain as you wait for them to think 'oh it's one of them from there.'"* (2012, 468; emphasis in original)

A striking trend is how certain places become associated with class position and how the names of stigmatized locales offer an alternative to the taboo against the word *class*. As Beverley Skeggs (2004, 112) pointed out in research on class inequality in English cities, "the term 'class' was rarely directly articulated . . . rather, local areas were continually used as shorthand to name those whose presence was seen to be potentially threatening." This politics of naming has been shown in several societies to have profound implications for labor market participation, interactions in daily encounters, and personal dignity (e.g., Brattbakk and Hansen 2004; Greenberg and Hollander 2006; Mood 2010; Morris 2013).

In Sweden, researchers who examined the implications of territorial stigmatization for the children of recent immigrants attending suburban schools found that it affected their life plans and educational prospects (Johansson and Olofsson 2011; Sernhede 2011). Because of the notoriety of their place of residence, youths were constantly having "to adjust to what they believe is the appropriate behaviour of a 'good Swedish student'" (Johansson and Olofsson 2011, 197). A policy of "equality" in the school curriculum (speaking, writing, and thinking in Swedish) had the effect of reinforcing the otherness of a "defective" and "problematic" immigrant cat-egory, one amplified by the stigma attached to certain suburban districts in Malmö and Stockholm. For the youths interviewed in these studies, school environments were far from a respite from living in stigmatized places; they unintentionally served as another context in which place stigma was experienced and served to aggravate the daily challenges of learning and assessment (a situation also analyzed by Eksner [2013] in Berlin).

A crucial question, then, is how residents of stigmatized territories deal with the denigration that affects their lives. Wacquant (2009: 177) remarked that in Chicago and Paris, residents "demarcated themselves from their neighbours and reassigned onto them the degraded image that public discourse gives them," and strategies for managing territorial stigma included "mutual distancing and lateral denigration, retreat into the private sphere, and flight into the outer world as soon as one acquires the means to move." He has consistently argued that various forms of *submission* tend to be the dominant (if not exclusive) strategies employed by residents of degraded urban zones. These strategies to deflect spatial disgrace include concealing the truth about place of residence from various public officials and private operators, rejecting being in any way like their neighbors and investing energy in spelling out micro-differences (e.g., Shildrick and MacDonald 2014), rejecting the public sphere as an arena for neighborhood sociability, and exiting the neighborhood as soon as possible (e.g., Keene and Padilla 2010, 2014).

Yet submissive strategies of *internalizing* stigma as the dominant response of residents have been called into question by scholars who have undertaken fieldwork approaches in other contexts. Sune Jensen and Ann-Dorte Christensen's (2012) scrutiny of data gathered in Aalborg East, a deprived area in the northern part of Denmark, revealed that the residents were not resigned to the defamation of their place of residence. They became sad or angry when confronted with the stigma, but they had either a positive or an ambivalent view of the area, and most were content to live there. Analyzing the deeply stigmatized district of St. Paul's in Bristol, England, Ntsiki Anderson and I explained that a strong sense of neighborhood pride among residents was a defensive response to external defamation (Slater and Anderson 2012). McKenzie's (2012) work in St. Ann's revealed a profound sense of "being and belonging to" the neighborhood, something common to different age groups and a resistant response to stigma. Similar conclusions were drawn by Paul Watt (2006, 786) from his work on housing estates in London, where "knowing people and being known were important in facilitating a sense of safety and belonging, even in estates which to outsiders could well be regarded as 'rough' or dangerous places."

Reporting on a study conducted on the very site where Wacquant formed the concept of territorial stigmatization, David Garbin and Gareth Millington's (2012, 2068) article on La Courneuve in Paris explored how residents "negotiate the grammars of marginalisation associated with their banlieue, how they live with the effects of territorial stigma." They found a variety of coping strategies, some submissive, others resistant.

Chief among them was recalcitrance, or "an assertion of the right to be other" (2075) via pride in La Courneuve's ethnic diversity. The authors' nuanced conclusion was that future research should not fall into the traps of "glibly celebrating 'resistance' or drawing overly pessimistic conclusions about the impact of place stigma," but should focus instead on the "ambiguities of domination/resistance" (2079).

This argument mirrors the work of Sean Purdy (2003, 97–98) in the public housing project of Regent Park, Toronto, who documented a place of "affirmative association" for many tenants, where a common response to defamation was "self-affirmation and pride of place . . . reflected eloquently in the themes of solidarity, friendship, and community in the face of economic devastation."[5] Whereas Wacquant (2010) reports that the internalization of territorial stigmatization has a dramatic effect on the collective psychology of place (to the extent that it undermines class solidarity and collective action), recent studies present a more positive picture of collective defiance and defense of residents in response to the denigration of their communities (dissected thoroughly in Nimes, France, by Kirkness [2014], and in Porto, Portugal, by Queiros and Pereira [2018]).

In sum, there is evidence that residents employ a variety of strategies of symbolic self-preservation in the face of territorial stigmatization, depending on class position, age/generation, lifecourse stage, type of employment, housing tenure, poverty status, and ethnic origin (to name but a few factors). James Rhodes (2012, 685) has shown that "while forms of contemporary stigma share commonalities[,] . . . they differ both within and between national contexts, influenced by patterns of governance, racial formation, demography, and urban geography." Many of the essays assembled in Paul Kirkness and Andreas Tije-Dra's book (2017) confirm this, as well as that history and geography matter vis-à-vis whether territorial stigma is internalized or resisted by residents of tainted places.

There is still much to learn about how focused stigmatizing images and discourses develop in the first place. Bruce Link and Jo C. Phelan's (2001) review and critique of social scientific treatments of numerous forms of stigma was propelled by their dissatisfaction with what they saw as the "decidedly individualistic focus" of published research: a focus that funnels analytic attention toward the stigma itself, rather than toward the *producers* of the stigma and the discursive and social strategies used to produce it. To gain a more complete understanding of stigmatization, they called for scholarship to scrutinize the numerous techniques of stereotyping, labeling, and "othering" that occur alongside the separation, loss of status, and discrimination felt by stigmatized individuals; in other words, a call for research on the stigmatizers, not just the stigmatized. In the diverse contexts in which place stigma is present, much work remains to be done to trace the practices of stigmatizing agents, institutions, and policies— what Sako Musterd (2008, 108) refers to as "the roles played by journalists, politicians, planners and intellectuals in the [social] construction process."

Surprisingly few studies have taken up directly the challenge of tracing the *production* of territorial stigmatization (Larsen and Delica 2019 provide a detailed overview). Robert Beauregard's landmark study *Voices of Decline* (1993) remains foundational in this respect: he illustrated that the fate of the US central city at the mid-twentieth century was not just a matter of structural causes and demographic shifts, but one of social and political construction. The decline of numerous cities was aggressively portrayed, often exaggerated and negatively branded in the mass media and think tanks of the time, which had material outcomes in terms of policy approaches. Georg Glasze and colleagues (2012, 1208) deployed lexicometric analysis to scrutinize how housing estates in Germany, France, and Poland were portrayed in major national newspapers, and in all these contexts they found "discursive demarcations which constitute and reproduce spatial and social structures." Various forms of media analysis vis-à-vis how places become denigrated (or further denigrated) have yielded some equally fascinating insights, such as Martin Power and colleagues' (2013) dissection of Google Street View's initial representations of the Moyross neighbourhood of Limerick, Ireland (only from a distance, and presenting only scenes of desolation, graffiti, abandonment, and neglect); Alice Butler's (2020a, 2020b) critical discourse analyses of decades of journalistic negativity directed at the neighborhood of Toxteth, Liverpool; and Kathy Arthurson, Michael Darcy, and Dallas Rogers's (2014) riveting exploration of "televised territorial stigma" in Australia via an analysis of the representations of social housing tenants in a popular TV show, *Housos* (they even discussed those representations with both tenants and outsiders, yielding fascinating insights on the differential impacts of symbolic structures).

To address the deficit of systematic research focusing on how certain areas become so widely shunned, feared, and condemned over time, and more particularly how negative terms and images circulate in everyday discourse as well as in the media and political discussion, I focus now on one stigmatizing term in the United Kingdom, especially in England, which has become the symbolic anchor for policies toward social housing that have resulted in considerable social suffering and intensified urban dislocation: the *sink estate*.

THE SINK ESTATE: THE GENEALOGY AND ANATOMY OF A SEMANTIC BATTERING RAM

Sink estate is a derogatory designator for large council housing estates in England and Wales (in Scotland it is less widespread than the equally derogatory designator *schemes* populated by *schemies*). It was invented by journalists, subsequently amplified and canonized by think tanks, and then converted into *doxa* or common sense by politicians. In January 2016, Prime Minister David Cameron announced plans to demolish the "worst 100 sink estates" in England and Wales, framed in these terms:

> Step outside in the worst sink estates, and you're confronted by brutal high-rise towers and dark alleyways that are a gift to criminals and drug dealers. . . . Decades of neglect have led to gangs, ghettos and anti-social behaviour. . . . One of the most concerning aspects of these estates is just how cut-off, self-governing and divorced from the mainstream these communities can become. . . . And that allows social problems to fester and grow unseen.

This was not the first time a British prime minister had used this term, and not the first time such stigma was activated for political ends. Tracing the genealogy of the sink estate category is instructive for any analysis of the plight of social housing estates in the United Kingdom. The etymology of *sink* dates back many centuries and refers to a cesspit for wastewater or sewage: a receptacle that collects and stores effluent. It would therefore be somewhat simplistic to see *sink* as a direct reference to something being poured down a kitchen sink, or just to the idea that people are sinking

rather than swimming in society. Wedding *sink* to a tract of council housing—an act of symbolic violence that turns a receptacle that collects and
stores effluent into a *place* that collects and stores the refuse of society—
is a journalistic invention and continues to be (though not exclusively) a
journalistic trait. The first use of *sink* by a UK newspaper to describe a
geographical area was on October 4, 1972, in the *Daily Mail*, a right-wing
tabloid newspaper: "The downward spiral of decline in these 'sink' areas
could be broken if the school led the way." However, it was journalist Jane
Morton who coined "sink estate," in November 1976, in a short piece for
New Society magazine, a short-lived left-wing publication (absorbed by
New Statesman magazine in 1988):

> Somewhere, in every town that has council houses at all, there's a sink
> estate—the roughest and shabbiest on the books, disproportionally tenanted
> by families with problems, and despised both by those who live there and the
> town at large. . . . As long as families on the margins of society are shunted
> into second best accommodation, there will be sinks. (Morton 1976, 356)

Although *sink estate* was first uttered in Parliament in 1983, the phrase
did not appear in British political debate until the late 1980s, when politicians began using it to make direct links between housing tenure and
deprivation, for example this statement by Labour MP Paul Boateng:
"They [the Conservative Government] have set their hands to a course
that is determined to create in our inner cities the development of welfare housing along American lines—sink estates to which people are condemned, with no prospect of getting out" (Boateng 2020).

The term cropped up occasionally after that in parliamentary debates,
but *sink estate* has circulated freely and widely since former prime minister Tony Blair visited the Aylesbury Estate in south London in May 1997
to make his very first speech as prime minister, an event that Ben Campkin (2013) analyzes as the symbolic watershed moment in the emerging
phenomenon of the sink estate spectacle. Blair spoke of an "underclass . . .
cut off from society's mainstream" and made a direct association between
sink estates and apparently self-inflicted poverty stemming from "fatal-
ism" and "the dead weight of low expectations" (quoted in Crossley 2017,
49).[6] Figure 7 shows the number of appearances of *sink estate* in major
UK newspapers over a thirty-year period.[7]

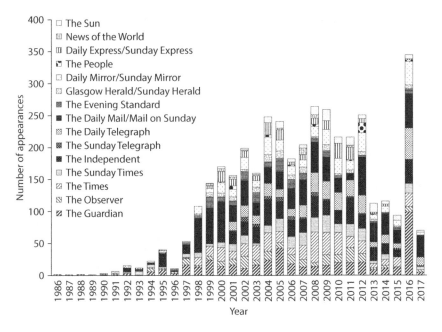

Figure 7. Number of appearances of *sink estate* in major UK newspapers, 1986–2017.

Campkin's assertion of the watershed moment is correct, as usage took off in 1997, and since then tabloids and broadsheets have used *sink estate* freely. It is noteworthy that while a majority of major UK newspapers are right wing in political orientation, center and left-wing newspapers have used the term just as frequently. One thing becomes very clear from even a cursory analysis of the reporting during this time frame: *sink estate* is used to describe an area of council housing where the behavior of tenants is, first, under intense moral condemnation, and second, both cause and symptom of poor housing conditions and neighborhood malaise. The *Oxford English Dictionary* in fact lists one meaning of *sink* as "a receptacle or gathering-place of vice, corruption, etc."

There is a very important intellectual precursor to *sink estate* that helps explain why the phrase has gained such currency. The American ethologist John B. Calhoun, based on his experiments with rodents in the 1950s, developed the concept of the *behavioral sink* to warn against the dangers of overpopulation in urban environments. After he put rats in an enclosure and supplied them with an ideal "rodent universe" (food, bedding, and shelter), the animals bred rapidly, and Calhoun (1962) documented how they behaved as their enclosure became more crowded. He produced a typology of pathological crowding behaviors and described the tendency to congregate in dense huddled knots of squalor and violence as the "behavioral sink." As Edmund Ramsden and Jon Adams (2009) explain in an article tellingly entitled "Escaping the Laboratory," Calhoun's concept was astonishingly influential, from its initial publication in the popular magazine *Scientific American*, where it remains one of the most-cited papers ever in the field of psychology; to its influence on a generation of scholars in human ecology, social epidemiology, and environmental psychology concerned with the problem of urban density; to its influence on urban planners and designers seeking physical solutions to social problems; to its popular uptake in science fiction, urban fiction (particularly the writings of Tom Wolfe), film, and comic books. As Ramsden and Adams explain:

> Calhoun's description of the behavioral sink not only captured the sense of the city as a destructive force, but further, seemed to explain why it was that such an horrific environment seemingly acted almost as an attractor, drawing and holding together large numbers of people. The process was one of "pathological togetherness," individuals conditioned to seek out the presence of others, even to the detriment of self and society. . . . Calhoun . . . had tapped into an extensive etymological precedent linking sinks with both cities and entropy. (2009, 773)

The authors were quick to point out that the diagnosis of problems was only one part of Calhoun's scientific life; he was convinced that within his experiments were possible solutions for the behaviors he had observed:

> [H]e thought his experiments underlined the need for a revolution in the way we organise our societies and our cities. . . . However, in the furore surrounding the grim spectacle of the "behavioral sink", Calhoun found that this ameliorative message was drowned out—everyone wanted to hear the diagnoses, no one wanted to hear the cure. (780)

The fact that Calhoun's behavioral sink concept was "extraordinarily appealing to popular audience[s]" (780) is not affirmation that the sink estate label derives directly from it. However, when a concept circulates so widely and resonates so strongly with multiple audiences, it makes it easier for concepts using the related phrases that follow to gain symbolic footholds.

The significant spike in usage of *sink estate* in 2016 (see figure 7) is directly attributable to the abovementioned speech made by Prime Minister Cameron in January of that year. As I demonstrate in the next section, the political embrace and policy deployment of the derogatory designator sink estate is a clear tactic in the ongoing condemnation of the very existence of social housing and in blaming poverty on the behavior/choices of tenants. However, it would be inaccurate to say that this is fueled by newspapers; rather, it is driven by free-market think tanks. It is one of these institutions in particular to which I now turn.

THE SINK ESTATE AND THE MARKETPLACE OF IGNORANCE PRODUCTION

Policy Exchange was established in 2002 and is probably best known as David Cameron's favorite think tank. It describes itself proudly as

> the UK's leading think tank. As an educational charity our mission is to develop and promote new policy ideas which deliver better public services, a stronger society and a more dynamic economy. The authority and credibility of our research is our greatest asset. Our research is independent and evidence-based and we share our ideas with policy makers from all sides of the political spectrum. Our research is strictly empirical and we do not take commissions. This allows us to be completely independent and make workable policy recommendations (Policy Exchange n.d.).

This description alone is enough material for an exegesis. "Research is evidence based," if we consider what else it could possibly be, is a bit like saying, "This water is wet." "Our research is strictly empirical" is the same. These two completely redundant sentences/tautologies are denegations of the deeply political nature of the knowledge produced, as indeed is "all sides of the political spectrum" and claims of being "completely independent." This description is therefore symptomatic of what think tanks actually are: mongrel institutions that claim to be knowledge producers (Medvetz 2012).

The claims of independence are also very bold, given that this "educational charity" was founded by three Conservative MPs. Perhaps unsurprisingly, the inaugural chairman of Policy Exchange was staunch Thatcherite Michael Gove, one of the two central political architects of Brexit (the other being Prime Minister Boris Johnson). Policy Exchange's claim that it does "not take commissions" is another denegation, and an interesting choice of wording. It was registered with the Charity Commission in 2003. Registering as a charity can provide numerous advantages for a think tank, as charities do not have to pay corporation tax or capital gains tax, and donations to charities are tax free. Most significantly, think tanks can also use their charitable status to refuse requests for transparency in terms of who donates to them. Who Funds You? is a campaign to make the so-called think tanks more transparent. Its methodology involves trawling through information provided on organizations' own websites or annual accounts where they are provided. Many think tanks across the political spectrum are registered charities and thus have the legal right not to disclose who funds them, but Who Funds You? offers unequivocal evidence that the more right wing and libertarian a think tank is, the less likely it is to show funding transparency. Policy Exchange is one of the least transparent of all think tanks in the United Kingdom. In 2007, Policy Exchange was investigated by the Charity Commission after a complaint was made that it was effectively a research branch of the Conservative Party. The investigation, remarkably, found "no evidence of party political bias" (Public Internet Investigations Powerbase 2019).

Policy Exchange is a very busy institution. It produces an astonishing number of reports—literally hundreds of them since it was founded it 2002—and it sponsors many events and public statements on various policy priorities like crime and justice; immigration; education; foreign affairs; and housing, planning, and urban regeneration. Its influence in all these spheres has been immense in the United Kingdom over the past decade—major political speeches and catchy slogans often originate from Policy Exchange reports—but in housing policy in particular it is possible to see a direct imprint of think tank writing on what has been happening to people living at the bottom of the class structure in UK cities. A report entitled *Making Housing Affordable*, written by neoclassical economist Alex Morton and published in 2010, is arguably the most influential document of all. Many of the proposals in this document quickly became housing policy under the Coalition government (2010–15) and subsequent Conservative governments, as did other work Morton authored, notably a report entitled *Ending Expensive Social Tenancies*. It was telling that, in December 2013, Alex Morton left Policy Exchange to become David Cameron's special adviser on housing policy, where he remained until Cameron resigned in June 2016.[8]

The *Making Housing Affordable* report argues that social housing of any form is a terrible disaster because it makes tenants unhappy, poor, unemployed, and welfare dependent. Not only is this baseline environmental determinism, it is a reversal of causation: a very substantial literature on social housing in the United Kingdom demonstrates that the reason people gain access to social housing is *precisely because* they are poor and in need, and that it was *not social housing that created poverty and need* in the first place (Forrest and Murie 1988; Malpass 2005; Hanley 2007). Nonetheless, here are just some of the things that Morton (2010) says about social housing in order to denigrate it:

"The real reason social housing fails is because of the incentives it creates" (12).

"[S]ocial housing will continually act to stop inactive tenants returning to work – essential to generate savings and reduce the welfare budget" (12).

"The current 'need' for social housing is not really a need for more social housing at all, but a need for new private housing" (42).

"Social housing has a substantial negative impact on employment per se over and above the characteristics of its tenants" (51).

"Social housing has always damaged equality of opportunity. . . . The effects of social housing are generally getting worse over time" (p.52).

"In the real world, it [prioritizing those in housing need] has acted as an extremely sharp poverty trap. Welfare dependency is rewarded while independence from the state is penalized" (59).

"If an area is becoming gentrified the worse thing to do in terms of creating future poverty is to increase the social housing element in the area" (61).

The bulk of these assertions come from cherry-picking various sound bites from a deeply problematic report on social housing written in 2007 by social policy professor John Hills (2007)—which embraces the "neighborhood effects" thesis (see chapter 5) while simultaneously ignoring the question of systematic disinvestment in social housing and in people's lives—and from numerous opinion polls commissioned by Policy Exchange, which are treated as robust evidence and the definitive verdict on the topic under scrutiny. Had Morton consulted the literature on low-income housing provision across Europe, he would have discovered that *nowhere* is low-income housing provided adequately by the market, and also that the countries with the largest social housing sectors (Sweden, France, Holland, etc.) are those with the *least* problematic social outcomes (e.g., Power 1997; van Kempen et al. 2005; Musterd and van Kempen 2007).

Having in effect argued that social housing is the scourge of British society, Morton then goes on to propose what he feels are solutions to the housing crisis. Predictably, they involve helping social tenants into home-ownership via the acquisition of considerable debt, as well as demolishing the "worst" social housing estates and selling the land to private sector housing developers. He also posits repeatedly the hegemonic view that the housing crisis is created by too much demand and not enough supply, ignoring the inconvenient existence of more than 750,000 empty homes across the United Kingdom. As discussed in chapter 4, if house prices were simply about supply and demand, then that massive surplus of homes would result in falling prices, but the opposite has happened, in that an oversupply of housing for purchase has led to unaffordability (Dorling 2014). Morton also ignores the land-banking epidemic facilitated by a system that actively rewards speculate-to-accumulate investment, and dismisses the importance of landownership, abundant mortgage credit, and consistently low interest rates as factors behind the crisis (Fernandez and Aalbers 2016). He asserts that the crisis is caused by a bloated local authority planning system aggravating NIMBYist tendencies and blocking the release of land for housing development, so he proposes that concerned local residents be given financial incentives by developers to give their blessing to proposed new housing developments nearby.

Most striking of all about this report is setting the content against its title: *Making Housing Affordable*. In addition to calling for the destruction of social housing and the removal of government support for housing associations, the report proposes numerous strategies to *make housing more expensive*:

> "What is needed are better quality developments that both increase housing supply and raise house prices and the quality of life for existing residents in the areas that they are built" (Morton 2010, 15).

> "The government should scrap all density and affordable housing targets and aspirations" (23).

> "It is a fallacy to assume that making new homes "low-cost" will help increase affordability—it makes no difference to house prices whether you build cheap or expensive new homes" (68).

> "Social rents should rise to meet market rents" (81).

It is difficult to imagine a more clear-cut case of agnotology than a report entitled *Making Housing Affordable* recommending that affordable housing targets and aspirations should be scrapped and social housing be demolished. The report won *Prospect Magazine*'s prestigious Think Tank Publication of the Year award in 2010 and, crucially, performed the ideological groundwork for the activation of the sink estate designator in the reports that followed, to which I now turn.

In 2012 Policy Exchange published a report jointly authored by Alex Morton and Nicholas Boys Smith, a director at Lloyds Banking Group with an interest in architecture. Boys Smith had just founded what he calls a "social enterprise and independent research institute," Create Streets, which has a mission to "encourage and facilitate the replacement of London's multi-storey housing and the development of brownfield sites with real houses in real streets" (Boys Smith and Morton 2013, 5). The inaugural *Create Streets* report castigated all high-rise social housing estates in London, in a spectacular torrent of unsubstantiated assertions:

> "Multi-storey housing is more risky and makes people sadder, badder and lonelier" (29).

> "The best predictor of juvenile delinquency was not population density but living in blocks of flats as opposed to houses" (30).

> "Multi-storey buildings create a myriad of opportunities for crime due to their hard to police semi-private corridors, walkways and multiple escape routes" (32).

"[T]he evidence also suggests that tower blocks might even encourage suicide. Without wishing to be glib, tower blocks don't just make you more depressed. They make it easier to kill yourself —you can jump" (30).

In a chapter entitled "Multi-story Housing Creates a Spiral of Decline," *sink estate* was used to describe the Aylesbury Estate in London, once again to illustrate that social housing fails regardless of the struggles to protect that estate from demolition (documented in Lees 2014). The authors even claimed that multi-story housing is bad for people regardless of income or social status, avoiding the question of how to account for the explosive growth and growing appeal of luxury condominium towers in many large cities globally. The question of how to account for any social problems in *low-rise* housing was studiously, perhaps judiciously, ignored. Boys Smith and Morton concluded by claiming that high-rise housing makes people "sadder" and low-rise housing makes people "happier." This fitted neatly with the Conservative government's embrace of "happiness" as a catch-all indicator of well-being in the austere times they had chosen (Davies 2016) and ensured that the Create Streets report was firmly on the political radar (as discussed later in this chapter).

The Create Streets report was followed two years later by another Policy Exchange report entitled *The Estate We're In: Lessons from the Front Line*, written by crime journalist Gavin Knight, author of a "nonfiction" book entitled *Hood Rat*, "an unflinching account of life and death in the sink estates of Britain" (Anthony 2011), for which he spent time "with dozens of violent criminals involved in gun and gang crime ... [and] accompanied detectives on a manhunt, firearms and drugs raids and was embedded with a CID unit over a lengthy drug surveillance operation" (Knight 2014b, 4). The report, which was launched with considerable fanfare, opens as follows: "The state of many of Britain's social housing estates is nothing short of a national embarrassment. Too often, crime, unemployment, gangs and violence are rife. The human cost is heart-breaking; the cost to the public purse immense" (7).[9]

A range of assertions is deployed to condemn both the design of the estates and the behavior of people living on them, furnished with interview quotations such as, "Sure, we have role models. Nelson Mandela.

Barack Obama. They just don't live around here" (13). The report con-
cocted a relationship between social housing estates and rioting:

> Let us state the obvious: the [2011 urban England] riots did not start in a
> street of Georgian houses with spacious sash windows and manicured
> lawns. The riots started on a social housing estate—Broadwater Farm Estate
> in Tottenham, to be exact. . . . The linking walkways between blocks were a
> gift to fleeing criminals. (13–14)

The 2011 riots did not start on the Broadwater Farm Estate. They began
following a peaceful evening protest outside a police station on Tottenham High Road in London against the police killing of Mark Duggan. Not
long after the protest concluded, a sixteen-year-old girl approached police
officers to voice her anger and was beaten back with batons (Eddo-Lodge
2011). Two police cars, a bus, and several shops were then attacked, looted,
and set ablaze in Tottenham, and the rioting then spread to several other
districts in the capital and beyond (Slater 2016). Social housing estates
did not cause rioting, nor did rioting occur on them; in fact, as well as the
looting and torching of stores and businesses, a large number of public
buildings—such as police stations, sports centers, municipal institutions,
and in a few cases schools—were targeted for attack (Sutterluty 2014).
Based on the unsubstantiated catalog of nefarious properties of social
housing, *The Estate We're In* report makes several predictable recommendations, best captured in this passage:

> Although Estate Recovery Plans will offer the opportunity to turn around
> social housing estates, we recognise that in some cases this may not be
> enough. In the long-term, where it is clear that an estate is beyond recovery,
> the government must commit to demolishing and replacing these estates.
> The replacement of high rise social housing must be the priority, given the
> strong evidence that tower blocks and multi-storey living leads to higher
> crime rates, weaker communities, and poorer health and education out-
> comes for residents. (50)

The "strong evidence" cited is a single source: the Create Streets report. In
addition, it is not just Policy Exchange elevating *sink estate* to semantic
battering ram: the former director of the Centre for Social Justice, the
think tank behind the current assault on the British welfare state (Slater
2014), wrote this while in that post:

2013 is the year to tackle the tyranny of sink estates, no-go neighbourhoods and child poverty. . . . Look a little closer at such neighbourhoods, and we see something deeper than physical dilapidation. Behind the front doors are far too many broken and chaotic families. . . . Many adults could work but don't because when they do the maths, there's nothing to be gained by coming off benefits. There's usually a local school where a culture of low expectations and high truancy rates is a catalyst for underachievement and future welfare dependency. Alcohol abuse and drug addiction tend to flow through these estates like a river. (Guy 2013, 10)

Tempting though it is to dismiss this sort of material as rhetorical ranting among like-minded free-market fanatics, it is worthy of analytic scrutiny given the policy implications. In April 2014 the Department for Communities and Local Government embraced many of Policy Exchange's recommendations in the three reports discussed and created a £140m Housing Estate Regeneration Fund. It then commissioned Savills, a global real estate corporation headquartered in London with expertise in high-end, elite markets, to investigate the potential of all Create Streets"'s proposals.

In January 2016 the Savills report was published (Savills 2016) and was used as evidence to support a government strategy pledging to demolish the "worst 100 sink estates" in England. Although the Savills report did not make a specific call for high-rise social housing demolition, it said, "We have assumed cleared sites." It points to the nature of housing policy priorities in the United Kingdom that Savills was even commissioned as an expert consultant on the matter of urban poverty on social housing estates, given that it stands to make vast profits from what replaces those estates. In addition to the phrasing, the strategy of demolishing social housing estates is guided by the simplistic, fictitious reasoning emanating from Policy Exchange, crystallized by the sink estate label: that people who live on those estates are trapped in the culture of poverty that such estates create and are an expensive, troublesome burden on "taxpayers" who do not live on such estates; therefore, the only feasible solution is to bulldoze the estates and rehouse people elsewhere. But if we were to take that same logic and apply it to, say, health care, it would be completely stranded. The argument would go: people in hospital tend to be less healthy than people who aren't in hospital, so to improve health, we should demolish hospitals in fairness to the taxpayer!

Although the "100 sink estates" proposals died a welcome death when David Cameron resigned in June 2016, the fact that a derogatory designator was activated in such a way in an attempt to justify demolishing people's homes shows that territorial stigma can become so powerful that it can shape the orientation of national housing and urban policies. Activating and amplifying the sink estate—repeatedly condemning social housing estates as precipitates that collect and incubate all the social ills of the world—makes it considerably easier to justify bulldozing those estates to the ground and displacing their residents (Wacquant 2008b). We can also see symbolic power in the 2016 Housing and Planning Act in England and Wales, which allowed social housing estates to be reclassified as "brownfield sites," a category normally reserved for *contaminated* former industrial land. The symbolic erasure of homes and entire communities thus paves the way for their literal erasure. One of the key teachings of Bourdieu's work is that symbolic systems—of which cities are major centers of production and diffusion—do not just mirror social relations but help constitute them.

The history and use of *sink estate* offers support for Imogen Tyler's (2013) argument that territorial stigmatization, amplified and activated, has become a device to procure consent for punitive policies directed at those living at the bottom of the class structure, policies that cause enormous disruption (Soederberg 2017). As discussed in chapter 3, numerous studies have revealed an intense and direct relationship between the defamation of place and processes of gentrification. The taint of place can become a target and rationale for "fixing" an area via its reincorporation into the real estate circuit of the city (Wacquant 2007), which can have major consequences for those least able to compete for housing. Symbolic defamation provides the groundwork and ideological justification for a thorough class transformation of urban space, usually involving housing demolition, dispersal of residents, land clearance, and the construction of housing and services aimed at a more affluent class of resident. A substantial body of scholarship on public housing demolitions in several societies illustrates how the frequent depiction of public housing complexes as obsolete, poverty-creating hellholes has justified the expulsion of people from their homes and the subsequent gentrification of valuable central city land tracts (e.g., Crump 2002; Imbroscio 2008; Steinberg 2010; Goetz 2013; Minton 2017). Wacquant summarizes this as follows:

> Once a place is publicly labelled as a "lawless zone" or "outlaw estate," outside the common norm, it is easy for the authorities to justify special measures, deviating from both law and custom, which can have the effect—if not the intention—of destabilizing and further marginalizing their occupants, subjecting them to the dictates of the deregulated labour market, and rendering them invisible or driving them out of a coveted space. (2007, 69)

If social housing estates become widely known and reviled as epicenters of self-inflicted and self-perpetuating destitution and depravity, opposing their demolition becomes significantly more challenging. The sink estate is thus a pure exemplar of what Wacquant (2012b, 17) calls a *categoreme*, "a term of accusation and alarm, pertaining not to social science but public polemic, that serves . . . to fuel the spiral of stigmatization enmeshing the impoverished districts of the urban periphery." Peter Marris offered a particularly succinct summary of the wider problem:

> Physical squalor is an affront to the order of society, which readily becomes associated with other signs of disorder in the public image. Crime, drunkenness, prostitution, feckless poverty, mental pathology do indeed cluster where housing is poorest—though not there only. Once this association has been taken for granted, any anomalous pattern of life embodied in shabby surroundings is easily assumed to be pathological, without much regard for the evidence. Bad housing thus becomes a symbol of complex discordances in the structure of society and so to be treated as if it were a cause of them. (1986, 53–54)

Think tanks have reframed a serious crisis of housing affordability as a crisis of housing supply caused by too much state interference in the market, which, inter alia, has trapped people in failed social housing estates that can never be improved. Viewed through the analytic lens of agnotology, we can see a complete inversion going on: the structural and political causes of the housing crisis—that is, deregulation, privatization, and attacks on the welfare state—are put forward as desirable and necessary remedies for the crisis that will squash an intrusive state apparatus. Viewed through the conceptual lens of symbolic power, we can see how the already intense stigma attached to social housing estates is vamped up by think tank writers and then by political elites. The framing of the sink estate filters societal attention toward family breakdown, worklessness, welfare dependency, antisocial behavior, and personal irresponsibility, and away from community, solidarity, shelter, and home.

NOT A NEIGHBORHOOD EFFECT, BUT A GAZE TRAINED ON THE NEIGHBORHOOD

The vast literature on neighborhood effects that I discussed in the previous chapter is sustained by a near-obsessive belief in the view that where you live affects your life chances. That literature usually (and surprisingly) ignores how the stigmatization of neighborhoods matters, and in some instances ends up contributing to that stigmatization. Even when the focus is on such stigmatization, analytic errors and misconstruals are commonplace. For example, Thomas Maloutas (2009, 830) has argued that when Wacquant writes of territorial stigmatization he is "definitely arguing about a growing neighbourhood effect." Yet what becomes clear from a close reading of studies of territorial stigmatization is that it is *not a property of the neighborhood, but rather a gaze trained on it—* and therefore definitely *not* a neighborhood effect. It is beyond dispute that the blemish of place affects life chances, but studying territorial stigmatization teaches us about the effects of symbolic structures applied *to* neighborhoods (or to other local geographies), which are not produced in neighborhoods and therefore are not neighborhood effects.

Failing to question the operation of a political-economic system that sorts people across metropolitan space based on their purchasing power in land and housing markets, and failing to question the role of symbolic structures in the production of inequality and marginality in the city, means that neighborhoods *become the problem* rather than the expression of the problems to be addressed. Health inequality researchers are especially prone to these failures; generally they tend to shy away from such structural and symbolic questions, preferring instead to focus on how neighborhoods are conducive to certain kinds of "health behaviors" like smoking, drinking alcohol, and unhealthy eating. Much of this stems from their lack of methodological self-consciousness in research on health and its social determinants, characterized by the refinement of measuring tools, boasting about the size and quality of data sets, and soporific use of terms such as *controlling* and *pathways*, all at the expense of theoretical vision and conceptual clarification. Thus, they often fail to uncover the mechanisms by which place and people are linked (ironically, the "black box" of neighborhood effects scholarship). A wonderful exception is to be found in the blend of ethnographic and survey work by Amber Wutich and colleagues (2014), who examined how neighborhood stigma and social bonding affected the physical and mental health of Latino immigrants in Phoenix, Arizona. The authors develop a fascinating "neighborhood stigma scale" designed to capture both "enacted stigma" (actual experience of discrimination) and "perceived stigma" (internalized or felt stigma), which includes shame, secrecy or withdrawal, and fear of discrimination.

If, as Wacquant (2010, 219) has argued, "the social psychology of place operates in the manner of a symbolic cog latching the macrodeterminants of urban political to the life options and strategies of the poor at ground level," then the study of territorial stigmatization provides propitious terrain for reformulating from "below," in empirical terms, the labels, discourses, and categories from "above" that have been shown in scholarship to have corrosive consequences. Such work is necessary to inform not only public policies designed to reduce the burden of material deprivation and the bruising of symbolic domination, but also grassroots campaigns and political struggles geared toward fighting the impact of social abjection in divided cities.

7 Ghetto Blasting

In this chapter I build on the critical interrogation of the phenomenon of territorial stigmatization in the preceding chapter in order to address the vexed question of the *ghetto*, focusing in particular on the dangerous mythology and political panic surrounding that term. I demonstrate how a robust conceptualization of the ghetto is essential to form a coherent and powerful response to the racialized denigration of people's lives, which cannot be separated from the racialized denigration of the places where they live. This thematic crescendo is offered as it speaks strongly to the core concerns of this book: the intentional production and circulation of ignorance, the rise of consequential categorization, and the importance of a critical approach deploying the concepts of agnotology and symbolic power in order to shake up mainstream understandings of urban inequalities that serve various vested interests.

"GHETTOS OF THE MIND"

Ghetto is without question one of the most misunderstood and inappropriately deployed terms both within and beyond the social sciences. It is regularly used (or abused) as a metaphor to describe the spatial clustering of *any* social category (student ghetto, immigrant ghetto), or indeed simply a dilapidated and/or poverty-stricken urban area, rather than used to account for and analyze the select few areas on the planet that exhibit *the involuntary spatial confinement of a single ethnoracial category* (in line with the history of the term). The paucity of research that is cognizant of the history of the term, together with qualitative disengagement and increasing confusion emanating from countless indices of segregation/isolation, means that analytical and policy errors concerning neighborhoods of relegation, whether ghettos or not, should come as little surprise. Two examples of the ghetto as a stigmatizing political myth, from Britain and Denmark, serve to illustrate why a firm grasp of historical realities is important.

   In a pivotal article, Ceri Peach (1996, 216) scrutinized the "recurrent fear expressed by politicians, journalists and scholars that Britain has ghettos or is developing towards the African American ghetto model." To define a ghetto, Peach drew on the classic work of Thomas L. Philpott (1978) in Chicago, who argued that a ghetto has "dual" characteristics: a single ethnic or racial group forms the whole population of the residential district, and most members of that group in the entire city are found in that district. The 1991 UK Census of Population (the first to include a question on ethnic identity) enabled Peach to use both the index of dissimilarity and Lieberson's P* index to measure the degree of ethnic segregation in British cities. He demonstrated that British levels of segregation were much lower than those found in the United States, and were declining for the Black Caribbean population. Crucially, no residential district conformed to the dual definition of the ghetto. Peach argued that the geography of ethnic minority disadvantage had been misdiagnosed, and despite "substantial evidence of continuing discrimination" (1996, 234), the evidence pointed toward ethnic mixing (and rising rates of interethnic marriage). Desegregation of Black Caribbeans, facilitated by entry to council housing since the 1970s (Peach and Byron 1994), and what Peach termed the "positive clustering" of the South Asian population (as opposed to involuntary spatial entrapment), were the explanations he put forward to refute academic and policy prophecies of a more ethnically segregated Britain. Nascent ghettos were urban mirages when ethnic segregation was subjected to careful empirical scrutiny.

Peach's article remains the major point of reference for any critique of the thesis of structural and functional equivalence between the multiethnic British inner city and the African American ghetto. This thesis was advanced once more in 2005, following a declamatory, high-profile speech entitled "After 7/7: Sleepwalking to Segregation" by Trevor Phillips, a Labour Party politician who was then director of the Commission for Racial Equality. Drawing particularly on a conference paper by geographer Mike Poulsen (2005), Phillips (2005) stated that Britain has some residential districts that are nearly as segregated as Chicago's South Side:

> Residentially, some districts are on their way to becoming fully fledged ghettos—black holes into which no-one goes without fear and trepidation, and from which no-one ever escapes undamaged. The walls are going up around many of our communities, and the bridges . . . are crumbling. If we allow this to continue, we could end up in 2048, a hundred years on from the Windrush, living in a New Orleans-style Britain of passively co-existing ethnic and religious communities, eyeing each other uneasily over the fences of our differences.

The national mainstream media picked up on these words and massaged an existing debate on ethnic segregation into a moral panic about "Ghetto Britain" and the perceived failures of multiculturalism, "integration," and immigration policy. Trevor Phillips delivered this now notorious speech at a crucial time in his career. Exercising symbolic power was important, for soon after the speech, he was appointed (and promoted to) chair of the Equalities and Human Rights Commission. He concluded the speech with these words: "[M]y job . . . cannot involve sitting on the sidelines when we are facing such a huge challenge. And you would rightly feel betrayed if we continued playing the same old, failed tunes while you are facing new realities."

The "new realities," to Phillips, were an "unconscious drift" toward an ethnically segregated Britain, with ghettos on the horizon. Phillips relied on a stream of work by geographers Ron Johnston, James Forrest, and Mike Poulsen, who had called into question the value of single-number indices of segregation (particularly the most commonly used index of dissimilarity) in several publications (Johnston, Forrest, and Poulsen 2002; Johnston, Poulsen, and Forrest 2005; Poulsen and Johnston 2006). The authors developed their own schema for measuring segregation, in which they defined a ghetto as an area or collection of areas within a city in which the white population is less than 30 percent, in which one minority group is twice the size of the next largest, and in which live at least 30 percent of all that minority group's residents in the city. Although this is far removed from the intensity of segregation seen in Philpott's original dual definition (on which it was purportedly based), Poulsen (2005) used the schema in a conference paper to argue that Indians in Leicester and Pakistanis in Bradford are living increasingly segregated lives, residing in areas where minorities form over 70 percent of the population. He also argued that Leicester and Bradford were almost as ethnically segregated as Chicago and Miami, which led Phillips to make the same assertions in his Manchester speech.

Peach (2009) subjected the schema designed by Johnston and colleagues, particularly the Poulsen (2005) arguments, to a careful yet hard-hitting critique, simultaneously reinstating the importance of indices of segregation by showing their epistemological and theoretical importance throughout twentieth-century segregation inquiry. Using those indices once more, he showed that segregation for all minority ethnic communities in Britain (with the exception of Bangladeshis) was *decreasing*, and argued that Johnston and colleagues had confused the ethnic enclave with the racial ghetto to the extent that they had "artificially manufactured ghettos."[1] Regarding the key claim that Bradford and Leicester were almost as segregated as Chicago or Miami, Peach responded that "this simply cannot be sustained" (2009, 1391) when examining the very different intensities of ethnic segregation in these cities. We can add to Peach's critique the fact that *there is not a single administrative ward* in Britain in which the population is 90–100 percent ethnic minority, whereas tracts with these percentages are commonplace in America. Peach rounded off his discussion by declaring that any mention of "British ghettos" "exaggerates British segregation and trivialises the severity of the African-American situation" (1388).

The most extensive critique of Phillips's speech can be found in Nissa Finney and Ludi Simpson's (2009) book, which carries the same title as the speech, but with the addition of the all-important question mark. They traced the moral panic about ethnic segregation and ghettoization back to uprisings in the northern English cities of Bradford, Burnley, and Oldham in the summer of 2001, in which mainly Pakistani young men battled with police following provocations by far-right political groups (Kundnani 2001). The immediate political reaction to these disturbances was to accuse minority groups of isolating themselves into ghettos and causing "indigenous" white families to flee to live with their own kind. Finney and Simpson showed that this was simply a damaging myth:

> [T]here is a formidable array of academic and political thought that fears segregation and sees it not as a result of inequality and injustice but as the result of a lack of cohesion and the cause of disadvantage.... [T]he evidence supports neither isolation nor flight, but the evidence is a minor inconvenience to political will with the bit between its teeth to pursue community cohesion. (2009, 119)

As well as showing that the index of dissimilarity *decreased* for every UK minority ethnic group in England and Wales between 1991 and 2001, they showed that the pattern in Bradford is in fact one of *increasing* ethnic mixing, particularly white movement into and minority movement out of the largest ethnic minority clusters in the city. Where there is growth of the ethnic minority population in a particular part of a UK city, the authors point to the benign dynamics of population growth (or "natural increase" as demographers call it) rather than the reactionary withdrawal into ghettos of a particular ethnic category. Reacting to Poulsen's classification of a ghetto, Finney and Simpson observed with incredulity that "one could have 30% White population, 25% Indian and 10% each of four other groups, and label this a ghetto" (134). Although they did acknowledge the limitations of their approach in a critical analysis of the politics of measurement vis-à-vis race/ethnicity, their arguments rested on an asociological and ahistorical (*gradational*) specification of a ghetto. They briefly mentioned the history of the term, but then stated that a ghetto "in more recent times refers to a considerable area of many streets in which one ethnic group forms 90-100% of the population.... [W]e are talking of areas with an unusually high proportion of a particular ethnic group" (120) This kind of definition is common among scholars who rely solely on quantitative measures of segregation to define a ghetto, but the problem with it is the dubious (and usually arbitrary) intellectual construction of ghetto boundaries. For example, how could an area containing 90.0 percent of one ethnic minority be a ghetto, but another area containing 89.9 percent not be a ghetto?

A much more sinister example of dubious ghetto construction comes from Denmark, the only European country that currently uses the term *ghetto* as an official classification of urban space.[2] In October 2010, then prime minister and leader of the center-right Venstre Party, Lars Lokke Rasmussen, addressed the opening of the Danish Parliament with a wide-ranging speech on his vision for Danish society, set against the backdrop of rising nationalist-communitarian sentiment in his party, which began to focus on the "cultural integration" as much as economic integration of minority groups:

> But black spots have appeared on the map of Denmark. Places where these fundamental Danish values obviously no longer are valid. . . . The problems are linked to particularly deprived housing areas. Areas called ghettos in our everyday language. The Government has identified 29 such ghetto areas with particular major challenges. These are areas where a large percentage of the residents are unemployed. Where many people with a criminal background live. And where many Danes with immigrant backgrounds live. We must take determined action. The time has come to put an end to a misguided tolerance for the intolerance which dominates in parts of the ghettos. Let us speak openly about it: in areas where Danish values do not have a firm foothold, ordinary solutions will be rendered completely inadequate. It does not help to pump more money into painting facades. We are facing special problems that require special solutions. We will tear the walls down. We will open the ghettos up to society. . . . They are stone deserts, without any lines of communication to the surrounding society. It is these fortresses we must break through. We must dare to say that some housing blocks need to be torn down. . . . The Government will release a comprehensive strategy for the ghettos before the autumn holiday. A strategy which addresses both the bricks and the people living behind the bricks."

Rasmussen's "ghetto list," as it became known, did considerable symbolic damage, but it largely remained at that level during his first (short) term as prime minister (2009–2011). Particularly striking in his 2010 speech was how a ghetto was defined not only as an un-Danish place, but as a sealed-off zone of housing deprivation, high unemployment, crime, and "immigration."

In the years that followed, the ghetto list became more than symbolic, becoming a reference point and benchmark for measuring the success of social housing programs and interventions under the social democratic government from 2011 to 2015, which retained the list (while muting some of the noisier terminology in public statements) in order to fend off criticism from the right-wing xenophobes of the advancing Danish People's Party. In fact, that government even enlarged the list with further variables targeting educational attainment and income. When Rasmussen came to power again for a second term (2015–2019), leading a coalition of right-wing parties, the exercise of symbolic power became more intense and much more damaging. The formal criteria for inclusion on the ghetto list have changed several times since 2010, but by 2017 a *ghetto* in Denmark was a not-for-profit housing estate with more than one thousand residents meeting three of the five following criteria:

- The share of inhabitants aged eighteen to sixty-four neither in employment nor education is higher than 40 percent, as an average over the span of two years.
- The share of immigrants and their descendants from non-Western countries is higher than 50 percent.
- The share of inhabitants aged eighteen and over convicted for infractions against the penal law, weapons law, or drug regulations is greater than 2.7 percent, as an average over the span of two years.
- The share of inhabitants aged thirty to fifty-nine with only primary education or less is greater than 50 percent.
- The average gross income for inhabitants aged eighteen to sixty-four, excluding those in education, is less than 55 percent of the average gross income for the region in question.

By 2017, twenty-two urban areas of Denmark were on this list. In a speech to Parliament in January 2018, the launchpad for his 2019 reelection campaign (integration being the central issue), Rasmussen turned up the volume:

Throughout the country there are parallel societies. Many people with the same problems are bunched together. That creates a downward spiral. A counter-culture. Where people do not take responsibility, do not participate, do not make use of the opportunities we have in Denmark—but stand outside the community. Cracks have appeared in the map of Denmark. I'm deeply concerned. Because the ghettos also reach out their tentacles into the streets where criminal gangs create insecurity. Into the schools where neglected children are teetering on the edge. Into local government coffers where revenue is smaller and expenditure larger than need be. And into society at large where Danish values such as equality, broad-mindedness and tolerance are losing ground. . . . We must set a new target of phasing out ghettos altogether. In some places by breaking up the concrete. By demolishing buildings. By spreading the inhabitants and rehousing them in different areas. In other places by taking full control over who moves in. We must close the cracks in the map of Denmark and restore the mixed neighbourhoods where we meet people from every walk of life.

In November 2018, the Danish Parliament passed the Rasmussen government's Ghetto Plan, aimed precisely at "phasing out ghettos altogether" and dissolving "parallel societies" by 2030. The plan, now a Danish law, even involves the designation of "hard ghettos": districts that remain on the ghetto list (in its many variants) for four years in a row (sixteen districts). It is now against the law for individuals on social welfare such as unemployment benefits, education aid, or integration aid to settle in these "hard ghettos." Perhaps more alarming is that social housing concentrations of 60 percent or more in any of the ghettos, hard or not, are now targeted for demolition or conversion in order to attract private investors and homeowners: a clear gentrification strategy. At the time of writing, approximately forty-five hundred people currently stand to lose their homes, which will be sold off to pension funds and private equity companies keen to exploit rent gaps on valuable urban land (see chapter 3).

Other measures in the plan require children to spend a minimum of twenty-five hours a week in state-approved, Danish-language childcare from the age of one, as well as harsher punishments for crimes committed inside "ghettos" and easier evictions of "ghetto" residents who have committed any crime. There has been a substantial backlash from neighborhood organizations and residents who bear the brunt of this state-imposed territorial stigmatization, but even with a new social democratic government in place since mid-2019, there are no signs that the Ghetto Plan will be rescinded. When a group of young women from a "hard-core ghetto area" wrote to the new housing minister, Kaare Dybvad, to complain about the intensity of stigmatization visited upon them and their neighbors, he replied:

> "I am sorry you feel stigmatized. The ghetto list is a tool to reduce the difference between the vulnerable residential areas and the more well-functioning residential areas. Therefore, we must create mixed cities and neighborhoods throughout the country. The agreements on combating parallel societies are a decisive factor to break the negative heritage." (Quoted in Hoffmann-Schroeder 2019)

In a sharp intervention some time ago, Simpson (2007) referred to the problems that emerge due to "ghettos of the mind": political and analytical constructions of urban space rooted in prejudice. To respond analytically to the political capacity for consequential categorization of *ghetto*, it is appropriate to turn to the birthplace of *ghetto*, both as a term and as a sociospatial device for containing a despised and stigmatized ethnoracial category.

CONTAINMENT AND EXTRACTION: WACQUANT'S CONCEPTUALIZATION

In a series of essays, Loïc Wacquant (2004, 2008c, 2010, 2012b) conceptualizes a ghetto as an instrument of ethnoracial closure and control, exhibiting four constituent elements: stigma, constraint, spatial confinement, and institutional parallelism.

> The ghetto is a social-organizational device that employs space to reconcile two antinomic functions: (1) to maximize the material profits extracted out of a category deemed defiled and defiling, and (2) to minimize intimate contact with its members so as to avert the threat of symbolic corrosion and contagion they are believed to carry. (2012b, 7)

Wacquant's conceptualization emerges from his dissection of three canonical cases: the sociospatial seclusion of African Americans in the Fordist industrial metropolis; the forced isolation and control of the Burakumin in Tokugawa-era Japan; and especially, the spatial containment of and economic extraction from the Jews in Renaissance Venice, from where the term *ghetto* comes. Following the defeat of the Venetians by the French

Figure 8. An entrance to the Jewish ghetto of Venice, September 2014.

at Agnadello (northern Italy) in 1509, Jews fled into Venice in increasing numbers, where they were well represented in the professions of, inter alia, moneylending, long-distance trade, and medicine. Fledgling fear and hatred of Jews by the ruling Christians was in part a consequence of a campaign for the moral reform of the city following the weakening of its regional power at the time. Jews were viewed by the Venetian authorities to be *the sole source* of moral corruption, as well as carriers of disease (the spread of syphilis was incorrectly attributed to Jewish religious practices, rather than to the growth of prostitution; ironically, Jews making profits through usury was seen as tantamount to prostitution, and thus disease). There were widespread calls for the expulsion of all Jews to save the city from further putative moral degeneracy and contamination, but that would have been economic suicide for Venice, which desperately needed the high taxes, rents, and especially professional skills that the Jewish population provided. The solution of the Senate of Venice was thus complete spatial segregation, not expulsion: in 1516 *all* Jews were rounded up into an abandoned foundry called *ghetto nuovo* (see figure 8). The ghetto was surrounded on all sides by water—not unusual in Venice—yet its walls were the highest in Venice, its outer windows and doors permanently sealed, its two bridges to the rest of the city guarded, and its surrounding canals patroled by police boat. Jews were allowed out into the city during daylight hours only for economic reasons, and they had to wear special yellow badges: the same color as the scarves that prostitutes were forced to wear. At dusk, Jews had to return to the ghetto or face serious consequences.

As noted by Wacquant, this inaugural ghetto was memorably described by Richard Sennett (1994, 237) as an "urban condom," a sociospatial device designed to protect Christian residents of the city from the perceived dangers of contact with the "diseased" yet economically essential bodies of an outcast category: "When they shut the Jews inside the Ghetto, the Venetians claimed and believed they were isolating a disease that had infected the Christian community.... The segregated space of the Ghetto represented a compromise between the economic needs of Jews and these aversions to them, between practical necessity and physical fear" (215–16).

The Venetian ghetto became a blueprint for cities throughout Europe. The same fears about disease and moral upheaval, in tandem with the same needs to retain and exploit a Jewish population for its economic function, saw the involuntary segregation of Jews in cities across the continent, as geographically distant as Rome, Frankfurt, Prague, and Amsterdam. While today they are often referred to as 'Jewish Quarters,' historically they were ghettos in both form and function. While featuring overcrowding, squalor, disease, and deprivation, they were also class-stratified zones of collective consciousness, solidarity, and social organization. Because ghettoized Jews were subject to territorial confinement by night and overt racial ostracization during the day, Jewish culture and community had no option but to develop in the densely packed ghetto. The peculiar combination of spatial entrapment and social cohesion saw the emergence of a "city within a city," with its own institutions and administrative priorities. Places of worship, presses, schools, medical clinics, businesses, and civic associations formed and developed behind ghetto walls, amplifying the rigid segregation of the Jews from the rest of society, yet strengthening bonds and kinship among ghetto dwellers, to the extent that strong divisions between Ashkenazic and Sephardic Jews collapsed in city after city under the experience of complete and involuntary ethnoracial containment.

If we adhere to these historical details—important if the ghetto is to be correctly distinguished from other marginal spaces that emerge from a different set of structural constraints (requiring a different set of analytical lenses)—then the ghetto can be defined as a space deployed by discriminatory authorities to isolate, contain, and exploit a single ethnoracial category, a place to cast out (yet paradoxically retain) a group that is already outcast from wider society. In all three canonical cases Wacquant analyzes, the parallel institutions that formed became at once a sword, effecting closure to the benefit of the dominant, and a shield, offering a protected space wherein the dominated could experience reciprocity and dignity; hence Wacquant's (2012b) characterization of the ghetto as "Janus-faced."

Why does this relational (as opposed to statistical/gradational) conceptualization of the ghetto matter? Against portrayals of the ghetto as a fearsome space of material destitution and social disintegration—which are hegemonic in large segments of urban research, journalism, and (as we saw in the British and Danish cases) politics—Wacquant shows that ghettoization typically (and unintentionally on the part of the oppressors) translates into the social strengthening and symbolic unification of the target population. He explains that, for the oppressed, the ghetto is "a protective and integrative device insofar as it relieves its members from constant contact with the dominant and fosters consociation and community-building within the constricted sphere of intercourse it creates. Enforced isolation from the outside leads to the intensification of social exchange and cultural sharing inside" (Wacquant 2012b, 10). What is more, the ghetto is "a cultural combustion engine that melts divisions among the confined population and fuels its collective pride even as it entrenches the stigma that hovers over it" and something that, at least in the Fordist cities of the United States, "turned racial consciousness into a mass phenomenon fueling community mobilization against continued caste exclusion" (12).

This analytic elaboration of the historical meaning and sociological contents of the ghetto proposed by Wacquant allows us to critique the loose or opportunistic use of *ghetto* to describe and/or condemn working-class territories and/or immigrant districts in the European urban periphery, which in fact sport remarkable ethnic diversity, usually without a strong collective ethnic identity. Wacquant also notes that "their inhabitants suffer not from institutional duplication and enclosure but, on the contrary, from the lack of an ingrown organization structure capable of sustaining them in the absence of gainful employment and adequate public services" (18). This led him to call these zones "anti-ghettos," as they move away from the pattern of the ghetto as conceptualized in the preceding: "[T]he immigrant neighbourhood and the ghetto serve diametrically opposed functions. . . . [O]ne is a springboard for *assimilation* via cultural learning and social-cum-spatial mobility, and the other is a material and symbolic isolation ward geared toward *dissimilation*. The former is best figured by a bridge, the latter by a wall" (21–22). There remains, however, an important question: What if people living in an area that does not fit within the preceding conceptualization nonetheless feel that they do live in a ghetto? Ntsiki Anderson and I addressed this very question many years ago in the neighborhood of St. Paul's in Bristol, England, when we spent time asking local residents about the ghetto reputation of the neighborhood and how it impacted upon their lives (Slater and Anderson 2012). One of the more absorbing interviews took place with a Jamaican-born pensioner who had moved to St. Paul's in 1963, during the period when the area became the locus of West Indian settlement in Bristol after World War II (rents were cheap in the multi-occupancy housing stock, and discrimination meant West Indians had difficulty finding accommodation elsewhere in the city). When we briefly summarized the gradational (statistical) view of the ghetto, he responded as follows:

> The ghetto is a state of mind, a way of life, not just a statistical thing. It has become a part of Black urban identity via culture, music, film, literature etc. and it has become part of Black British culture. St Paul's has things similar to American ghettos, not just because we have incorporated the ghetto into our culture. I mean, if you listen to Black, actually not just Black, but British urban music, literature etc. how can you deny that ghettos exist in this country?

This reaction (he was one of several residents we encountered to use and even embrace the term *ghetto* in relation to St. Paul's) presents analytic challenges to the many scholars who have refuted claims that Britain has ghettos (or is moving toward ghettoization). If residents believe they live in a ghetto and use that term in their everyday vocabulary (several residents, unprompted, spoke of "ghetto life"), how does the analyst refuting the existence of ghettos in Britain (due to concerns about stigmatization and any policy blunders that follow) respond? Rather than *accept* and *adopt* resident vocabulary, as Didier Lapeyronnie (2007) does in his discussion of French banlieues, it becomes essential to maintain a critical analytical distance and *interpret* and *scrutinize* resident vocabulary.

With this distance, *ghetto* among St. Paul's residents can be seen as an appropriated label used varyingly as a synonym for ethnic and neighborhood pride, for social status and solidarity, for cultural difference from a perceived mainstream, and sometimes to capture the shared feeling of living at the bottom of the hierarchy of places that constitute central Bristol. In this respect, St. Paul's exhibited a crucial difference from Wacquant's conceptualizations of both territorial stigmatization (see chapter 6) and the anti-ghetto. There was a strong sense of shared identity and collective pride in the neighborhood, often in response to external defamation. This identity was something that residents were determined to protect, and the way many did this was to resist the stigma the ghetto label carries by turning that label on its head in an attempt to make it something positive. Among the residents we encountered, hardly any engaged in the strategies of "mutual distancing and lateral denigration" identified by Wacquant (2008b, 116). Instead, there was a discernible protectionism in respect of what St. Paul's stands for: collective struggle against adversity, a phoenix from the ashes of postwar economic malaise, and strong neighborhood organizations.

Notwithstanding residents' appropriations of stigmatizing labels, there can be little doubt that external imposition of the idea of ghetto has deeply damaging consequences. A brief and final example comes from Belgium. The worldwide attention visited upon the Brussels neighborhood of Sint-Jans Molenbeek (known simply as Molenbeek) in late 2015 and early 2016 showed just how powerful the ghetto designator has become for politicians, journalists, and assorted pundits keen to resuscitate long-running debates over immigration policy and the failures of assimilation ideology; the tensions between Islam and the secular policies of European states; and in particular the deepening misery of marginal districts, which in demographic composition (large ethnic and religious minority population)

and socioeconomic condition (crushing poverty and widespread unemployment) are viewed to be European urban ghettos. The context for the
panic over Molenbeek was two brutal terrorist attacks orchestrated by the
Islamic State of Iraq and the Levant (ISIL): on November 13, 2015, at
several venues across central Paris, and on March 22, 2016, in Brussels
Airport and a Brussels metro station. Following police investigations, several of the terrorists were found to have links to Molenbeek (from being
born and raised there to having visited it once). Molenbeek subsequently
found itself portrayed by journalists and politicians alike as, inter alia,
"Europe's jihadi central" (Traynor 2015), "the Islamic State of Molenbeek"
(Cohen 2016), "the most notorious postcode in Western Europe" (Chalmers 2017), and "some seething Middle-Eastern or North African ghetto"
(Jones 2015).

To be sure, the terrorists did have links to Molenbeek, but contrary to
simplistic exercises in symbolic power, it was not Molenbeek that made
them terrorists. While the deterioration of living conditions and declining
life chances in the Brussels periphery since the advent of the intertwined
processes of postindustrialization and neoliberalization cannot be dis-
puted, to designate as ghettos neighborhoods like Molenbeek robs these
areas of an appropriate conceptual and analytical framework that otherwise may go some way toward explaining their plight, for two reasons.
First, a brief glimpse at censuses of population, or even a few hours spent
there, will reveal that the population residing within Molenbeek, just like
in many other "notorious neighborhoods" in European cities, is characterized by remarkable ethnic *heterogeneity*, as opposed to the strictly
enforced (from without) ethnic homogeneity of ghettos. The population of
Molenbeek is repeatedly described as "mainly" or "entirely" Muslim in the
mainstream media; however, the actual figure hovers around 40 percent.
Second, residents of Molenbeek have regular contact with and dependency
on (through employment and consumption practices) residents of adja-
cent neighborhoods or those in the central city. With the possible exception of religious institutions, a rigorous analyst will not find evidence of a
set of parallel institutions forming to serve the basic needs of the excluded
population; by contrast with what is common to all ghettos, the same analyst will quickly discover that these are areas where the tentacles of the
welfare state, though shorter than in previous decades, still stretch into

and attempt to assist those for whom employment is precarious or absent, and for whom opportunities for upward mobility are limited by language, skills, and discrimination. In sum, analysts who deploy the trope of the ghetto for rhetorical dramatization in hopes of inciting progressive policy intervention actually contribute to the further symbolic degradation of dispossessed districts and thus to the very phenomenon they should be dissecting.

BLACK LIVES MATTER AGAINST URBAN AGNOTOLOGY

One of the more memorable essays in Robert Proctor and Londa Schiebinger's foundational edited collection on agnotology is Charles Mills's "White Ignorance." Mills articulates his understanding of "an ignorance, a non-knowing, that is not contingent, but in which race—white racism or white racial domination and their ramifications—is central to its origins" (2008, 233). He outlines ten features of this white ignorance, most of which are to do with the systematic silencing of Black intellectuals, before bringing them together with this conclusion: "White ignorance has been able to flourish all these years because a white epistemology of ignorance has safeguarded it against the dangers of an illuminating Blackness . . . protecting those who for 'racial' reasons have needed not to know" (247).

I read these words at around the time protests were erupting in Minneapolis in late May 2020 in response to the brutal killing of George Floyd, a Black man stopped on suspicion of having a counterfeit $20 bill, by a white police officer. These protests, which very quickly spread nationwide and triggered massive solidarity protests in dozens of cities across the globe, amplified and extended the Black Lives Matter movement that was born in 2013 via the online activism of three Black queer women in response to multiple police murders of Black people on US streets or in US prisons (and which had come to international prominence in the summer of 2014 following the police murder of Michael Brown in Ferguson, Missouri). On June 7, 2020, activists in Bristol, England, pulled down the statue of seventeenth-century slave owner Edward Colston in solidarity with the Black Lives Matter movement, triggering an overdue debate about the celebratory way that the history of the British Empire is taught in UK high schools. A hopeful interpretation of the rapid surge of the Black Lives Matter movement is that we are at the beginning of an era of "illuminating Blackness" or "the long process that will lead to the eventual overcoming of this white darkness and the achievement of an enlightenment that is genuinely multiracial" (Mills, 247).

Tragically there is nothing new about the racial violence of the police in the United States (and beyond), and nothing new in uprisings against racial oppression and systematic/institutional discrimination. But given the discussion in this chapter on the agnotology surrounding the spaces in which marginalized urban dwellers live, and the harmful racialized categorizations that have material consequences, it seems important to close it with a consideration (albeit brief) of the emerging geographies of racial oppression. Ferguson is a small city on the outskirts of St. Louis with a majority African American population; George Floyd was killed at the intersection of four multiethnic neighborhoods only three miles south of downtown Minneapolis. Neither of these places is a ghetto in the sociological sense (via Wacquant) that I have outlined here, even though both have been stigmatized as such. In fact, according to Wacquant (2008b), the African American ghetto in the United States is long gone, having either gentrified, or (by contrast) having mutated into what he calls a "hyperghetto," a place in which the supportive parallel institutions have disappeared and where there is no collective economic function (for the oppressors) of the resident population. In Ferguson and Powderhorn Park, however, there appears to be a relationship between gentrification, displacement, and police violence against Black people. In a striking analysis of Ferguson, Deborah Cowen and Nemoy Lewis (2018) draw upon critical race theory to argue that we are witnessing the consequences of *internal colonialism*, where "empire oppresses, exploits, disciplines and dispossesses populations internal to its territorial core" (271). The authors argue that Neil Smith's rent gap theory (see chapter 3) was "about geopolitical economy, where the specificities of who and where matter, and where the market relies on violent force" and contend that "the rent gap in American cities should be understood as a profoundly racial and violent effect of internal colonialism" (272). The spatial manifestations of this internal colonialism are as follows: "Ferguson has become a majority Black suburb as a result of gentrification and displacement in St. Louis and surrounding areas—although this shift is not reflected in the political leadership or police force, which remain almost entirely white." For Cowen and Lewis, Ferguson is best understood and conceptualized as an *internal colony*, with its white leadership functioning as an "internal colonial administration" (276). This argument is supported by Keeanga-Yamahtta Taylor (2015):

> No one would have anticipated that a small city on the outskirts of St. Louis would become the epicenter of the "rising up" against police terrorism in the United States. At the same time, it is easy to see why Ferguson exploded. Racist police not only routinely harassed African Americans, but the city also relied on citing the Black majority for a range of minor offenses to generate income—fines from tickets became the second leading source of revenue for Ferguson. The antagonism between a white, racist police force and the Black majority was literally institutionalized. . . . These problems will continue to be exacerbated as the destruction of the public sector, urban restructuring and gentrification, and the limited prospects for work in private job market leaves millions of working class African Americans in a precarious state.

Six years after Michael Brown was murdered, George Floyd was murdered outside an Arab American mom-and-pop store on the corner of 38th and Chicago Streets in the Southside of Minneapolis, literally at the point where four neighborhoods meet (Central, Bryant, Bancroft, and Powderhorn Park). Central and Bryant are historically poor African American neighborhoods; Bancroft and Powderhorn Park are historically middle-class white neighborhoods. This segregation was the outcome of a familiar story: racial covenants (redlining) added by real estate developers in the first half of the twentieth century that prevented the sale or lease of land to people of color, trapping Black people in neighborhoods with no chance of living elsewhere in the city. Central and Bryant are now more mixed, with majority working-class white and Latino residents, and Bancroft and Powderhorn Park have gentrified significantly in the past decade. According to a community organizer interviewed by a reporter for the Minneapolis *Star-Tribune*: "Chicago was the divide, which is why 38th and Chicago has been battled over. It's where a historic white and a historic Black community meet," he said. "This is an old battle for land; it goes back 400 years on this continent" (quoted in Otarola 2020).

It is no coincidence that Floyd was murdered by a white police officer where very different worlds collide under racial capitalism, and where city council members in recent years have been trying to attract investment (gentrification) in the hope that the relative affluence of Bancroft and Powderhorn Park will cross Chicago Street. The analytic and political lesson here is that understanding contemporary spaces of racial oppression as internal colonies seems necessary in the face of ongoing white ignorance, visible in stigmatizing labels such as *ghetto* and in the violent processes of predatory capitalism, dehumanization of Black lives, and land dispossession that are behind the internal colonies' formation (Adamson 2019).

8 Some Possibilities for Critical Urban Studies

I submitted the first draft of this book to the publisher at the end of February 2020, a time when COVID-19 was transmitting rapidly from humans to humans across borders, with very limited government action anywhere to contain it. A month later, it was too late to contain it; most of the world's population was placed in lockdown in response to the World Health Organization's declaration of a global pandemic, as the seriousness and deadliness of this highly infectious virus overwhelmed hospitals and completely devastated families, communities, and economies. It turned out that, as a species, we were not as "resilient" to crises as many city managers would have us believe (see chapter 2). As I write these words, many months later, it is clear that this ongoing tragedy is not going to end any time soon, and that the presence of the virus is something to which we will have to adjust our lives for as long as it takes vaccination programs to have their desired effects. Given the staggering death toll in countries led by free-market ideologues who prioritize individual freedoms over collective public health, it did seem, at times, as if the world were witnessing the bitter, deathly harvest of neoliberal capitalism, weaponized with a complex virus that could have been contained (and its impacts softened) through coordinated decision-making and collective action informed by a range of expert knowledge.

I am neither an epidemiologist nor someone who studies diseases and urban environments, and therefore I am not qualified to offer any analysis here of what some observers were quickly describing (rather opportunistically) as "pandemic urbanisms." However, it is of relevance to this book and my own expertise that the politically charged production of ignorance was suddenly everywhere as the pandemic unfolded. This took the form of predictably dangerous statements and (in)actions of world leaders, such as the claim (most frequently uttered by public health officials without any training in structural or political analysis, or by people speaking from positions of immense privilege) that the virus "doesn't discriminate." This claim, usually justified by the simplistic statement that "anyone can catch it," received a devastating rebuke in a series of tweets on March 23, 2020, by a medical doctor in India, Jaradish J. Hiramath:

> Social distancing is a privilege. It means you live in a house large enough to practise it. Hand washing is a privilege too. It means you have access to running water. Hand sanitisers are a privilege. It means you have money to buy them. Lockdowns are a privilege. It means you can afford to be at home. Most of the ways to ward off Corona are accessible only to the affluent. In essence, a disease that was spread by the rich as they flew around the globe will now kill millions of the poor. All those who are practising social distancing & imposing a lockdown on themselves must appreciate how privileged they are.

While it is of course the case that anyone can catch the virus, it is most certainly not the case that the risks of catching it are the same for all human beings, nor is it the case that the experience of the disease and the pandemic is somehow uniform. There is no shortage of examples of the unfolding public health calamities that are fueled by agnotology, especially in the United States, the United Kingdom, and Brazil, countries governed by right-wing populist-authoritarian administrations that have demonstrated callous disregard for the lives of citizens, especially those in Black, minority ethnic, and Indigenous communities, which are most exposed to and hardest hit by the virus (Ortega and Orsini 2020). The stunning disregard of scientific expertise that was demonstrated by Donald Trump, Boris Johnson, and Jair Bolsonaro is perhaps to be expected, but their ignorance has been engineered quite deliberately to deflect attention away from what the pandemic has so clearly exposed and exacerbated: the massive social divisions and inequalities that exist within those nations (Lee 2020), which are experienced most acutely in cities, with marked spatialities:

> COVID-19 proliferates in extended forms of urbanization and in the urban periphery that have characterized recent urbanization trends. Traditionally a metaphor of escape—as a place of refuge, of backyards and fresh air, away from the dense, sick city centre—the global urban periphery has become the epicentre of zoonotic transmission, infection through travel (e.g. airports), community spread and new forms of health governance. Furthermore, vulnerabilities have been particularly pronounced in this new urban world where spatial peripherality has coincided with social marginality both in institutional and community contexts. Our argument is not that this is a suburban virus. Rather, we point to the fact that where the virus is concentrated, you find the peripheral, in the city and in society. (Biglieri, De Vidovich, and Keil 2020, 2)

Although it is too soon to add detailed empirical substance to these important observations, one thing seems clear from the COVID-19 pandemic at this juncture: inequalities and their specific geographies are now impossible to ignore, despite the best attempts of politicians to plant ignorance and doubt among the populace.

In the preceding chapters I have demonstrated a critical approach to urban studies that guards against the subordination of scholarly to policy agendas and challenges the rise of policy-driven research at the expense of research-driven policy, in the broader context of the growing heteronomy of urban research. This has been a 'double move' approach, one that weds social critique with epistemological critique: I have addressed the causal mechanisms behind different forms of urban inequality, while scrutinizing how knowledge (and all too often ignorance) on these issues is produced. I have deployed two concepts along the way: agnotology (the intentional production of ignorance) and symbolic power (the capacity for consequential categorization). In this closing chapter, I present a conclusion in the form of some possible pathways for critical urban studies, positioned against vested interest urbanism and against the prevailing political wind of the steady erosion of intellectual autonomy. My main purpose is to think carefully about the relationships between urban knowledges, urban ignorances, and urban struggles, and to suggest that the analysis of urban inequalities along these lines carries some interesting possibilities for critical urban studies as a vibrant and multidisciplinary intellectual field.

In multiple international contexts, but especially in the United Kingdom where I work, urban research has been taking place in the context of universities that have neoliberalized with stunning celerity, where the pressure of finding research funds to recover the costs of ever-increasing expenditure by university managers has come to dominate the functioning of academic departments, so much so that the award of a massive research grant carrying institutional overheads is usually a fast track to academic promotion (often regardless of the relevance and influence of the research or the quality of publications arising from the project). Universities have become "ever more grotesque parodies of businesses" (Smith 2001, 146), competing against each other for footloose capital, or as antigentrification activists fighting Columbia University's expansion into Harlem once put it, they are "multibillion-dollar, multinational corporations with major interests in the global equity markets and in local real estate development which also happen to give out degrees every May" (quoted in Smith 2008, 264).

This context means that scholars are under greater pressure than ever before to secure substantial external funding, and it is to government funding bodies that most social scientists apply. As I outlined in chapter 1, the outcome has been the serious subordination of scholarly to policy agendas and the rise of policy-driven research at the expense of research-driven policy (and with it, decision-based evidence making instead of evidence-based decision-making). The autonomous scholar, conducting research for reasons arrived at in the course of their engagements with knowledge, politics, and society, is increasingly a challenging role to fulfill in the context of the rise to prominence of scholars guided primarily by the priorities and categories of state managers and the worries of the mainstream media. Loïc Wacquant (2009, 124) has elaborated on this trend:

> On both sides of the Atlantic, autonomous researchers are also increasingly supplanted by bureaucratic experts, those shadowy scholars who deliver to government the answers that officials wish for and who, above all, accept the questions posed by politicians. In point of fact . . . there is a huge deficit of collective reflection on the collective organization of scientific work and on the changing nexus between research, the media, money, and politics. This

deficit fosters scientific heteronomy and, through it, the diffusion of the monopoly of neoliberal "one-way thinking" which has truncated and paralysed public debate for the past decade.

Rob Imrie (2004, 706) urged urban scholars to ask *how* and *why* certain types of urban knowledge have "filtrated into public policy institutions and gained 'good currency.'" The implications of this filtration are without doubt serious: take, for instance, the demolitions of public housing projects in the United States under the federal government HOPE VI program, in which academic discourses of "concentrated poverty," which completely ignored the roles of racial and gendered domination and systematic state disinvestment in creating brutal conditions for tenants, were used to justify the displacement of thousands of low-income, predominantly female-headed, African American families against their wishes, with little concern for their future housing situation (Crump 2002; Goetz 2003, 2013). The discourse of "concentrated poverty" also precludes consideration of concentrations of *affluence* and the kinds of subsidised housing within them:

> Most Americans think that federal housing assistance is a poor people's program. In fact, relatively few low-income Americans receive federal housing subsidies. In contrast, about three-fourths of wealthy Americans—many living in very large homes—get housing subsidies from Washington in the form of tax breaks. These tax breaks subsidize many households who can afford to buy homes without it. (Dreier 2006, 105)

Furthermore, these subsidised housing developments of the rich are characterized by high levels of criminality (of a different kind), antisocial behavior, and declining social capital; in short, they are microcosms of some of worst societal problems of our age, but nobody ever seems to call for policies aimed at dispersing the rich.

To overthrow the hegemonic view—the 'dispersal consensus' (Imbroscio 2008)—that people within poor neighborhoods should be moved for the greater good of society, it is necessary to correct what Imbroscio identifies as one of the fundamental starting premises of that consensus: "that helping the poor where they live—through place-based economic (or community) development—is destined to be of limited success" (121–22). The policy-scholarly fusion that has strengthened in neoliberalized

universities holds immense career prestige for those who embrace it, making the leap of perspective required to see the world from the standpoint
of those experiencing social suffering ever more unlikely among the mainstream. Policy-relevant research need not be policy-*driven* research (Wyly
2004), but there are many scholars in positions of power (e.g., on grant
funding panels, journal editorial boards, and professional associations)
who do not see it that way. A *critical* urban studies involves the intense
scrutiny of any grant application or well-promoted funded project boasting "policy relevance" stemming from conceptualizations imposed by policy elites; moreover, it involves the sustained critique of the structural and
institutional arrangements under which a great deal of urban research
and publication takes place.

The political philosopher G. A. Cohen once remarked:

> The point of theory is not to generate a comprehensive social design which
> the politician then seeks to implement. Things don't work that way, because
> implementing a design requires whole cloth, and nothing in contemporary
> politics is made out of whole cloth. Politics is an endless struggle, and theory
> serves as a weapon in that struggle, because it provides a characterization of
> its direction, and of its controlling purpose. (1994, 4)

This important reminder of the political uses of theory brings me to the
current state of theoretical and methodological debates *within* critical
urban studies. Some of these debates, to be frank, are increasingly tautological and exhausting. One illustration is the back and forth between
those who work with Henri Lefebvre's "problematique" of *planetary
urbanization* to understand the scalar transformations, violences and
injustices vis-à-vis the mutations of contemporary capitalist exploitation
(e.g., Brenner 2014; Brenner and Schmid 2015), and those who work
with feminist, queer, and postcolonial approaches to urban questions,
who argue that the planetary urbanization thesis does not leave adequate
room for equally important considerations of racism, coloniality, patriar-
chy, heteronormativity, and nationalism (Derickson 2018; McLean 2018;
Oswin 2018). These debates recently appeared in a special issue of a leading geography journal (*Environment and Planning D: Society and Space*
36, no. 3 [2018]) and then became particularly tense on Twitter. My own
reaction to those exchanges was a sense of frustration that scholars who

all have in common deep political commitments to progressive left politics were expending energy arguing against each other (often with arguments they have made before in multiple forums), when it could be expended on praxis, that is, actually doing different kinds of critical urban research in solidarity with each other, against all kinds of disturbing developments roiling unequal cities at a time of surging populisms, right-wing nationalisms, and the diffusion of all manner of racist/sexist/colonialist ideologies. Furthermore, as Hillary Angelo and Kian Goh (2020) argue and demonstrate, the planetary urbanization approach is not at all incompatible with questions of difference.

To clarify, I am not dismissing theoretical debates and disagreements in critical urban studies as somehow pointless, nor am I saying that a wide range of different theoretical interventions does not help us understand and explain urban problems in more depth. But theoretical *debates* can so easily become narcissistic and totally disconnected from urban struggles. Professors endlessly criticizing each other about who has the best critical approach is really not a good look when low-income people are being evicted; when the cost of housing is becoming absolutely ruinous; when women, people of color, and Indigenous people are disproportionately banished from public and residential spaces; when welfare institutions are being systematically dismantled; when climate crisis hits marginalized people hardest; and when there is just so much injustice to fight against and radically open futures to fight for.

When scholars on the left engaged in critical urban studies spend more time arguing among and against each other than they spend calling into question scholarship that, inter alia, promotes "resilient cities," embraces gentrification, trashes rent control, uncritically parrots neighborhood effects, and stigmatizes the places where marginalized people live, then urban ignorance will have an even smoother journey into policy circles than it currently does. While theoretical and epistemological jousting continues among the academic left, free-market think tanks will continue to amplify their convictions that market-driven initiatives are desirable and necessary solutions for urban (and especially housing) problems. In a thorough analysis of the history and sociology of think tanks in the United States, Tom Medvetz (2012, 226) argues that their rise and influence must be set analytically "against the backdrop of a series of processes that have contributed to the growing subordination of knowledge to political and economic demand." The neoliberalization of universities is undoubtedly one of those processes, but so too is that peculiar academic left trait of always finding opponents where there are political allies, and thus going after the wrong targets.

Given the thematic content I have addressed in this book, it seems appropriate to close it with some observations regarding the importance of two issues at the core of every chapter: urban housing and urban land. Housing—having a roof over one's head—is absolutely central to human dignity, community, family, solidarity, and life chances (Madden and Marcuse 2016). One of the more arresting statistics I have ever come across is that if food prices in the United Kingdom had risen at the same rate as house prices since 1971, a fresh chicken purchased in a supermarket would cost over £50 (Carylon 2013). The mainstream/hegemonic argument critiqued in chapters 4 and 6 is that statistics like this are the outcome of an imbalance between housing supply and housing demand. This argument hides the articulation of deregulation, privatization, and attacks on the welfare state that have led to such a serious crisis of affordability. As I have shown, the mainstream/hegemonic argument is hardly confined to the United Kingdom, and the unrelenting dissemination and circulation of ignorance vis-à-vis housing (agnotology) is a major obstruction in terms of thinking critically about the question of land: *who owns it, and how they got it.* The institution of (and inequities in) landownership, together with speculative landed developer interests, constitute the major determinants not only of the cost of housing, but also of the enormous disparities in living standards and life chances in cities across multiple international contexts.

In this respect I think David M. Smith's (very underrated) arguments on territorial social justice are especially helpful. Most of his teachings and writings were motivated by a simple question: *Who gets what where (and how)?* (Smith 1977, 1987, 1994). Given the uneven geographical distribution of needs, resources, and rights, with some places far better served than others, territorial social justice would entail addressing the structural and institutional arrangements that block a more even distribution. Animating Smith's work was a deep conviction about the necessity and importance of place for human existence, not as some kind of neighborhood effect like those I critiqued in chapter 5, but as something that goes beyond other basic needs, such as food and clothing, and indeed beyond the physical occupation of space and of a structure thereon. Our place, and sense of geographical space or territory, merges imperceptibly with a broader sense of identity, of who we are, of position in the general scheme of things. (Smith 1994, 253)

Such a conviction led to an equally powerful argument about the injustice of displacement (see chapter 4), something that Smith framed as "part of the human struggle that should not be overlooked in pursuit of social justice in a geographical context" (254).

Smith argued that, given the chance of birth (that is, the chance of *to whom* we are born and particularly *where* we are born), and given such grotesque inequalities between people and places, social justice should be a process of equalization. Guided by his extensive engagement with moral and political philosophy, he argued that this process must start by arresting the private inheritance of advantages such as wealth, land, and political power; in terms of other spheres like education, health care, and the law, a principle of strict equality according to human need should apply, so as to give people the same capabilities in society. So, informed by decades of mixed-methods research in very different urban contexts (North and South), Smith's argument became: the more equal a society, the better for everyone in that society (and the converse is true vis-à-vis inequality). Crucially, Smith's was also a deeply geographical argument, for social justice as *spatial* equalization. It was a critique of uneven development that recognized and respected that places are shaped by radically different histories and political structures, but it was anchored in a universal commitment to the equal realization of what is minimally required to be, and to feel, human. As all human beings have no choice but to occupy a place in the world, and as place is so central to human existence in so many ways, Smith argued that *not being involuntarily banished from a place* is a very solid principle and a building block for social justice.

It is interesting to consider these powerful arguments vis-à-vis urban land and social justice in relation to some equally compelling, more recent interventions from scholars working with settler-colonial and decolonial theory. As Libby Porter and Oren Yiftachel (2019, 177) explain, critical urban theory has "generally overlooked the skewed dynamics of power in settler-colonial contexts as a key dimension for theorizing contemporary cities." This means that critical urban studies, as a multidisciplinary field, has largely seen "the perceptions, logic and mobilizations of Indigenous people as apparently irrelevant to contemporary forms of urbanization" (177). This is an oversight in multiple respects, not least because it is via the foregrounding of Indigenous knowledges and struggles that radically different, politically progressive understandings of land can be gained, which could prove useful far beyond settler-colonial contexts (Blomley 2004).

Especially important about the literature working with settler-colonial theory (Wolfe 1999; Edmonds 2010; Coulthard 2014: Veracini 2015) is its articulation of the land relation in settler-colonial contexts as the organizing principle that really matters (more so than the labor relation, which is the primary mode of power in other types of colonial projects). Naama Blatman-Thomas and Libby Porter (2019, 31) remind us that, in settler colonialism, "colonists and their colonizing processes came to stay, rendering necessary (if unattainable) the erasure of Indigenous lands and peoples as on ongoing project." Land dispossession in settler societies is especially painful for Indigenous peoples, not only because of the violence of usurpation and theft, but because land, among Indigenous peoples, tends to be "constituted quite differently" from European white possession. For example, in urban Xhosa communities in South Africa, activities on the land occur via "various stages of negotiation amongst all residents until a consensus is reached by all before community elders grant individual land-use rights, [which] are also only granted with the spiritual blessing from ancestors" (Winkler 2018, 597). This points to how land is regarded among many Indigenous peoples as the genesis of being:

> This is an ontology of land and belonging that performs a repertoire of *being with* and *coming from* a place, and in so doing, knowing, practicing and imagining place as a relationship where place and subject constitute each other. Land is a material being that *through its being* creates the world and the subjects (human and non-human) of that world. . . . For Indigenous sovereignty, property as land is corporeal, inscribed in and through Indigenous bodies and emanating from land in itself. (Blatman-Thomas and Porter 2019, 40)

These authors are very clear that Indigeneity is not a singular experience, and that there are protracted, gendered struggles over power and authority in Indigenous communities, but their point is that particular Indigenous ontologies have tremendous potential for reconsidering land and land struggles not only in settler societies, but in any society where the exchange value of land (and housing) has been naturalized to the extent that it squashes any consideration of any other understanding of land.

Therefore, "Indigenous epistemologies and philosophies for reading place, belonging and identity" (Porter and Yiftachel 2019, 180–81) can guide a critical urban studies concerned with not only who gets what where (and how), but, as Winkler (2017) argues, with unsettling and unlearning the guiding logics of commodification and marketization that remain naturalized and unquestioned in mainstream urban studies and planning. There are large and interconnected literatures on the right to housing, the right to place, and the right to the city that have provided profound insights on the repertoires of tactics deployed by social movements in order to fight for democratized and decommodified futures, yet relatively few of these writings consider radically different understandings of land that can help rehumanize oppressed peoples against classism, racism, and sexism (Cupples 2019). Critical urban studies tends to identify the social sources of critique in the perspectives of social movements, marginalized communities, and politicized workers, but there is an even wider world of alternative territorial perspectives from which to derive insights about urban inequalities and how to address them.

The point here is not that certain modes of critical thought are outdated, nor that certain Eurocentric or Western thinkers are not worth engaging with or citing, but that new pictures of emancipation and *dis*-alienation are possible if we consider multiple worldviews, in what is known among decolonial philosophers as epistemic pluriversalism (Grosfoguel 2007). As Julie Cupples has pointed out, the "engaged pluralism" advocated by Michiel van Meeteren, Ben Derudder, and David Bassens (2016) and Neil Brenner (2018) "does not merely involve incorporating poststructuralist, feminist and queer approaches into (Marxist) urban theorizing" but rather should involve "urban scholarship that is attentive to the relational, communitarian, indigenous and rural elements that compose political struggles in cities today" (Cupples 2019, 221). Decolonial approaches to land involve asserting and reinstating much more *social* logics, for colonization required logics of dispossession, alienation, and commodification that attempted to destroy them. These social logics are by no means incompatible with the Marxist theories I have articulated in various chapters of this book; indeed, there is a well-established literature on Black Marxism, with a landmark text (Robinson 1983), that demonstrates their compatibility. Cupples's point, which I think is very well made, is that critical urban studies has been rather slow to catch on.

Epistemic pluriversalism can advance hand in hand with epistemic reflexivity, a practice that constantly seeks to question the *doxas*—commonsense assumptions—that permeate academic labor and production in a systematic manner. As Troels Schultz Larsen (2018, 1133–34) has noted, this requires "historicizing and contextualizing the research problematics and the core categories and concepts"—that is, "reconstructing the specific history, context, and institutional and social conditions of our core problems and concepts." Henceforth it seems very important to ask critical questions about the pertinence—and especially history and geography—of certain concepts, and to ask whether they are helpful or not in dissecting urban processes beyond the time and place where those concepts were formed. Concepts are devices of explanatory utility. They are there to be useful to us if we need them: to bring things to light that we did not see before or know about and to help explain phenomena that require careful and sometimes urgent scrutiny. They may or may not have utility across geographical and historical contexts, but if they help explain social phenomena and help us answer questions we have asked about the world, and maybe even help us make and inform political interventions, then they should be retained. But there may be even more powerful concepts available to us, from sources we may not have considered, if we take the trouble to look closely.

Notes

1. For a vivid illustration of this contrast, compare Glaeser (2011) with Graham (2010).

CHAPTER 1. CHALLENGING HETERONOMY
OF URBAN RESEARCH

1. Robinson et al. (2017). Thank you to Phil Lawton for alerting me to this document.

2. Alexander (2018) provides an excellent analysis of heteronomy as state penetration into the arts field in the United Kingdom.

3. See the organization's website at www.radstats.org.uk.

4. See a discussion of the programmable city at https://progcity.maynooth university.ie/.

5. A fascinating example of community resistance to this kind of abuse of big data to punish the poor can be found in the work of the Los Angeles–based Stop LAPD Spying Coalition, whose vision is the dismantling of government-sanctioned spying and intelligence gathering, in all its multiple forms. See the organization's website at https://stoplapdspying.org/.

CHAPTER 2. THE RESILIENCE
OF NEOLIBERAL URBANISM

1. Fortunately the "Guardian Cities" section improved significantly from this shaky start and became an excellent resource full of superb journalism on urban issues, until it was discontinued in January 2020, when Rockefeller's sponsorship ended.

CHAPTER 3. BEYOND FALSE CHOICE URBANISM

1. Thank you to Mathieu van Criekingen for this excellent point.

2. Neil Smith nailed this embrace:

> A predictably populist symbolism underlies the hoopla and boosterism with which gentrification is marketed. It focuses on "making cities liveable," meaning liveable for the middle class. In fact, of necessity, they have always been "liveable" for the working class. The so-called renaissance is advertised and sold as bringing benefits to everyone regardless of class, but available evidence suggests otherwise. (Smith 1982, 152)

3. Contrary to the "back to the city" rhetoric of the 1970s (see Laska and Spain 1980), most gentrifiers came from other central city neighborhoods, not the suburbs.

4. An immediate reaction I had to this argument was that the privatization of nonprivate land tenures could be analyzed as a gentrification strategy, when gentrification is defined appropriately as the class transformation of space and not defined as Ghertner's "nothing more than a rising rent environment and associated forms of market-induced displacement" (2015, 552).

5. *USA Today* ran the headline "Studies: Gentrification a Boost for Everyone" (Hampson 2005), under which coverage of Lance Freeman's (2005) work appeared. *Time* magazine featured the study by McKinnish, Walsh, and White (2008) under the headline "Gentrification: Not Ousting the Poor?" (Kiviat 2008).

6. Sandra Annunziata was a brilliant young Italian scholar-activist who died suddenly at the beginning of 2019. I hope she would have enjoyed reading this chapter, and I hope that highlighting her work encourages others to read it closely.

CHAPTER 4. DISPLACEMENT, RENT CONTROL,
HOUSING JUSTICE

1. The use of the word *artificially* is revealing; neoclassical economists are especially prone to viewing a competitive market as a natural evolution that is best left alone if equilibrium and growth are to be achieved.

2. I am grateful to Elvin Wyly for pointing this out.

3. This discussion of rent control myths and realities draws upon and extends an earlier essay I wrote with Hamish Kallin (Kallin and Slater 2018), from whom I always learn so much about housing issues.

4. Mason (2019). Reproduced with permission of the author.

CHAPTER 5. NEIGHBORHOOD EFFECTS
AS TAUTOLOGICAL URBANISM

1. David Imbroscio (2008, 114) advanced a fascinating critique of how mainstream housing policy researchers in the United States treat choice in respect of low-income categories: "The expansion of residential choices for the urban poor only exists when the ability to exit is enhanced; it does not include enhancing—in Chester Hartman's (1984) useful phrase—'the right [or ability] to stay put.'"

2. As Sampson (2012, 46) commented when reflecting on his 2002 review of neighborhood effects studies, "It was impossible to review them all then and would be even more so now."

CHAPTER 6. PRODUCTION OF TERRITORIAL STIGMA

1. For an intricate dissection of the history and politics of "sensitive neighborhoods" policies in France, see Dikeç (2007).

2. Tyler (2018) has recently advanced a compelling critical dissection of some of the more problematic aspects of Goffman's framework in *Stigma*, not least its politics and some of the terminology Goffman used.

3. Wacquant's claim that territorial stigma is novel and distinctive has led to criticism. For example, Loyd and Bonds (2018) take issue with what they see as the "historical break" in Wacquant's conceptualization, arguing that territorial stigma is "neutralising" and leaves no room for an understanding of the historical continuities underpinning contemporary racial capitalism in the United States.

4. The book-length treatment of this estate is McKenzie's *Getting By* (2015), a stirring ethnographic study of St. Ann's that offers a fine-grained portrait of the lived experience of territorial stigmatization and class prejudice.

5. This has been partially demolished and radically transformed, not without dislocation and controversy, into a mixed-income development (combining public and condominium housing with commercial development).

6. Lees (2014, 928) has demonstrated that the repeated media categorization of Aylesbury as a sink estate was a crucial tactic in "branding both the community and its residents as deviant and untrustworthy and thus justified

paternalistic treatment of them," resulting in a massive regeneration project that has displaced many of those residents against their wishes.

7. The first appearance in a UK newspaper article was in the *Guardian* in 1982, when columnist Polly Toynbee (1982) said that the Tulse Hill estate in Brixton, London, "used to be a rock bottom sink estate."

8. Morton is now head of policy at the Centre for Policy Studies, a free-market think tank closely associated with the late 1970s rise to power of Margaret Thatcher.

9. For example, Knight (2014a) wrote a short piece for right-wing mouthpiece *Conservative Home* entitled "Britain's Sink Estates Can—and Must—Be Turned Around," stating: "Britain's most deprived housing estates are a time-bomb of social decay. Decades of neglect and ghettoisation have led to acute, entrenched social problems that cost billions to the public purse: gang warfare, knife crime, domestic violence, illiteracy, unemployment and child neglect."

CHAPTER 7. GHETTO BLASTING

1. They continue to do this in their response to Peach: "Peach argues that the major difference between ghettos and enclaves is that, in the former, nearly all members of the group concerned are 'forced' to live in the ghetto (a definition at odds with the OED's)" (Johnston, Poulsen, and Forrest 2010, 698). But that *Oxford English Dictionary* definition is of *segregation*, not ghetto, and the two are not the same.

2. I am exceptionally grateful to Troels Schultz Larsen and Kristian Nagel Delica for some informative correspondence about the Danish case.

References

Aalbers, Manuel. 2016. *The Financialization of Housing: A Political Economy Approach*. London: Routledge.

Acuto, Michel, Susan Parnell, and Karen Seto. 2018. "Building a Global Urban Science." *Nature Sustainability* 1 (1): 2–4.

Adamson, Morgan. 2019. "Internal Colony as Political Perspective: Counterinsurgency, Extraction, and Anticolonial Legacies of '68 in the United States." *Cultural Politics* 15 (3): 343–57.

Aiello, Daniela, Lisa Bates, Terra Graziani, Christopher Herring, Manissa Maharawal, Erin McElroy, Pamela Phan, and Gretchen Purser. 2018. "Eviction Lab Misses the Mark." *Shelterforce*, August 22. https://shelterforce.org/2018/08/22/eviction-lab-misses-the-mark/.

Albon, Robert P., and David C. Stafford. 1990. "Rent Control and Housing Maintenance." *Urban Studies* 27 (3): 233–40.

Alexander, Victoria. 2018. "Heteronomy in the Arts Field: State Funding and British Arts Organizations." *British Journal of Sociology* 69 (1): 23–43.

Allen, Irving Lewis. 1995. *The City in Slang: New York Life and Popular Speech*. New York: Oxford University Press.

Alonso, William. 1964. *Location and Land Use*. Cambridge, MA: Harvard University Press.

Alston, Richard M., J. R. Kearl, and Michael B. Vaughan. 1992. "Is There a Consensus among Economists in the 1990s?" *American Economic Review* 82: 203–9.

Ambrosius, Joshua D., John I. Gilderbloom, William J. Steele, Wesley L. Meares, and Dennis Keating. 2015. "Forty Years of Rent Control: Reexamining New Jersey's Moderate Local Policies after the Great Recession." *Cities* 49: 121–33.

Anas, Alex. 1997. "Rent Control with Matching Economies: A Model of European Housing Market Regulation." *Journal of Real Estate Finance and Economics* 15: 111–37.

Andersson, Roger, and Sako Musterd. 2005. "Area-Based Policies: A Critical Appraisal." *Tijdschrift voor Economische en Sociale Geografie* 96: 377–89.

Angelo, Hillary, and Kian Goh. 2020. "Out in Space: Difference and Abstraction in Planetary Urbanization." *International Journal of Urban and Regional Research* (early view, May 8). onlinelibrary.wiley.com/doi/abs/10.1111/1468-2427.12911.

Anguelovski, Isabelle. 2015. "From Toxic Sites to Parks as (Green) LULUs? New Challenges of Inequity, Privilege, Gentrification, and Exclusion for Urban Environmental Justice." *Journal of Planning Literature* 31 (1): 23–36.

Annunziata, Sandra, and Clara Rivas-Alonso. 2018. "Resisting Gentrification." In *The Handbook of Gentrification Studies*, edited by Loretta Lees with Martin Phillips, 393–412. London: Edward Elgar.

Anthony, Andrew. 2011. "Review of 'Hood Rat' by Gavin Knight." *Guardian*, July 10.

Arbaci, Sonia. 2019. *Paradoxes of Segregation: Housing Systems, Welfare Regimes and Ethnic Residential Change in Southern European Cities.* Oxford: Wiley-Blackwell.

Arnott, Richard. 1995. "Time for Revisionism on Rent Control?" *Journal of Economic Perspectives* 9 (1): 99–120.

———. 2003. "Tenancy Rent Control." *Swedish Economic Policy Review* 10: 89–121.

Arnott, Richard, and Masahiro Igarashi. 2000. "Rent Control, Mismatch Costs and Search Efficiency." *Regional Science and Urban Economics* 30 (3): 249–88.

Arthurson, Kathy, Michael Darcy, and Dallas Rogers. 2014. "Televised Territorial Stigma: How Social Housing Tenants Experience the Fictional Media Representation of Estates in Australia." *Environment and Planning A* 46 (6): 1334–50.

Atkinson, Rowland, and Gary Bridge. 2005. *Gentrification in a Global Context: The New Urban Colonialism.* London: Routledge.

August, Martine. 2014. "Challenging the Rhetoric of Stigmatization: the Benefits of Concentrated Poverty in Toronto's Regent Park." *Environment and Planning A* 46 (6): 1317–33.

Autor, David H., Christopher J. Palmer, and Parag A. Pathak. 2014. "Housing Market Spillovers: Evidence from the End of Rent Control in Cambridge, Massachusetts." *Journal of Political Economy* 122 (3): 661–717.

Auyero, Javier. 2012. *Patients of the State*. Durham, NC: Duke University Press.

Bacque, Marie-Helene, Gary Bridge, Michaela Benson, Tim Butler, Eric Charmes, Yankel Fijalkow, Emma Jackson, Lydie Launay, and Stephanie Vermeersch. 2015. *The Middle Classes and the City: A Study of Paris and London*. Basingstoke: Palgrave Macmillan.

Badger, Emily, and Quoctrung Bui. 2018. "Detailed Maps Show How Neighborhoods Shape Children for Life." *New York Times*, October 1.

Baldwin, James. 1972. *No Name in the Street*. New York: Doubleday.

Ball, Philip. 2014. "Gentrification Is a Natural Evolution." *Guardian*, November 19.

Barrett, Liz Cox. 2004. "Deadline Looming? Taxi!" *Columbia Journalism Review* (July 24). https://archives.cjr.org/politics/deadline_looming_taxi.php.

Basu, Kaushik, and Patrick M. Emerson. 2003. "Efficiency Pricing, Tenancy Rent Control and Monopolistic Landlords." *Economica* 70 (278): 223–32.

Battersby, Jane. 2011. "Urban Food Insecurity in Cape Town, South Africa: An Alternative Approach to Food Access." *Development Southern Africa* 28 (4): 545–61.

Bauder, Harold. 2002. "Neighbourhood Effects and Cultural Exclusion." *Urban Studies* 39 (1): 85–93.

Beauregard, Robert. 1993. *Voices of Decline: The Postwar Fate of U.S. Cities*. Oxford: Blackwell.

Benach, Nuria, and Abel Albet. 2018. "Gentrification and the Urban Struggle: Neil Smith and Beyond." In *Gentrification as a Global Strategy: Neil Smith and Beyond*, edited by Abel Albet and Nuria Benach, 282–96. London: Routledge.

Bernt, Matthias. 2016. "Very Particular, or Rather Universal? Gentrification through the Lenses of Ghertner and López-Morales." *CITY* 20 (4): 637–44.

Berube, Alan. 2005. *Mixed Communities in England: A US Perspective on Evidence and Policy Prospects*. York: Joseph Rowntree Foundation.

Biglieri, Samantha, Lorenzo De Vidovich, and Roger Keil. 2020. "City as the Core of Contagion? Repositioning COVID-19 at the Social and Spatial Periphery of Urban Society." *Cities and Health* (July 28). www.tandfonline.com/doi/full/10.1080/23748834.2020.1788320.

Blatman-Thomas, Naama, and Libby Porter. 2019. "Placing Property: Theorizing the Urban from Settler Colonial Cities." *International Journal of Urban and Regional Research* 43 (1): 30–45.

Blomley, Nicholas. 2004. *Unsettling the City: Urban Land and the Politics of Property*. London: Routledge.

Boateng, Paul. 2020. "1987 Maiden Speech in the House of Commons." January 2. www.ukpol.co.uk/paul-boateng-1987-maiden-speech-in-the-house-of-commons/.

Boddy, Martin. 2007. "Designer Neighbourhoods: New-Build Residential Development in Non-metropolitan UK Cities—the Case of Bristol." *Environment and Planning A* 39: 86–105.

Bonneval, Loïc. 2019. "Does Rent Control Prevent Investment in Real Estate?" *Metropolitics*, February 8. www.metropolitiques.eu/Does-Rent-Control -Prevent-Investment-in-Real-Estate.html.

Bourdieu, Pierre. 1988. *Homo Academicus*. Stanford, CA: Stanford University Press.

———. 1991. *Language and Symbolic Power*. Cambridge, UK: Polity Press.

———. 1993. *The Field of Cultural Production*. Cambridge, UK: Polity Press.

———. 1996a. *The Rules of Art: The Genesis and Structure of the Literary Field*. Stanford, CA: Stanford University Press.

———. 1996b. "On the Family as a Realized Category." *Theory Culture & Society* 13 (3): 19–26.

———. (2001) 2004. *Science of Science and Reflexivity*. Cambridge, UK: Polity Press.

Bourgois, Phillipe. 2003. *In Search of Respect: Selling Crack in El Barrio*. 2nd ed. Cambridge, UK: Cambridge University Press.

Bourne, Ryan. 2014. *The Flaws in Rent Ceilings*. London: Institute of Economic Affairs.

Bourne, Ryan, and Jasmine Stone. 2014. Interview by Matt Frei. *Channel 4 News*, December 19. http://t.co/ZLzoiHp2Su.

Boys Smith, Nicholas, and Alex Morton. 2013. *Create Streets, Not Just Multi-Storey Estates* www.policyexchange.org.uk/images/publications/create %20streets.pdf.

Brattbakk, Ingar, and Thorbjorn Hansen. 2004. "Post-war Large Housing Estates in Norway: Well-Kept Residential Areas Still Stigmatised?" *Journal of Housing and the Built Environment* 19: 311–32.

Brenner, Neil, ed. 2014. *Imposions/Explosions: Towards a Study of Planetary Urbanization*. Berlin: Jovis.

———. 2018. "Debating Planetary Urbanization: Towards an Engaged Pluralism." *Environment and Planning D: Society and Space* 36 (3): 570–90.

Brenner, Neil, Peter Marcuse, and Margit Mayer. 2009. In "Cities for People, Not for Profit," special issue, *CITY* 13 (2–3): 176–84.

Brenner, Neil, Jamie Peck, and Nik Theodore. 2010. "Variegated Neoliberalization: Geographies, Modalities, Pathways." *Global Networks* 10 (2): 182–222.

Brenner, Neil, and Christian Schmid. 2015. "Towards a New Epistemology of the Urban?" *CITY* 19 (2–3): 151–82.

Brenner, Neil, and Nik Theodore. 2002. "Cities and the Geographies of 'Actually Existing Neoliberalism.'" *Antipode* 34: 349–79.

Briggs, Xavier de Sousa, Susan Popkin, and John Goering. 2010. *Moving to Opportunity: The Story of an American Experiment to Fight Ghetto Poverty.* New York: Oxford University Press.

Brummet, Quentin, and Davin Reed. 2019. "The Effects of Gentrification on the Well-Being and Opportunity of Original Resident Adults and Children." Federal Reserve Bank of Philadelphia Working Paper No. 19-30. https://papers.ssrn.com/sol3/papers.cfm?abstract_id=3421581.

Burawoy, Michael. 2017. "On Desmond: The Limits of Spontaneous Sociology." *Theory and Society* 46: 261–84.

Butler, Alice. 2020a. "Toxic Toxteth: Understanding Press Stigmatization of Toxteth during the 1981 Uprising." *Journalism* 21 (4): 541–56.

———. 2020b. "Foundational Stigma: Place-Based Stigma in the Age before Advanced Marginality." *British Journal of Sociology* 71 (1): 140–52.

Butler, Tim. 1997. *Gentrification and the Middle Classes.* Aldershot: Ashgate.

Butler, Tim, and Garry Robson. 2003. *London Calling: The Middle Classes and the Global City.* London: Berg.

Calhoun, John B. 1962. "Population Density and Social Pathology." *Scientific American*, February, 139–48.

Cameron, David. 2016. "I Will Bulldoze Sink Estates." *Sunday Times*, January 10.

Campkin, Ben. 2013. *Remaking London: Decline and Regeneration in Urban Culture.* London: I. B. Tauris.

Carlyon, Tristan. 2013. "Food for Thought: Applying House Price Inflation to Grocery Prices." Shelter, February. http://england.shelter.org.uk/professional_resources/policy_and_research/policy_library/policy_library_folder/food_for_thought.

Causa Justa/Just Cause. 2018. *Development without Displacement: Resisting Gentrification in the San Francisco Bay Area.* https://cjjc.org/wp-content/uploads/2015/11/development-without-displacement.pdf.

Chalmers, Robert. 2017. "Is Molenbeek Really a No-Go Zone?" *GQ Magazine*, June 21.

Chetty, Raj, John Friedman, Nathaniel Hendren, Maggie R. Jones, and Sonya R. Porter. 2018a. "The Opportunity Atlas: Mapping the Childhood Roots of Social Mobility." National Bureau of Economic Research Working Paper No. 25147.

———. 2018b. *The Opportunity Atlas: Mapping the Childhood Roots of Social Mobility—Executive Summary.* https://opportunityinsights.org/wp-content/uploads/2018/10/atlas_summary.pdf.

Christophers, Brett. 2018. *The New Enclosure: The Appropriation of Public Land in Neoliberal Britain.* London: Verso.

City Region Deal. n.d. Home page. Edinburgh & South East Scotland. http://esescityregiondeal.org.uk/about-us.

———. 2018. "What's Been Happening with the City Region Deal since the Official Signing Three Months Ago?" Edinburgh & South East Scotland, November 8. http://esescityregiondeal.org.uk/new-blog/2018/11/8/whats-been-happening -with-the-city-region-deal-since-the-official-signing-three-months-ago.

Clark, Eric. 1987. *The Rent Gap and Urban Change: Case Studies in Malmö 1860–1985*. Lund: Lund University Press.

———. 2011. "Dispossession, Displacement and Human Security." Paper presented at the International Conference on Industrial Transformation, Urbanization, and Human Security in the Asia Pacific, Taiwan, January 14–15.

Clemens, Tom, Chris Dibben, Jamie Pearce, and Niamh Shortt. 2020. "Neighbourhood Tobacco Supply and Individual Maternal Smoking During Pregnancy: A Fixed-Effects Longitudinal Analysis Using Routine Data." *Tobacco Control* 29: 7–14.

Cohen, G. A. 1994. "Back to Socialist Basics." *New Left Review* 1 (207): 3–16.

Cohen, Roger. 2016. "The Islamic State of Molenbeek." *New York Times*, April 16.

Coulthard, Glen S. 2014. *Red Skin, White Masks. Rejecting the Colonial Politics of Recognition*. Minneapolis: University of Minnesota Press.

Cowen, Deborah, and Nemoy Lewis. 2018. "Revanchism and the Racial State: Ferguson as 'Internal Colony.'" In *Gentrification as a Global Strategy: Neil Smith and Beyond*, edited by Abel Albet and Nuria Benach, 269–79. London: Routledge.

Crookes, Lee. 2017. "The 'Not So Good', the 'Bad' and the 'Ugly': Scripting the 'Badlands' of Housing Market Renewal." In *Negative Neighbourhood Reputation and Place Attachment: The Production and Contestation of Territorial Stigma*, edited by Paul Kirkness and Andreas Tije-Dra, 81–101. London: Routledge.

Crossley, Stephen. 2017. *In Their Place: The Imagined Geographies of Poverty*. London: Pluto Press.

Crump, Jeff. 2002. "Deconcentration by Demolition: Public Housing, Poverty and Urban Policy." *Environment and Planning D: Society and Space* 20: 581–96.

Cupples, Julie. 2019. "Urban Research and the Pluriverse: Analytical and Political Lesson from Scholarship in Varied Margins." In *Producing and Contesting Urban Marginality: Interdisciplinary and Comparative Dialogues*, edited by Julie Cupples and Tom Slater, 205–26. Basingstoke: Rowman and Littlefield.

Cupples, Julie, and Kevin Glynn. 2018. *Shifting Nicaraguan Mediascapes: Authoritarianism and the Struggle for Social Justice*. New York: Springer.

Curran, Winifred. 2018. *Gender and Gentrification*. New York: Routledge.

Danewid, Ida. 2020. "The Fire This Time: Grenfell, Racial Capitalism and the Urbanisation of Empire." *European Journal of International Relations* 26 (1): 289–313.

Davidson, Justin. 2014. "Is Gentrification All Bad?" *New York Magazine*, February 2. http://nymag.com/news/features/gentrification-2014-2/.

Davidson, Mark, and Loretta Lees. 2005. "New-Build 'Gentrification' and London's Riverside Renaissance." *Environment and Planning A* 37 (7): 1165–90.

Davies, Will. 2016. *The Happiness Industry*. London: Verso.

DeFilippis, James. 2004. *Unmaking Goliath: Community Control in the Face of Global Capital*. New York: Routledge.

DeFilippis, James, and James Fraser. 2010. "Why Do We Want Mixed-Income Housing and Neighbourhoods?" In *Critical Urban Studies: New Directions*, edited by Jonathan Davies and David Imbroscio, 135–49. Albany: State University of New York Press.

Derickson, Kate Driscoll. 2016. "Resilience Is Not Enough." *CITY* 20 (1): 161–66.

———. 2018. "Masters of the Universe." *Environment and Planning D: Society and Space* 36 (3): 556–62.

Derudder, Ben, and Michiel van Meeteren. 2019. "Engaging with 'Urban Science.'" *Urban Geography* 40 (4): 555–64.

Desmond, Matthew. 2012. "Eviction and the Reproduction of Urban Poverty." *American Journal of Sociology* 118 (1): 88–133.

———. 2016. *Evicted: Poverty and Profit in the American City*. London: Penguin.

DeVerteuil, Geoffrey. 2011. "Evidence of Gentrification-Induced Displacement among Social Services in London and Los Angeles." *Urban Studies* 48 (8): 1563–80.

DeVerteuil, Geoffrey, and Oleg Golubchikov. 2016. "Can Resilience Be Redeemed? Resilience as a Metaphor for Change, Not against Change." *CITY* 20 (1): 143–51.

Diamond, Rebecca, Timothy McQuade, and Franklin Qian. 2019. "The Effects of Rent Control Expansion on Tenants, Landlords, and Inequality: Evidence from San Francisco." National Bureau of Economic Research Working Paper No. 24181.

Dikec, Mustafa. 2007. *Badlands of the Republic: Space, Politics and Urban Policy*. Oxford: Wiley-Blackwell.

Diprose, Kristina. 2015. "Resilience Is Futile." *Soundings* 58 (5): 44–56.

Dorling, Danny. 2014. *All That Is Solid: The Great Housing Disaster*. London: Penguin.

———. 2016. "Has Brexit Burst the British Housing Bubble?" *New Statesman*, October 21. www.newstatesman.com/politics/uk/2016/10/has-brexit-burst-british-housing-bubble.

Dreier, Peter. 2006. "Federal Housing Subsidies: Who Benefits and Why?" In *A Right to Housing: Foundation for a New Social Agenda*, edited by Rachel G. Bratt, Michael E. Stone, and Chester Hartman, 105–38. Philadelphia: Temple University Press.

Duany, Andres. 2001. "Three Cheers for Gentrification." *American Enterprise Magazine*, April, 38–39.

Dumbledon, Bob. 2006. *'Help Us, Somebody': The Demolition of the Elderly*. London: London Press.

Eddo-Lodge, Reni. 2011. "Twitter Didn't Fuel the Tottenham Riot." *Guardian*, August 8.

Edinburgh Futures Institute. n.d. Home page. https://efi.ed.ac.uk/.

Edmonds, Penelope. 2010. *Urbanizing Frontiers: Indigenous Peoples and Settlers in 19th-Century Pacific Rim Cities*. Vancouver: University of British Columbia Press.

Eksner, H. Julia. 2013. "Revisiting the 'Ghetto' in the New Berlin Republic: Immigrant Youths, Territorial Stigmatisation and the Devaluation of Local Educational Capital, 1999–2010." *Social Anthropology* 21 (3): 336–55.

Engels, Benno. 1994. "Capital Flows, Redlining and Gentrification: The Pattern of Mortgage Lending and Social Change in Glebe, Sydney, 1960–1984." *International Journal of Urban and Regional Research* 18 (4): 628–57.

Engels, Friedrich. 1845. *The Condition of the Working Class in England*. London: Penguin Classics.

———. 1872. *The Housing Question*. www.marxists.org/archive/marx/works/1872/housing-question/index.htm.

Ernstson, Henrik. 2014. "Stop Calling Me RESILIENT: Comment on Tom Slater's Blog Post 'The Resilience of Neoliberal Urbanism.'" www.rhizomia.net/2014/02/comment-on-tom-slaters-blog-post.html.

Eubanks, Virginia. 2017. *Automating Inequality: How High-Tech Tools Profile, Police, and Punish the Poor*. New York: St. Martin's Press.

Fainstein, Susan S. 2010. *The Just City*. Ithaca, NY: Cornell University Press.

Fairbanks, Eve. 2018. "Dry, the Beloved Country." *Huffington Post*, April 19. https://highline.huffingtonpost.com/articles/en/cape-town-drought/.

Fernandez, Rodrigo, and Manuel Aalbers. 2016. "Financialization and Housing: Between Globalization and Varieties of Capitalism." *Competition and Change* 20 (2): 71–88.

Fields, Desiree. 2017. "Urban Struggles with Financialization." *Geography Compass* 11 (11): e12334.

Finney, Nissa, and Ludi Simpson. 2009. *Sleepwalking to Segregation: Challenging Myths about Race and Migration*. Bristol: Policy Press.

Florida, Richard. 2017. *The New Urban Crisis*. London: One World.

Forrest, Ray, and Alan Murie. 1988. *Selling the Welfare State: The Privatisation of Public Housing*. London: Routledge.

Freeman, Lance. 2005. "Displacement or Succession? Residential Mobility in Gentrifying Neighborhoods." *Urban Affairs Review* 40: 463–91.

Freeman, Lance, and Frank Braconi. 2004. "Gentrification and Displacement: New York City in the 1990s." *Journal of the American Planning Association* 70 (1): 39–52.

Fried, Marc. 1966. "Grieving for a Lost Home: Psychological Costs of Relocation." In *Urban Renewal: The Record and the Controversy*, edited by James Q. Wilson, 359–79. Cambridge, MA: MIT Press.

Fullilove, Mindy T. 2004. *Root Shock: How Tearing Up City Neighborhoods Hurts America and What We Can Do about It*. New York: One World.

Galster, George, Roger Andersson, Sako Musterd, and T. M. Kauppinen. 2008. "Does Neighborhood Income Mix Affect Earnings of Adults? New Evidence from Sweden." *Journal of Urban Economics* 63: 858–70.

Garbin, David, and Gareth Millington. 2012. "Territorial Stigma and the Politics of Resistance in a Parisian Banlieue: La Courneuve and Beyond." *Urban Studies* 49 (10): 2067–83.

García-Lamarca, Melissa, and Maria Kaika. 2016. "'Mortgaged Lives': The Biopolitics of Debt and Housing Financialisation." *Transactions of the Institute of British Geographers* 41 (3): 313–27.

Ghertner, D. Asher. 2014. "India's Urban Revolution: Geographies of Displacement beyond Gentrification." *Environment and Planning A* 46 (7): 1554–71.

———. 2015. "Why Gentrification Theory Fails in 'Much of the World.'" *CITY* 19 (4): 552–63.

Gilbert, Alan. 2003. *Rental Housing—An Essential Option for the Urban Poor in Developing Countries*. Nairobi: UN-Habitat.

Gilderbloom, John I., and Lin Ye. 2007. "Thirty Years of Rent Control: A Survey of New Jersey Cities." *Journal of Urban Affairs* 29 (2): 207–20.

Gilroy, Paul. 2009. "The Death of Multiculturalism?" Paper presented to Parallel Lives Conference, London School of Economics, May 20. http://mcincrisis.podomatic.com/entry/index/2009-05-20T10_43_44-07_00.

Glaeser, Edward L. 2002. "Does Rent Control Reduce Segregation?" Harvard Institute of Economic Research Discussion Paper No. 1985, Harvard University, Cambridge, MA.

———. 2011. *Triumph of the City: How Our Greatest Invention Makes Us Richer, Smarter, Greener, Healthier, and Happier*. New York: Penguin.

———. 2013. "Ease Housing Regulation to Increase Supply." *New York Times*, October 16.

Glaeser, Edward L., and Erzo F. P. Luttmer. 2003. "The Misallocation of Housing under Rent Control." *American Economic Review* 93 (4): 1027–46.

Glasgow City Council. 2016a. "Glasgow Places People and Communities at Heart of Resilience Strategy." *Glasgow City Council News Archives*, September 1. https://glasgow.gov.uk/article/19981/Glasgow-places-people-and-communities-at-heart-of-resilience-strategy

———. 2016b. "Our Resilient Glasgow." https://www.glasgow.gov.uk/resilience.

Glass, Ruth. 1964. "Introduction: Aspects of Change." In *London: Aspects of Change*, edited by Centre for Urban Studies, xiii–xlii. London: MacKibbon and Kee.

Glasze, Georg, Robert Putz, Melina Germes, Henning Schirmel, and Adam Brailich. 2012. "'The Same But Not the Same': The Discursive Constitution of

Large Housing Estates in Germany, France and Poland." *Urban Geography* 33 (8): 1192–211.

Glynn, Sarah. 2008. "Soft-Selling Gentrification?" *Urban Research & Practice* 1: 164–80.

Goering, John. 2003. "Comments on Future Research and Housing Policy." In *Choosing a Better Life: Evaluating the Moving to Opportunity Social Experiment*, edited by John Goering and Judith Feins, 383–407. Washington, DC: Urban Institute Press.

Goetz, Edward. 2003. *Clearing the Way: Deconcentrating the Poor in Urban America*. Washington, DC: Urban Institute Press.

———. 2013. "The Audacity of HOPE VI: Discourse and the Dismantling of Public Housing." *Cities* 35: 342–48.

Goffman, Erving. 1963. *Stigma: Notes on the Management of Spoiled Identity.* New York: Simon & Schuster.

Graham, Stephen. 2010. *Cities under Siege: The New Military Urbanism.* New York: Verso.

Gray, Neil. 2018. "Introduction: Rent Unrest; From the 1915 Rent Strikes to Contemporary Housing Struggles." In *Rent and Its Discontents: A Century of Housing Struggle*, edited by Neil Gray, xvii–xxxix. London: Rowman and Littlefield.

Gray, Neil, and Gerry Mooney. 2011. "Glasgow's New Urban Frontier: 'Civilising' the Population of 'Glasgow East.'" *CITY* 15: 1–24.

Greenberg, Michael, and Justin Hollander. 2006. "Neighborhood Stigma Twenty Years Later: Revisiting Superfund Sites in Suburban New Jersey." *Appraisal Journal* 74 (2): 161–73.

Grier, George, and Eunice Grier. 1978. *Urban Displacement: A Reconnaissance.* Washington, DC: US Department of Housing and Urban Development.

Grosfoguel, Ramon. 2007. "The Epistemic Decolonial Turn." *Cultural Studies* 21 (2–3): 211–23.

Gross, Matthias, and Linsey McGoey, eds. 2015. *The Routledge International Handbook of Ignorance Studies.* London: Routledge.

Gunderson, Lance, and Crawford Holling. 2002. *Panarchy: Understanding Tranformations in Human and Natural Systems.* Washington, DC: Island Press.

Gurian, Craig. 2003. "Let Them Rent Cake: George Pataki, Market Ideology, and the Attempt to Dismantle Rent Regulation in New York." *Fordham Urban Law Journal* 31 (2): 339–411.

Guy, Christian. 2013. "Two Nations, One Mission." *Total Politics*, February.

Hackner, Jonas, and Sten Nyberg. 2000. "Rent Control and Prices of Owner-Occupied Housing." *Scandinavian Journal of Economics* 102(2): 311–24.

Hackworth, Jason. 2006. *The Neoliberal City.* Ithaca, NY: Cornell University Press.

Hammel, Daniel. 1999. "Re-establishing the Rent Gap: An Alternative View of Capitalised Land Rent." *Urban Studies* 36: 1283–93.

———. 2006. "Public Housing Chicago-Style: Transformation or Elimination?" In *Chicago's Geographies: Metropolis for the 21st Century*, edited by Richard P. Greene, 172–88. Washington, DC: Association of American Geographers.

Hamnett, Chris. 1991. "The Blind Men and the Elephant: The Explanation of Gentrification." *Transactions of the Institute of British Geographers* 17: 173–89.

———. 2008. "The Regeneration Game." *Guardian*, June 11.

———. 2010. "Moving the Poor out of Central London? The Implications of the Coalition Government 2010 Cuts to Housing Benefits." *Environment and Planning A* 42 (12): 2809–19.

Hampson, Rick. 2005. "Studies: Gentrification a Boost for Everyone." *USA Today*, April 20.

Hanley, Lynsey. 2007. *Estates: An Intimate History*. London: Granta.

Hart, Deborah. 1988. "Political Manipulation of Urban Space: The Razing of District Six, Cape Town." *Urban Geography* 9 (6): 603–28.

Hartman, Chester. 1974. *Yerba Buena: Land Grab and Community Resistance in San Francisco*. San Francisco: Glebe Books.

———. 1984. "The Right to Stay Put." In *Land Reform, American Style*, edited by Charles Geisler and Frank Popper, 302–18. Totowa, NJ: Rowman and Allanheld.

Hartman, Chester, Dennis Keating, and Richard LeGates. 1982. *Displacement: How to Fight It*. Washington, DC: National Housing Law Project.

Hartman, Chester, and David Robinson. 2003. "Evictions: The Hidden Housing Problem. *Housing Policy Debate* 14: 461–501.

Harvey, David. 1973. *Social Justice and the City*. London: Edward Arnold.

———. 1978. "The Urban Process under Capitalism: A Framework for Analysis." *International Journal of Urban and Regional Research* 2: 101–31.

———. 1982. *The Limits to Capital*. Oxford: Blackwell.

———. 1989. "From Managerialism to Entrepreneurialism: The Transformation of Urban Governance in Late Capitalism." *Geografiska Annaler B* 71: 3–17.

———. 2002. "Memories and Desires." In *Geographical Voices: Fourteen Autobiographical Essays*, edited by Peter Gould and Forrest R. Pitts, 149–88. Syracuse, NY: Syracuse University Press.

———. 2010. *The Enigma of Capital and the Crises of Capitalism*. London: Profile Books.

———. 2014. *Seventeen Contradictions and the End of Capitalism*. London: Profile Books.

Hayek, Friedrich A., Milton Friedman, George J. Stigler, Bertrand de Jouvenel, F. W. Paish, Sven Rydenfelt, and F. G. Pennance. 1972. *Verdict on Rent Control*. London: Institute of Economic Affairs.

Heffley, Dennis. 1998. "Landlords, Tenants and the Public Sector in a Spatial Equilibrium Model of Rent Control." *Regional Science and Urban Economics* 28 (6): 745–72.

Herd, Mike. 2014. "What Makes Your City So Special?" *Guardian*, January 27.

Hills, John. 2007. *Ends and Means: The Future Role of Social Housing in England*. London School of Economics, Centre for the Analysis of Social Exclusion.

Ho, Lok Sang. 1992. "Rent Control: Its Rationale and Effects." *Urban Studies* 29 (7): 1183–90.

Hodkinson, Stuart. 2012. "The New Urban Enclosures." *CITY* 16 (5): 500–18.

———. 2019. *Safe as Houses: Private Greed, Political Negligence and Housing Policy After Grenfell*. Manchester: Manchester University Press.

Hoffmann -Schroeder, Anne Sofie. 2019. "Young Women Fight the Government's Ghetto List." *Deutsche Welle (DW)*, December 30. www.dw.com/en/denmark-young-women-fight-the-governments-ghetto-list/a-51833223.

Holling, Crawford S. 1973. "Resilience and Stability of Ecological Systems." *Annual Review of Ecology and Systematics* 4: 1–23.

Hoyt, Homer. 1933. *One Hundred Years of Land Values in Chicago*. Chicago: University of Chicago Press.

Hua, Dominique. 2018. "Five Rent Strikes Which Changed the Game." *Red Pepper*, January 30. www.redpepper.org.uk/five-rent-strikes-which-changed-the-game/.

Hunt, Tristram. 2009. *Marx's General: The Revolutionary Life of Friedrich Engels*. London: Holt McDougal.

Hutchinson, Brian. 2015. "'Disabled' Undercover Cop Waits for Robbers in Vancouver But Finds Only Kindness." *National Post*, July 16.

Hyötyläinen, Mika. 2019. "Divided by Policy: Urban Inequality in Finland." PhD thesis, University of Helsinki.

Imbroscio, David. 2008. "Challenging the Dispersal Consensus in American Housing Policy Research." *Journal of Urban Affairs* 30 (2): 111–30.

Imrie, Rob. 2004. "Urban Geography, Relevance, and Resistance to the 'Policy Turn'." *Urban Geography* 25: 697–708.

International Expert Panel (IEP). 2018. *Science and the Future of Cities: A Report on the Global State of the Urban Science-Policy Interface*. www.nature.com/documents/Science_and_the_future_of_cites.pdf.

Janoschka, Michael, and Jorge Sequera. 2016. "Gentrification in Latin America: Addressing the Politics and Geographies of Displacement." *Urban Geography* 37 (8): 1175–94.

Jeffries, Stuart. 2006. "On Your Marx." *Guardian*, February 4. www.guardian.co.uk/news/2006/feb/04/mainsection.stuartjeffries.

Jenkins, Blair. 2009. "Rent Control: Do Economists Agree?" *Econ Journal Watch* 6: 73–112.

Jensen, Steffan. 2008. *Gangs, Politics and Dignity in Cape Town*. Chicago: University of Chicago Press.

Jensen, Sune Qvotrup, and Ann-Dorte Christensen. 2012. "Territorial Stigmatization and Local Belonging: A Study of the Danish Neighbourhood Aalborg East." *CITY* 16 (1–2): 74–92.

Johansson, Thomas, and Rita Olofsson. 2011. "The Art of Becoming 'Swedish': Immigrant Youth, School Careers and Life Plans." *Ethnicities* 11 (2): 184–201.

Johnston, Ron, James Forrest, and Mike Poulsen. 2002. "Are There Ethnic Enclaves/Ghettos in English Cities?" *Urban Studies* 39 (4): 591–618.

Johnston, Ron, Mike Poulsen, and James Forrest. 2005. "On the Measurement and Meaning of Residential Segregation: A Response to Simpson." *Urban Studies* 42 (7): 1221–7.

———. 2010. "Moving on from Indices, Refocusing on Mix: On Measuring and Understanding Ethnic Patterns of Residential Segregation." *Journal of Ethnic and Migration Studies* 36 (4): 697–706.

Jokela, Markus. 2014. "Are Neighborhood Health Associations Causal? A 10-Year Prospective Cohort Study with Repeated Measurements." *American Journal of Epidemiology* 180 (8): 776–84.

Jones, David. 2015. "Europe's Crucible of Terror." *Daily Mail*, November 16.

Kaika, Maria. 2017. "'Don't Call Me Resilient Again!': The New Urban Agenda as Immunology . . . or . . . What Happens When Communities Refuse to Be Vaccinated with 'Smart Cities' and Indicators." *Environment and Urbanization* 29 (1): 89–102.

Kallin, Hamish. 2017. "Opening the Reputational Gap." In *Negative Neighbourhood Reputation and Place Attachment: The Production and Contestation of Territorial Stigma*, edited by Paul Kirkness and Andreas Tije-Dra, 102–18. London: Routledge.

———. 2018. "The State of Gentrification Has Always Been Extra-Economic." In *Gentrification as a Global Strategy: Neil Smith and Beyond*, edited by Nuria Benach and Abel Albet, 43–55. London: Routledge.

Kallin, Hamish, and Tom Slater. 2014. "Activating Territorial Stigma: Gentrifying Marginality on Edinburgh's Periphery." *Environment and Planning A* 46 (6): 1351–68.

———. 2018. "The Myths and Realities of Rent Control." In *Rent and Its Discontents: A Century of Housing Struggle*, edited by Neil Gray, 139–52. London: Rowman and Littlefield.

Katz, Cindi. 2004. *Growing up Global: Economic Restructuring and Children's Everyday Lives*. Minneapolis: University of Minnesota Press.

Keene, Danya E., and Mark Padilla. 2010. "Race, Class, and the Stigma of Place: Moving to 'Opportunity' in Eastern Iowa." *Health & Place* 16 (6): 1216–23.

———. 2014. "Spatial Stigma and Health Inequality." *Critical Public Health* 24 (4): 392–404.

Keene, Danya E., and Erin Ruel. 2013. "'Everyone Called Me Grandma': Public Housing Demolition and Relocation among Older Adults in Atlanta." *Cities* 35: 359–64.

Keil, Roger. 2014. "Resilience: Not a Cuddly Kitten, More Like a Beastly Cat." *Global Suburbanisms* (blog), February 24. https://suburbs.info.yorku.ca /2014/02/resilience-not-a-cuddly-kitten-more-like-a-beastly-cat/.

Kern, Clifford R. 1981. "Upper-Income Renaissance in the City: Its Sources and Implications for the City's Future." *Journal of Urban Economics* 9: 106–24.

Kirkness, Paul. 2014. "The Cités Strike Back: Restive Responses to Territorial Taint in the French Banlieues." *Environment and Planning A* 46 (6): 1281–96.

Kirkness, Paul, and Andreas Tije-Dra, eds. 2017. *Negative Neighbourhood Reputation and Place Attachment: The Production and Contestation of Territorial Stigma*. London: Routledge.

Kiviat, Barbara. 2008. "Gentrification: Not Ousting the Poor?" *Time*, June 29.

Klein, Naomi. 2007. *The Shock Doctrine: The Rise of Disaster Capitalism*. New York: Metropolitan.

Knight, Gavin. 2014a. "Britain's Sink Estates Can—and Must—Be Turned Around." *Conservative Home*, August 22. www.conservativehome.com /platform/2014/08/gavin-knight-britains-sink-estates-can-and-must-be -turned-around.html.

Knight, Gavin. 2014b. "The Estate We're In: Lessons from the Front Line." Policy Exchange. https://policyexchange.org.uk/wp-content/uploads/2016 /09/the-estate-were-in.pdf.

Korsgaard, Christine M. 1996. *Creating the Kingdom of Ends*. Cambridge, UK: Cambridge University Press.

Krijnen, Marieke. 2018a. "Beirut and the Creation of the Rent Gap." *Urban Geography* 39 (7): 1041–59.

Krijnen, Marieke. 2018b. "Gentrification and the Creation and Formation of Rent Gaps." *CITY* 22 (3): 437–46.

Krol, Robert, and Shirley Svorny. 2005. "The Effect of Rent Control on Commute Times." *Journal of Urban Economics* 58 (3): 421–36.

Krugman, Paul. 2000. "Reckonings: A Rent Affair." *New York Times*, June 7. www.nytimes.com/2000/06/07/opinion/reckonings-a-rent-affair.html

Kundnani, Arun. 2001. "From Oldham to Bradford: the Violence of the Violated." *Race and Class* 43 (2): 105–31.

Kutty, Nandinee. 1996. "The Impact of Rent Control on Housing Maintenance: A Dynamic Analysis Incorporating European and North American Rent Regulations." *Housing Studies* 11: 69–88.

Lansley, Stewart, and Joanna Mack. 2015. *Breadline Britain: The Rise of Mass Poverty*. London: One World.

Lapeyronnie, Didier. 2007. *Ghetto Urbain: Segregation, Violence, Pauvrete en France aujourd'hui*. Paris: Robert Laffont.

Larsen, Troels Schultz. 2018. "Advanced Marginality as a Comparative Research Strategy in Praxis: The Danish 'Grey Belt' in Conversation with the French 'Red Belt.'" *Urban Geography* 39 (8): 1131–51.

Larsen, Troels Schultz, and Kristian Nagel Delica. 2019. "The Production of Territorial Stigmatisation: A Conceptual Cartography." *CITY* 23 (4–5): 540–63.

Laska, Shirley Bradway, and Daphne Spain. 1980. *Back to the City: Issues in Neighborhood Renovation*. Oxford: Pergamon Press

Lawton, Philip. 2020. "Unbounding Gentrification Theory: Multidimensional Space, Networks and Relational Approaches." *Regional Studies* 54 (2): 268–79.

Leary, John Patrick. 2018. *Keywords: The New Language of Capitalism*. Chicago: Haymarket Books.

Lee, Monica M. 2020. "Covid-19: Agnotology, Inequality, and Leadership." *Human Resource Development International* 23 (4): 333–46.

Lees, Loretta. 2014. "The Urban Injustices of New Labour's 'New Urban Renewal': The Case of the Aylesbury Estate in London." *Antipode* 46 (4): 921–47.

Lees, Loretta, Hyun Bang Shin, and Ernesto Lopez-Morales, eds. 2015. *Global Gentrifications*. Bristol: Policy Press.

———. 2016. *Planetary Gentrification*. Cambridge, UK: Polity Press.

Lees, Loretta, Tom Slater, and Elvin Wyly, eds. 2008. *Gentrification*. New York: Routledge.

Lefebvre, Henri. (1970). 2003. *The Urban Revolution*. Minneapolis: University of Minnesota Press.

LeGates, Richard, and Chester Hartman. 1981. "Displacement." *Clearinghouse Review* 15 (July): 207–49.

Leitner, Helga, and Eric Sheppard. 2013. "Unbounding Critical Geographic Research on Cities: The 1990s and Beyond." *Urban Geography* 24 (6): 510–28.

Lemanski, Charlotte. 2014. "Hybrid Gentrification in South Africa: Theorising Across Southern and Northern Cities." *Urban Studies* 51 (14): 2943–60.

LeRoy, Stephen, and Jon Sonstelie. 1983. "Paradise Lost and Regained: Transportation Innovation, Income, and Residential Location." *Journal of Urban Economics* 13: 67–89.

Ley, David. 1996. *The New Middle Class and the Remaking of the Central City*. Oxford: Oxford University Press.

Lind, Hans. 2001. "Rent Regulation: A Conceptual and Comparative Analysis." *European Journal of Housing Policy* 1 (1): 41–57.

Lindbeck, Assar. 1971. *The Political Economy of the New Left*. New York: Harper & Row.

Link, Bruce, and Jo C. Phelan. 2001. "Conceptualizing Stigma." *Annual Review of Sociology* 27: 365–85.

Lipton, S. Gregory. 1977. "Evidence of Central City Revival." *Journal of the American Institute of Planners* 43: 136–47.

Liu, Ying, Shuangshuang Tang, Stan Geertman, Yanliu Lin, and Frank van Oort. 2017. "The Chain Effects of Property-Led Redevelopment in Shenzhen: Price-Shadowing and Indirect Displacement." *Cities* 67: 31–42.

Logan, John R., and Harvey L. Molotch. 2007. *Urban Fortunes: The Political Economy of Place, 20th Anniversary Edition*. Berkeley, CA: University of California Press.

López-Morales, Ernesto. 2010. "Real Estate Market, State Entrepreneurialism and Urban Policy in the Gentrification by Ground Rent Dispossession of Santiago de Chile." *Journal of Latin American Geography* 9 (1): 145–73.

———. 2011. "Gentrification by Ground Rent Dispossession: The Shadows Cast by Large Scale Urban Renewal in Santiago de Chile." *International Journal of Urban and Regional Research* 35 (2): 330–57.

———. 2016. "Assessing Exclusionary Displacement through Rent Gap Analysis in the High-Rise Redevelopment of Santiago, Chile." *Housing Studies* 31 (5): 540–59.

Loyd, Jenna, and Anne Bonds. 2018. "Where Do Black Lives Matter? Race, Stigma, and Place in Milwaukee, Wisconsin." *Sociological Review* 66 (4): 898–918.

Lupton, Ruth, and Crispian Fuller. 2009. "Mixed Communities: A New Approach to Spatially Concentrated Poverty in England." *International Journal of Urban and Regional Research* 33 (4): 1014–28.

MacKinnon, Danny, and Kate Driscoll Derickson. 2012. "From Resilience to Resourcefulness: A Critique of Resilience Policy and Activism." *Progress in Human Geography* 37 (2): 253–70.

MacLeod, Gordon. 2013. "New Urbanism/Smart Growth in the Scottish Highlands: Mobile Policies and Post-Politics in Local Development Planning." *Urban Studies* 50: 2196–221.

Madden, David, and Peter Marcuse. 2016. *In Defence of Housing*. London: Verso.

Maloutas, Thomas. 2009. "Urban Outcasts: A Contextualized Outlook on Advanced Marginality." *International Journal of Urban and Regional Research* 33 (3): 828–34.

———. 2011. "Contextual Diversity in Gentrification Research." *Critical Sociology* 38: 33–48.

Malpass, Peter. 2005. *Housing and the Welfare State: The Development of Housing Policy in Britain*. Basingstoke: Macmillan.

Manley, David, Maarten van Ham, and Joe Doherty. 2011. "Social Mixing as a Cure for Negative Neighbourhood Effects: Evidence-Based Policy or Urban Myth?" In *Mixed Communities: Gentrification by Stealth?*, edited by Gary Bridge, Tim Butler, and Loretta Lees, 151–68. Bristol: Policy Press.

Marcuse, Peter. 1985a. "Gentrification, Abandonment and Displacement: Connections, Causes and Policy Responses in New York City." *Journal of Urban and Contemporary Law* 28: 195–240.

———. 1985b. "To Control Gentrification: Anti-displacement Zoning and Planning for Stable Residential Districts." *Review of Law and Social Change* 13: 931–45.

———. 1986. "Abandonment, Gentrification and Displacement: The Linkages in New York City." In *Gentrification of the City*, edited by Neil Smith and Peter Williams, 153–77. London: Unwin Hyman.

Marris, Peter. 1986. *Loss and Change*. Rev. ed. London: Routledge.

Marshall, Aarian. 2018. "Cities Are Watching You—Urban Sciences Graduates Watch Back." *Wired*, June 25. www.wired.com/story/mit-urban-sciences -program/.

Mason, Joshua W. 2019. "Considerations on Rent Control." Testimony before Jersey City Council on Rent Control, November 13. https://jwmason.org /slackwire/considerations-on-rent-control/.

Mattern, Shannon. 2018. "Databodies in Codespace." *Places Journal* (April). https://placesjournal.org/article/databodies-in-codespace/.

Mayer, Margit. 2013. "First-World Urban Activism: Beyond Austerity Urbanism and Creative City Politics." *CITY* 17 (1): 5–19.

McCrone, David, and Brian Elliot. 1989. *Property and Power in a City: The Sociological Significance of Landlordism*. Basingstoke: MacMillan.

McFarlane, Alastair. 2003. "Rent Stabilization and the Long-Run Supply of Housing." *Regional Science and Urban Economics* 33 (3): 305–33.

McGoey, Linsey. 2019. *The Unknowers: How Strategic Ignorance Rules The World*. London: Zed Books.

McKenzie, Lisa. 2012. "A Narrative from the Inside, Studying St. Ann's in Nottingham: Belonging, Continuity and Change." *Sociological Review* 60: 457–75.

———. 2015. *Getting By: Estates, Class and Culture in Austerity Britain*. Bristol: Policy Press.

McKinnish, Terra, Randall Walsh, and Kirk White. 2008. "Who Gentrifies Low-Income Neighborhoods?" National Bureau of Economic Research Working Paper No. W14036. www.nber.org/papers/w14036.

McLean, Heather. 2018. "In Praise of Chaotic Research Pathways: A Feminist Response to Planetary Urbanization." *Environment and Planning D: Society and Space* 36 (3): 547–55.

Medvetz, Tom. 2012. *Think Tanks in America*. Chicago: University of Chicago Press.

Mendes, Luis. 2018. "Requiem for Neil Smith: A Retrospective of the Author's Thought on Gentrification from the Lens of Critical Geography." *ACME: An International Journal for Critical Geographies* 17 (3): 618–33.

Merrifield, Andy. 2014. *The New Urban Question.* London: Pluto Press.

Metzger, John T. 2000. "Planned Abandonment: The Neighbourhood Life-Cycle Theory and National Urban Policy." *Housing Policy Debate* 11 (1): 7–40.

Michael, Chris, and Ellie Violet Bramley. 2014. "Spike Lee's Gentrification Rant: 'Fort Greene Park Is Like the Westminster Dog Show.'" *Guardian,* February 26. www.theguardian.com/cities/2014/feb/26/spike-lee-gentrification-rant -transcript.

Millington, Nate, and Suraya Scheba. 2021. "Day Zero and the Infrastructures of Climate Change: Water Governance, Inequality, and Temporality in Cape Town's Water Crisis." *International Journal of Urban and Regional Research* 45 (1): 116–32.

Mills, Charles. 2008. "White Ignorance." In *Agnotology: The Making and Unmaking of Ignorance,* edited by Robert N. Proctor and Londa Schiebinger, 230–49. Stanford, CA: Stanford University Press.

Minton, Anna. 2017. *Big Capital: Who Is London For?* London: Penguin.

Mirowski, Philip. 2013. *Never Let a Serious Crisis Go to Waste: How Neoliberalism Survived the Financial Meltdown.* London: Verso.

Montgomery, Alesia. 2016. "Reappearance of the Public: Placemaking, Minoritization and Resistance in Detroit." *International Journal of Urban and Regional Research* 40 (4): 776–99.

Mood, Carina. 2010. "Neighborhood Social Influence and Welfare Receipt in Sweden: A Panel Data Analysis." *Social Forces* 88 (3): 1331–56.

Moon, Graham, Ross Barnett, Jamie Pearce, Lee Thompson, and Liz Twigg. 2018. "The Tobacco Endgame: The Neglected Role of Place and Environment." *Health and Place* 53: 271–78.

Moreno, Louis. 2014. "The Urban Process under Financialised Capitalism." *CITY* 18 (3): 244–68.

Morris, Alan. 1997. "Physical Decline in an Inner-City Neighbourhood: A Case Study of Hillbrow: Johannesburg." *Urban Forum* 8 (2): 153–75.

———. 2013. "Public Housing in Australia: A Case of Advanced Urban Marginality?" *Economic and Labour Relations Review* 24 (1): 80–96.

Morton, Alex. 2010. *Making Housing Affordable: A New Vision for Housing Policy.* Policy Exchange. www.policyexchange.org.uk/wp-content/uploads /2016/09/making-housing-affordable-aug-10.pdf.

Morton, Jane. 1976. "Tough Estates." *New Society,* November 18, 365.

Munch, Jakob Roland, and Michael Svarer. 2002. "Rent Control and Tenancy Duration." *Journal of Urban Economics* 52 (3): 542–60.

Musterd, Sako. 2008. "Diverse Poverty Neighbourhoods: Reflections on Urban Outcasts." *CITY* 12 (1): 107–14.

Musterd, Sako, and Ronald Van Kempen. 2007. Trapped or on the Springboard? Housing Careers in Large Housing Estates in European Cities." *Journal of Urban Affairs* 29 (3): 311–29.

Muth, Richard F. 1969. *Cities and Housing*. Chicago: University of Chicago Press.

Myrdal, Gunnar. 1965. "Opening Address to the Council of International Building Research in Copenhagen." *Dagens Nyheter*, August 25, 12.

Neocleous, Mark. 2013. "Resisting Resilience." *Radical Philosophy* 178 (March/April): 2–7.

Neuhouser, Frederick. 2011. "Jean-Jacques Rousseau and the Origins of Autonomy" *Inquiry* 54 (5): 478–93.

Newman, Kathe, and Elvin Wyly. 2006. "The Right to Stay Put, Revisited: Gentrification and Resistance to Displacement in New York City." *Urban Studies* 43 (1): 23–57.

Newman, Katherine. 2001. *No Shame in My Game: The Working Poor in the Inner City*. New York: Russell Sage Foundation.

Observatorio Metropolitano. 2013. *Crisis and Revolution in Europe: People of Europe, Rise Up!* Madrid: Traficantes de Suenos.

Olivier, David W. 2017. "Cape Town's Water Crisis: Driven by Politics More Than Drought." The Conversation, December 12. http://theconversation.com/cape-towns-water-crisis-driven-by-politics-more-than-drought-88191.

Olsen, Edgar. 1988. "What Do Economists Know about the Effect of Rent Control on Housing Maintenance?" *Journal of Real Estate Finance and Economics* 1: 295–307.

Olver, Crispian. 2019. *A House Divided: The Feud That Took Cape Town to the Brink*. Johannesburg: Jonathan Ball Publishers.

Ortega, Francisco, and Michael Orsini. 2020. "Governing Covid-19 without Government in Brazil: Ignorance, Neoliberal Authoritarianism, and the Collapse of Public Health Leadership." *Global Public Health* 15 (9): 1257–77.

Oswin, Natalie. 2018. "Planetary Urbanization: A View from Outside." *Environment and Planning D: Society and Space* 36 (3): 540–46.

Otarola, Miguel. 2020. "After George Floyd's Death, South Minneapolis Asks: Who Does 38th and Chicago Belong To?" *Star-Tribune*, July 4. www.startribune.com/after-floyd-s-death-who-does-38th-and-chicago-belong-to/571616872/.

Otto, Friederike, et al. 2018. "Anthropogenic Influence on the Drivers of the Western Cape Drought 2015–2017." *Environmental Research Letters* 13 (12): 124010.

Overman, Henry G. 2002. "Neighbourhood Effects in Large and Small Neighbourhoods." *Urban Studies* 39: 117–30.

Paton, Kirsteen. 2010. "Creating the Neoliberal City and Citizen: The Use of
    Gentrification as Urban Policy in Glasgow." In *Neoliberal Scotland: Class and
    Society in a Stateless Nation*, edited by Neil Davidson, Patricia McCafferty,
    and David Miller, 203–24. Newcastle: Cambridge Scholars Publishing.

Paton, Kirsteen, Vikki McCall, and Gerry Mooney. 2017. "Place Revisited: Class,
    Stigma and Urban Restructuring in the Case of Glasgow's Commonwealth
    Games." *Sociological Review* 65 (4): 578–94.

Peach, Ceri. 1996. "Does Britain Have Ghettos?" *Transactions of the Institute of
    British Geographers* 21 (1): 216–35.

———. 2009. "Slippery Segregation: Discovering or Manufacturing Ghettos?"
    Journal of Ethnic and Migration Studies 35 (9): 1381–95.

Peach, Ceri, and Margaret Byron. 1994. "Council House Sales, Residualisation
    and Afro-Caribbean Tenants." *Journal of Social Policy* 23 (3): 363–83.

Pearce, Jamie, Esther Rind, Niamh Shortt, Catherine Tisch, and Richard
    Mitchell. 2016. "Tobacco Retail Environments and Social Inequalities in
    Individual-Level Smoking and Cessation among Scottish Adults." *Nicotine
    and Tobacco Research* 18: 138–46.

Peck, Jamie. 2005. "Struggling with the Creative Class." *International Journal
    of Urban and Regional Research* 29 (4): 740–70.

———. 2010a. "Zombie Neoliberalism and the Ambidextrous State." *Theoretical
    Criminology* 14 (1): 104–10.

———. 2010b. *Constructions of Neoliberal Reason*. Oxford: Oxford University
    Press.

———. 2016. "Economic Rationality Meets Celebrity Urbanology: Exploring
    Edward Glaeser's City." *International Journal of Urban and Regional
    Research* 40 (1): 1–30.

Peck, Jamie, Neil Brenner, and Nik Theodore. 2009. "Neoliberal Urbanism:
    Models, Moments, Mutations." *SAIS Review of International Affairs* 29 (1):
    49–66.

Philpott, Thomas L. 1978. *The Slum and the Ghetto: Neighbourhood Deteriora-
    tion and Middle-Class Reform, Chicago 1880–1930*. New York: Oxford
    University Press.

Phillips, Trevor. 2005. "After 7/7: Sleepwalking to Segregation." Speech delivered
    at Manchester Town Hall, September 22.

Pinnock, Don. 2016. *Gang Town*. Cape Town: Tafelberg Press.

Policy Exchange. n.n. "About Us." https://policyexchange.org.uk/about-us.

PolicyLink, the Centre for Popular Democracy, and the Right to the City
    Alliance. 2019. *Our Homes, Our Future: How Rent Control Can Build
    Healthy, Stable Communities*. www.policylink.org/resources-tools/our
    -homes-our-future.

Porteous, J. Douglas, and Sandra Smith. 2001. *Domicide: The Global Destruc-
    tion of Home*. Montreal: McGill-Queens University Press.

Porter, Libby. 2009. "Planning Displacement: The Real Legacy of Major Sporting Events." *Planning Theory & Practice* 10 (3): 395–418.

Porter, Libby, and Simin Davoudi. 2012. "The Politics of Resilience for Planning: A Cautionary Note." *Planning Theory and Practice* 13 (2): 329–33.

Porter, Libby, and Oren Yiftachel. 2019. "Urbanizing Settler-Colonial Studies: Introduction to the Special Issue." *Settler Colonial Studies* 9 (2): 177–86.

Poulsen, Mike. 2005. "The 'New Geography' of Ethnicity in Britain." Paper delivered to the Annual Conference of the Royal Geographical Society-Institute of British Geographers, August 31.

Poulsen, Mike, and Ron Johnston. 2006. "Ethnic Residential Segregation in England: Getting the Right Message Across." *Environment and Planning A* 38: 2195–99.

Power, Anne. 1997. *Estates on the Edge: The Social Consequences of Mass Housing in Europe.* Basingstoke: Macmillan.

Power, Martin, Patricia Neville, Eoin Devereux, Amanda Haynes, and Cliona Barnes. 2013. "'Why Bother Seeing the World for Real?': Google Street View and the Representation of a Stigmatised Neighbourhood." *New Media and Society* 15 (7): 1022–40.

Proctor, Robert. 1995. *The Cancer Wars: How Politics Shapes What We Know and Don't Know about Cancer.* New York: Basic Books.

———. 2008. "Agnotology: A Missing Term to Describe the Cultural Production of Ignorance (and Its Study)." In *Agnotology: The Making and Unmaking of Ignorance,* edited by Robert Proctor and Londa Schiebinger, 1–36. Stanford, CA: Stanford University Press.

Proctor, Robert, and Londa Schiebinger, eds. 2008. *Agnotology: The Making and Unmaking of Ignorance.* Stanford, CA: Stanford University Press.

Project for Public Spaces. n.d. "What Is Placemaking?" www.pps.org/article /what-is-placemaking.

Public Internet Investigations Powerbase. 2019. "Policy Exchange." July 19. http://powerbase.info/index.php/Policy_Exchange.

Purdy, Sean. 2003. "'Ripped Off' by the System: Housing Policy, Poverty, and Territorial Stigmatization in Regent Park Housing Project, 1951–1991." *Labour/La Travail* 52: 45–108.

Purser, Gretchen. 2016. "The Circle of Dispossession: Evicting the Urban Poor in Baltimore." *Critical Sociology* 42 (3): 393–415.

Queiros, Joao, and Virgilio Borges Pereira. 2018. "Voices in the Revolution: Resisting Territorial Stigma and Social Relegation in Porto's Historic Centre (1974–1976)." *Sociological Review* 66 (4): 857–76.

Ramaswamy, V., and Manish Chakravarti. 1997. "Falahak, Inshallah (Flowering—God's Will): The Struggle of the Labouring Poor and a Vision, Strategy and Programme for Tenant-Led *Basti* and City Renewal." *Environment and Urbanization* 9 (2): 63–80.

Ramsden, Edmund, and Jon Adams. 2009. "Escaping the Laboratory: The Rodent Experiments of John B. Calhoun and Their Cultural Influence." *Journal of Social History* 42 (3): 761–92.

Ramsey, Joseph. 2016. "Evict the Landlords." *Jacobin*, June 9. www.jacobinmag .com/2016/09/evicted-landlords-tenants-rent-housing-milwaukee-racism/.

Ranganathan, Malini, and Eve Bratman. 2021. "From Urban Resilience to Abolitionist Climate Justice in Washington, DC." *Antipode* 53 (1): 115–37.

Rasmussen, Lars L. 2010. "Opening Speech to the Parliament," October 5. Copenhagen: The Danish Department of State.

———. 2018. "New Year Speech to the Parliament," January 1. Copenhagen: The Danish Department of State.

Rassool, Ciraj, and Sandra Prosalendis. 2001. *Recalling Community in Cape Town: Creating and Curating the District Six Museum*. Cape Town: District Six Museum Press.

Rawls, John. 1971. *A Theory of Justice*. Cambridge, MA: Harvard University Press.

Reid, Julian. 2013. "Interrogating the Neoliberal Biopolitics of the Sustainable Development-Resilience Nexus." *International Political Sociology* 7 (4): 353–67.

Rhodes, James. 2012. "Stigmatization, Space, and Boundaries in De-industrial Burnley." *Ethnic & Racial Studies* 35 (4): 684–703.

Right to the City (RTTC) Alliance. 2010. *We Call These Projects Home: Solving the Housing Crisis from the Ground Up*. https://righttothecity.org/wp -content/uploads/2014/02/We_Call_These_Projects_Home-2.pdf.

Rive, Richard. 1986. *Buckingham Palace, District Six*. Cape Town: David Philip Press.

Robinson, Cedric J. 1983. *Black Marxism: The Making of the Black Radical Tradition*. Chapel Hill: University of North Carolina Press.

Robinson, Jennifer. 2006. *Ordinary Cities: Between Modernity and Development*. London: Routledge.

———. 2011. "Cities in a World of Cities: The Comparative Gesture." *International Journal of Urban and Regional Research* 35 (1): 1–23.

Robinson, Stuart et al. 2017. "Placemaking: Value and the Public Realm." CBRE. www.cbre.com/research-and-reports/Global-Placemaking-Value-and -the-Public-Realm-May-2017.

Rockefeller Foundation, The. 2019. *Resilient Cities, Resilient Lives: Learning from the 100 RC Network*. https://resilientcitiesnetwork.org/urban _resiliences/resilient-cities-resilient-lives-learnings-from-100rc-network.

Rodger, Richard. 1989. "Crisis and Confrontation in Scottish Housing 1880–1914." In *Scottish Housing in the Twentieth Century*, edited by Richard Rodger, 25–53. Leicester: Leicester University Press.

Rolnik, Raquel. 2019. *Urban Warfare: Housing under the Empire of Finance*. London: Verso.

Romero, Gustavo. 1990. "Rented Housing in Mexico City." In *Rental Housing: Proceedings of an Expert Group Meeting*, 197–203. Nairobi: UNCHS.

Roy, Ananya. 2017. "Dis/possessive Collectivism: Property and Personhood at City's End. *Geoforum* 80: 1–11.

Sakizlioğlu, Bahar. 2014. "Inserting Temporality into the Analysis of Displacement: Living under the Threat of Displacement." *Tijdschrift Voor Economische En Sociale Geografie* 105 (2): 206–20.

———. 2018. "Rethinking the Gender-Gentrification Nexus." In *The Handbook of Gentrification Studies*, edited by Loretta Lees with Martin Phillips, 205–24. London: Edward Elgar.

Salins, Peter. 1999. "Reviving New York City's Housing Market." In *Housing and Community Development in New York City: Facing the Future*, edited by Michael H. Schill, 53–72. Albany: State University of New York Press.

Salo, Elaine R. 2018. *Respectable Mothers, Tough Men and Good Daughters: Producing Persons in Manenberg Township South Africa*. Bamenda, Cameroon: Langaa Research and Publishing.

Samara, Tony. 2011. *Cape Town After Apartheid: Crime and Governance in the Divided City*. Minneapolis: University of Minnesota Press.

Sampson, Robert. 2012. *Great American City: Chicago and the Enduring Neighborhood Effect*. Chicago: University of Chicago Press.

———. 2013. "The Place of Context: A Theory and Strategy for Criminology's Hard Problems." *Criminology* 51: 1–31.

———. 2018. "Neighbourhood Effects and Beyond: Explaining the Paradoxes of Inequality in the Changing American Metropolis." *Urban Studies* 56 (1): 3–32.

Sampson, Robert, Jeffrey D. Morenoff, and Thomas Gannon-Rowley. 2002. "Assessing 'Neighbourhood Effects': Social Processes and New Directions." *Annual Review of Sociology* 28: 443–78.

Saunders, Emma, Kate Samuels, and Dave Statham. 2018. "Rebuilding a Shattered Housing Movement: Living Rent and Contemporary Private Tenant Struggles in Scotland." In *Rent and Its Discontents: A Century of Housing Struggle*, edited by Neil Gray, 101–16. London: Rowman and Littlefield.

Savills. 2016. *Completing London's Streets*. Report to the UK Cabinet Office. http://pdf.euro.savills.co.uk/uk/residential---other/completing-london-s-streets-080116.pdf.

Sayer, Andrew. 2015. *Why We Can't Afford the Rich*. Bristol: Policy Press.

Scheba, Suraya, and Nate Millington. 2018a. "Crisis Temporalities: Intersections between Infrastructure and Inequality in the Cape Town Water Crisis."

IJURR blog. www.ijurr.org/spotlight-on/parched-cities-parched-citizens
/crisis-temporalities-intersections-between-infrastructure-and-inequality
-in-the-cape-town-water-crisis/.

———. 2018b. "Temporalities of Crisis: On Cape Town's Day Zero." *Situated Urban Political Ecology* (blog), April 3. www.situatedupe.net/temporalities -of-crisis-on-cape-towns-day-zero/.

Schill, Michael, and Richard Nathan. 1983. *Revitalizing America's Cities: Neighborhood Reinvestment and Displacement.* Albany: State University of New York Press.

Schmitt, Patrick. 2018. "Drought Forcing Cape wine Industry to 'Rightsize.'" *The Drinks Business,* February 6. www.thedrinksbusiness.com/2018/02 /drought-forcing-cape-wine-industry-to-rightsize/.

Schrecker, Ted, and Clare Bambra. 2015. *How Politics Makes Us Sick: Neoliberal Epidemics.* Basingstoke: Palgrave Macmillan.

Sennett, Richard. 1994. *Flesh and Stone: The Body and the City in Western Civilization* London: Faber & Faber.

Sernhede, Ove. 2011. "School, Youth Culture and Territorial Stigmatization in Swedish Metropolitan Districts." *Young* 19 (2): 159–80.

Sharkey, Patrick, and Jacob W. Faber. 2014. "Where, When, Why, and for Whom Do Residential Contexts Matter? Moving Away from the Dichotomous Understanding of Neighborhood Effects." *Annual Review of Sociology* 40: 559–79.

Shaw, Kate, and Iris Hagemans. 2015. "'Gentrification without Displacement' and the Consequent Loss of Place: The Effects of Class Transition on Low-income Residents of Secure Housing in Gentrifying Areas." *International Journal of Urban and Regional Research* 39 (2): 323–41.

Sheppard, Eric. 2001. "Quantitative Geography: Representations, Practices, and Possibilities." *Environment and Planning D: Society & Space* 19: 535–54.

Shildrick, Tracy, and Rob MacDonald. 2014. "Poverty Talk: How People Experiencing Poverty Deny Their Poverty and Why They Blame 'The Poor.'" *Sociological Review* 61: 285–303.

Shortt, Niamh, Esther Rind, Jamie Pearce, Richard Mitchell, and Sarah Curtis. 2018. "Alcohol Risk Environments, Vulnerability and Social Inequalities in Alcohol Consumption." *Annals of the American Association of Geographers* 108: 1210–27.

Simpson, Ludi. 2007. "Ghettos of the Mind: The Empirical Behaviour of Indices of Segregation and Diversity." *Journal of the Royal Statistical Society* 170 (2): 405–24.

Sims, David P. 2007. "Out of Control: What Can We Learn from the End of Massachusetts Rent Control?" *Journal of Urban Economics* 61 (1): 129–51.

Skeggs, Beverley. 2004. *Class, Self and Culture*. London: Routledge.

Slater, Tom. 2006. "The Eviction of Critical Perspectives from Gentrification Research." *International Journal of Urban and Regional Research* 30 (4): 737–57.

———. 2014. "The Myth of 'Broken Britain': Welfare Reform and the Production of Ignorance." *Antipode* 46 (4): 948–69.

———. 2016. "The Neoliberal State and the 2011 English Riots: A Class Analysis." In *Urban Uprisings: Challenging Neoliberal Urbanism in Europe*, edited by Margit Mayer, Catharina Thörn, and Hakan Thörn, 121–48. Basingstoke: Palgrave Macmillan.

Slater, Tom, and Ntsiki Anderson. 2012. "The Reputational Ghetto: Territorial Stigmatisation in St. Paul's, Bristol." *Transactions of the Institute of British Geographers* 37 (4): 530–46.

Small, Mario Luis. 2007. "Racial Differences in Networks: Do Neighborhood Conditions Matter?" *Social Science Quarterly* 88 (2): 320–43.

Small, Mario Luis, Erin Jacobs, and Rebecca P. Massengil. 2008. "Why Organizational Ties Matter for Neighborhood Effects: A Study of Resource Access through Childcare Centers." *Social Forces* 87 (1): 387–414.

Smith, David M. 1977. *Human Geography: A Welfare Approach*. London: Hodder Arnold.

———. 1987. *Geography, Inequality and Society*. Cambridge, UK: Cambridge University Press.

———. 1994. *Geography and Social Justice*. Oxford: Blackwell.

———. 2001. "On Performing Geography." *Antipode* 33: 141–46.

Smith, Neil. 1978. "Gentrification and Capital: Practice and Ideology in Society Hill." *Antipode* 11: 24–35.

———. 1979. "Toward a Theory of Gentrification: A Back to the City Movement by Capital, Not People." *Journal of the American Planning Association* 45 (4): 538–48.

———. 1982. "Gentrification and Uneven Development." *Economic Geography* 58 (2): 139–55.

———. 1984. *Uneven Development: Nature, Capital and the Production of Space*. Oxford: Blackwell.

———. 1992. "Blind Man's Bluff, or Hamnett's Philosophical Individualism in Search of Gentrification?" *Transactions of the Institute of British Geographers* 17 (1): 110–15.

———. 1996. *The New Urban Frontier: Gentrification and the Revanchist City*. London: Routledge.

———. 2006. "There's No Such Thing as a Natural Disaster." *Social Science Research Council* blog, June 11. https://items.ssrc.org/understanding-katrina/theres-no-such-thing-as-a-natural-disaster/.

———. 2008. *Uneven Development: Nature, Capital and the Production of Space*, 3rd Edition. Athens: University of Georgia Press.

Smith, Neil, and Scott Larson. 2007. "Beyond Moses and Jacobs." *Planetizen*, August 13. www.planetizen.com/node/26287.

Smith, Neil, and Peter Williams. 1986. "Alternatives to Orthodoxy: Invitation to a Debate." In *Gentrification of the City*, edited by Neil Smith and Peter Williams, 1–10. London: Allen & Unwin.

Smith, Susan J., and Donna Easterlow. 2005. "The Strange Geography of Health Inequalities." *Transactions of the Institute of British Geographers* 30 (2): 173–90.

Soederberg, Susanne. 2017. "Governing Stigmatised Space: The Case of the 'Slums' of Berlin-Neukölln." *New Political Economy* 22 (5): 478–95.

———. 2018. "Evictions: A Global Capitalist Phenomenon." *Development and Change* 49 (2): 286–301.

Soliman, Ahmed. 2002. "Typology of Informal Housing in Egyptian Cities." *International Development Planning Review* 24: 177–202.

Sommers, Jeff, and Nicholas Blomley. 2002. "'The Worst Block in Vancouver.'" In *Every Building on 100 West Hastings*, edited by Stan Douglas, 18–61. Vancouver: Contemporary Art Gallery.

Soudien, Crain. 1990. "District Six: From Protest to Protest." In *The Struggle for District Six, Past and Present*, edited by Shamil Jeppie and Crain Soudien, 143–84. Cape Town: Buchu Books.

Stabrowski, Filip. 2014. "New-Build Gentrification and the Everyday Displacement of Polish Immigrant Tenants in Greenpoint, Brooklyn." *Antipode* 46 (3): 794–815.

Stavrides, Stavros. 2016. *Common Space: The City as Commons*. London: Zed Books.

Steinberg, Stephen. 2010. "The Myth of Concentrated Poverty." In *The Integration Debate: Competing Futures for American Cities*, edited by Chester Hartman and Gregory D. Squires, 213–27. New York: Routledge.

Stel, Nora. 2016. "The Agnotology of Eviction in South Lebanon's Palestinian Gatherings: How Institutional Ambiguity and Deliberate Ignorance Shape Sensitive Spaces." *Antipode* 48 (5): 1400–419.

Sullivan, Esther. 2018. *Manufactured Insecurity: Mobile Home Parks and Americans' Tenuous Right to Place*. Berkeley: University of California Press.

Sultana, Farhana. 2015. "Governance Failures in Neoliberal Times." *International Journal of Urban and Regional Research* 30 (5): 1047–8.

Sutterluty, Ferdinand. 2014. "The Hidden Morale of the 2005 French and 2011 English Riots." *Thesis Eleven* 121 (1): 38–56.

Swanson, Felicity, and Jane Harries. 2001. "Ja! So was District Six: But It Was a Beautiful Place." In *Lost Communities, Living Memories: Remembering*

Forced Removals in Cape Town, edited by Sean Field, 62–80. Cape Town: David Philip.

Taylor, Keeanga-Yamahtta. 2015. "The Rise of the #BlackLivesMatter Movement." *Socialist Worker*, January 13. https://socialistworker.org/2015/01/13/the-rise-of-blacklivesmatter.

Taylor, Zac, and Alex Schafran. 2016. "Can Resilience Be Redeemed?" *CITY* 20 (1): 142.

Tempelhoff, Johann. 2019. "The Rise (and Fall?) of Resilience in Dealing with Cape Town's Water Crisis." In *Resilient Water Services and Systems: The Foundation of Wellbeing*, edited by Petri Juuti, Harri Matilla, Riikka Rajala, Klaas Schwartz, and Chad Staddon, 111–48. London: IWA Publishing.

Teresa, Benjamin F. 2019. "New Dynamics of Rent Gap Formation in New York City Rent-Regulated Housing: Privatization, Financialization, and Uneven Development." *Urban Geography* 40 (10): 1399–421.

Thörn, Catharina, and Helena Holgersson. 2016. "Revisiting the Urban Frontier through the Case of New Kvillebäcken, Gothenburg." *CITY* 20 (5): 663–84.

Tierney, Kathleen. 2015. "Resilience and the Neoliberal Project: Discourses, Critiques, and Practices—and Katrina." *American Behavioural Scientist* 59 (10): 1327–42.

Toynbee, Polly. 1982. "Once No One Wanted to Live There: Now, Thanks to Anne Power, the Estate Has Been Pulled Back into Shape." *Guardian*, February 19.

Traynor, Ian. 2015. "Molenbeek: The Brussels Borough Becoming Known as Europe's Jihadi Central." *Guardian*, November 15.

Turner, Bengt, and Stephen Malpezzi. 2003. "A Review of Empirical Evidence on the Costs and Benefits of Rent Control." *Swedish Economic Policy Review* 10 (1): 11–56.

Tyler, Imogen. 2013. *Revolting Subjects: Social Abjection and Resistance in Neoliberal Britain*. London: Zed Books.

———. 2018. "Resituating Erving Goffman: From Stigma Power to Black Power." *Sociological Review* 66 (4): 744–65.

Uitermark, Justus, Jan Willem Duyvendak, and Reinout Kleinhans. 2007. "Gentrification as a Governmental Strategy: Social Control and Social Cohesion in Hoogvliet, Rotterdam." *Environment and Planning A* 39: 125–41.

UK Parliament. 2016. *Housing and Planning Bill: Written Evidence Submitted by Crisis*. www.publications.parliament.uk/pa/cm201516/cmpublic/housingplanning/memo/hpb04.htm.

University of Edinburgh. n.d. "City Region Deal." www.ed.ac.uk/local/city-region-deal.

Valli, Chiara. 2015. "A Sense of Displacement: Long-Time Residents' Feelings of Displacement in Gentrifying Bushwick, New York." *International Journal of Urban and Regional Research* 39 (6): 1191–208.

van der Klaauw, Bas, and Jan van Ours. 2003. "From Welfare to Work: Does the Neighborhood Matter?" *Journal of Public Economics* 87: 957–85.

van Kempen, Ronald, Karien Dekker, Stephen Hall, and Ivan Tosics, eds. 2005. *Restructuring Large Housing Estates in Europe*. Bristol: Policy Press.

van Meeteren, Michiel, Ben Derudder, and David Bassens. 2016. "Can the Straw Man Speak? An Engagement with Postcolonial Critiques of 'Global Cities Research.'" *Dialogues in Human Geography* 6 (3): 247–67.

Venkatesh, Sudhir. 2006. *Off the Books: The Underground Economy of the Urban Poor*. Cambridge, MA: Harvard University Press.

Veracini, Lorenzo. 2015. *The Settler Colonial Present*. Basingstoke: Palgrave Macmillan.

Vigdor, Jacob. 2002. "Does Gentrification Harm the Poor?" *Brookings-Wharton Papers on Urban* Affairs, 133–73.

Wachsmuth, David, and Alexander Weisler. 2018. "Airbnb and the Rent Gap: Gentrification Through the Sharing Economy." *Environment and Planning A* 50 (6): 1147–70.

Wacquant, Loïc. 1996. "L''Underclass' Urbaine dans L'imaginaire Social et Scientifique Américain." In *L'Exclusion. L'état des Savoirs*, edited by Serge Paugam, 248–62. Paris: La Découverte.

———. 2004. "Ghetto." In *International Encyclopedia of the Social and Behavioural Sciences*, edited by Neil Smelser and Paul Baltes. London: Pergamon Press.

———. 2007. "Territorial Stigmatization in the Age of Advanced Marginality." *Thesis Eleven* 91 (1): 66–77.

———. 2008a. "Relocating Gentrification: The Working Class, Science, and the State in Recent Urban Research." *International Journal of Urban and Regional Research* 32: 198–205.

———. 2008b. *Urban Outcasts: A Comparative Sociology of Advanced Marginality*. Cambridge, UK: Polity Press.

———. 2008c. "Ghettos and Anti-Ghettos: An Anatomy of the New Urban Poverty." *Thesis Eleven* 94: 113–18.

———. 2009. "The Body, the Ghetto and the Penal State." *Qualitative Sociology* 32: 101–29.

———. 2010. "Urban Desolation and Symbolic Denigration in the Hyperghetto." *Social Psychology Quarterly* 73 (3): 215–19.

———. 2012a. "Three Steps to a Historical Anthropology of Actually Existing Neoliberalism." *Social Anthropology* 20 (1): 66–79.

———. 2012b "A Janus-Faced Institution of Ethnoracial Closure: A Sociological Specification of the Ghetto." In *The Ghetto: Contemporary Global Issues and Controversies*, edited by Ray Hutchison and Bruce Haynes, 1–31. Boulder, CO: Westview Press.

———. 2017. "Practice and Symbolic Power in Bourdieu: The View from Berkeley." *Journal of Classical Sociology* 17 (1): 55–69.

Wacquant, Loïc, Tom Slater, and Virgilio Borges Pereira. 2014. "Territorial Stigmatization in Action." *Environment and Planning A* 46 (6): 1270–80.

Wainwright, Oliver. 2014 "Guardian Cities: Welcome to Our Past, Present, and Future." *Guardian*, January 27.

Walker, Jeremy, and Melinda Cooper. 2011. "Genealogies of Resilience: From Systems Ecology to the Political Economy of Crisis Adaptation." *Security Dialogue* 42 (2): 143–60.

Walker, Sylvia. 2018. *Dealing in Death: Ellen Pakkies and a Community's Struggle with Tik*. Cape Town: Penguin Random House.

Watson, Bruce. 2014. "What Makes a City Resilient?" *Guardian*, January 27.

Watt, Paul. 2006. "Respectability, Roughness and 'Race': Neighbourhood Place Images and the Making of Working-Class Social Distinctions in London." *International Journal of Urban and Regional Research* 30 (4): 776–97.

Weber, Rachel. 2010. "Selling City Futures: The Financialization of Urban Redevelopment Policy." *Economic Geography* 86 (3): 251–74.

West, Cornel. 2008. *Hope on a Tightrope: Words and Wisdom*. Carlsbad, CA: Hay House.

Western, John. 1996. *Outcast Cape Town*. 2nd ed. Berkeley: University of California Press.

Wheaton, William C. 1977. "Income and Urban Residence: An Analysis of Consumer Demand for Location." *American Economic Review* 67: 620–31.

Whitehead, Judy, and Nitim More. 2007. "Revanchism in Mumbai? Political Economy of Rent Gaps and Urban Restructuring in a Global City." *Economic and Political Weekly*, June 23, 2428–34.

Wilson, William J. 1987. *The Truly Disadvantaged*. Chicago: University of Chicago Press.

———. 1991. "Another Look at the Truly Disadvantaged." *Political Science Quarterly* 106: 639–56.

Winkler, Tanja. 2018. "Black Texts on White Paper: Learning to See Resistant Texts as an Approach towards Decolonising Planning." *Planning Theory* 17 (4): 588–604.

Wolfe, Patrick. 1999. *Settler Colonialism and the Transformation of Anthropology*. London and New York: Cassell.

Wright, Melissa. 2014. "Gentrification, Assassination and Forgetting in Mexico: A Feminist-Marxist Tale." *Gender, Place & Culture* 21 (1): 1–16.

Wutich, Amber, Alissa Ruth, Alexandra Brewis, and Christopher Boone. 2014. "Stigmatized Neighborhoods, Social Bonding, and Health." *Medical Anthropology Quarterly* 28 (4): 556–77.

Wyly, Elvin. 2004. "The Accidental Relevance of American Urban Geography." *Urban Geography* 25: 738–41.

———. 2009. "Strategic Positivism." *Professional Geographer* 61 (3): 310–22.

———. 2011. "Positively Radical." *International Journal of Urban and Regional Research* 35 (5): 889–912.

———. 2015. "Gentrification on the Planetary Urban Frontier: The Evolution of Turner's Noosphere." *Urban Studies* 52 (14): 2515–50.

Wyly, Elvin, and Daniel Hammel. 2000. "Capital's Metropolis: Chicago and the Transformation of American Housing Policy." *Geografiska Annaler B* 82 (4): 181–206.

Wyly, Elvin, and C. S. Ponder. 2011. "Gender, Age, and Race in Subprime America." *Housing Policy Debate* 21 (4): 529–64.

Zhang, Yunpeng. 2016. "Domicide, Social Suffering and Symbolic Violence in Contemporary Shanghai, China." *Urban Geography* 39 (2): 190–213.

Ziervogel, Gina. 2019. *Unpacking the Cape Town Drought: Lessons Learned.* African Centre for Cities, University of Cape Town. www .africancentreforcities.net/wp-content/uploads/2019/02/Ziervogel-2019 -Lessons-from-Cape-Town-Drought_A.pdf.

Index

Founded in 1893,
UNIVERSITY OF CALIFORNIA PRESS
publishes bold, progressive books and journals
on topics in the arts, humanities, social sciences,
and natural sciences—with a focus on social
justice issues—that inspire thought and action
among readers worldwide.

The UC PRESS FOUNDATION
raises funds to uphold the press's vital role
as an independent, nonprofit publisher, and
receives philanthropic support from a wide
range of individuals and institutions—and from
committed readers like you. To learn more, visit
ucpress.edu/supportus.

Made in the USA
Las Vegas, NV
17 September 2023

77720511R00152